Critical Social Psychology

Studies in the
Postmodern Theory of Education

Joe L. Kincheloe and Shirley R. Steinberg
General Editors

Vol. 16

PETER LANG
New York • Washington, D.C./Baltimore
Bern • Frankfurt am Main • Berlin • Vienna • Paris

Philip Wexler

Critical Social Psychology

PETER LANG
New York • Washington, D.C./Baltimore
Bern • Frankfurt am Main • Berlin • Vienna • Paris

Library of Congress Cataloging-in-Publication Data

Wexler, Philip.
Critical social psychology/ Philip Wexler.
p. cm. — (Counterpoints; vol. 16)
Includes bibliographical references (p.   ) and index.
1. Social psychology. I. Title. II. Series.
HM251.W575   302—dc20   95-52853
ISBN 0-8204-3148-6
ISSN 1058-1634

Die Deutsche Bibliothek-CIP-Einheitsaufnahme

Wexler, Philip:
Critical social psychology/ Philip Wexler–New York; Washington,
D.C./Baltimore; Bern; Frankfurt am Main; Berlin; Vienna; Paris: Lang.
(Counterpoints; Vol. 16)
ISBN 0-8204-3148-6
NE: GT

Grateful acknowledgment is also made for permission to reprint extracts from
the following copyrighted material: Wexler, *American Journal of Sociology*,
83 (1977): 178–185. Copyright © 1977 by The University of Chicago Press.
Reprinted by permission of The University of Chicago Press. Excerpts from
Critical Social Psychology. Reprinted by permission of *Psychology and Social
Theory*. Knud S. Larsen, *Social Psychology: Crisis or Failure*, pp. 52–82.
Reprinted by permission of the author.

Cover art by Helen Wexler.
Cover design by James F. Brisson.

The paper in this book meets the guidelines for permanence and durability
of the Committee on Production Guidelines for Book Longevity
of the Council of Library Resources.

© 1996 Peter Lang Publishing, Inc., New York

Printed in the United States of America.

I saw the best minds of my generation destroyed by madness, starving hysterical naked,

—Allen Ginsberg

Acknowledgments

Many friends and colleagues have read various versions of parts of the manuscript. I cannot thank them all here, but I have tried to thank them along the way. I hope that they find the book improved by their comments.

I want to thank Margaret Zaccone for her administrative and typing assistance as well as her friendly but determined struggle at the site of word production. I thank Betty Drysdale and Jo Minges for shouldering the major typing burden. My thanks also to: Frances Crawford, Bill De Angelis, Nancy Fruchtman, Judy Gueli, Rose Mancini, Marjorie Shannon, Cindi Venable.

Without the help of several friends and colleagues, I doubt that the book would have been possible. My heartfelt thanks to: Michael Apple, Elaine Hatfield, Laurence Parker, William Pinar, and Ilene Zipkin.
A special added thanks to Laurence Parker for his dedicated and inspired editorial help.

Thanks to Ari and Michael Wexler for more than I can say here.

Acknowledgments
to the second edition

In addition to the acknowledgments for the earlier publication, I want to express my particular appreciation to Shirley Steinberg for making this volume possible. Shirley Steinberg and Joe Kincheloe have both taken a keen interest in my work, which I appreciate. I am grateful for Shirley's faith that a number of lonely readers of *Critical Social Psychology* can now be joined by a wider audience in this Peter Lang publication.

Table of Contents

Preface

I have long resisted both neo-Marxist and psychoanalytic explanations of social life—both of which are pivotal to Wexler's *Critical Social Psychology*. Some of my writings have even been inimical to these ventures. Yet, I view the present volume as a landmark contribution to social psychology and count it as an honor to serve as the trumpeter for its timely republication. I share with Philip a deep investment in social psychological inquiry, and for many of the same reasons illuminated in this work. And, like Philip, I believe that the traditional hypothetico-deductive orientation to social inquiry is deeply flawed—intellectually, politically, and in terms of its potential contribution to cultural life. In effect, *Critical Social Psychology* grows from a profound commitment to intellectual work in the service of the greater good, a commitment that is so strong that it demands placing in critical perspective the very grounds of one's endeavors. Such bold honesty was at stake when Philip placed his own career in jeopardy publishing this volume in its original, and it remains robust in his invitation to me now.

To be sure, those who labor in the liberal-individualist tradition, with its emphasis on human experimentation and truth through method, share the desire for a broadly beneficial discipline. However, the field has taken very little interest in reflexive questioning of its own activities. To raise such questions is to interfere with the smooth functioning of research programs and the accumulation of personal publications. Further, there are few resources for asking reflexive questions about the discipline's taken-for-granted construction of the subject, along with its weaknesses and potentials vis à vis societal needs. It is also a field whose political and ethical commitments are obscured by its claims to value neutrality; it can locate no alternatives—intellectual or passionate—with which to bring itself to account. It is precisely these reflexive resources that Wexler provides in this work—aggravating, unsettling, and provocative. While I may not agree with all the particulars of Wexler's analysis, I value enormously the dialogue that it initiates.

This new edition breaks upon an intellectual landscape far different from that confronted on its first appearance. On the one hand, the targeted tradition of social psychology is—at its core—even more deeply entrenched in its assumptions, methods, and central concepts. If anything, the state of "ignorant expertise," of which Serge Moscovici spoke over 20 years ago (quoted in Wexler's Introduction), has only intensified. Experimental research is now so remote from the central concerns of the society, and its intellectual deliberations so isolated from the current dialogues of the social sciences, that the field is in danger of becoming an antiquarian curiosity. Few of the committed will be able to hear Wexler's message. I fear that hope must now be placed in the younger ranks—those whose earlier backgrounds in the broader dialogues of the social sciences will have sensitized them to the intellectual tidal waves now sweeping across the academy.

For as we find, the broader intellectual ethos has been virtually transformed over the past two decades. When *Critical Social Psychology* was initially published, sensitivities to movements variously labeled as post-empiricist, post-structuralist, and postmodernist were only beginning to make their way into common consciousness. Terms such as deconstruction, hermeneutics, neo-pragmatism, interpretive community, dialogism, the imaginary, cyborgology, capillary power, the rhetoric of inquiry, narratology, discursive pragmatics, multiculturalism, identity politics, and social construction were largely in incubation. Academic programs in women's studies, queer studies, interpretation studies, and cultural studies were rare. These movements, concepts, and programs—all interwoven—are engendering a profound transformation in our conceptions of social science, the place of research, the function of theory, and the place of the scholar in cultural life. The entire scientific tradition, as it has emerged and flourished in Western culture—along with its presumptions of truth, objectivity, and foundational rationality—has come under sharp attack. The future course of social inquiry is radically open, and the atmosphere is both daunting and exhilarating.

For scholars in this context, the new edition of Wexler's work will not speak with the same voice that it did in the early 1980s. Consider first the sea-change that has occurred in both Marxist and psychoanalytic thought. In both cases, major theoretical movements

xii

have "gone post-structural." Thus, in the Marxist case, theory has largely shifted its concern from the material conditions of labor that manifest themselves in societal relations, to economies of signification—to styles, artifacts, publications, music, and other forms of symbolic capital endemic to post-industrial culture. Traditional views of stratified structures of power have given way to conceptions of multiple, distributed, and dynamic processes of power relations. Neo-analytic theory now largely ignores processes of repression and instinctual desire to focus on the imprint of the symbolic or linguistic register on object relations. For these endeavors, the reappearance of Wexler's book will serve as an important voice of conscience. Do these various analyses, on the one hand, signal a loss of critical concern with the increasing conservativism of government, the global expansion of capitalist enterprise, the conditions of labor and poverty, and the quality of everyday intimacy—along with the continued rationalization of these endeavors by major academic institutions? Does "going post-structural" mean "going literary," "going pop," and resultantly, going politically flat? And, when psychoanalytic thought abandons concern with repression, denial, and the elements of passion, does it also remove itself from deep engagement with human experience and the emancipation of the spirit? The volume warns us, then, to beware the loss of rebellious innocence.

Further, as Wexler notes in his introduction to the re-edition, the ethos of critique has also changed substantially. Where critical voices were once confined to the domains of class and race, the chorus has increased dramatically. Ideological critiques of the kind that once threatened Wexler with marginalization are now shared by myriad minorities spanning the political spectrum. Many of these groups will surely find Wexler's an affirmative voice; his challenges to the status quo, and his concerns with domination, ideological blindness, and exploitation, will expand the resources available in the quest. However, more importantly, Wexler's is also a call for unity. As he sees it, the fragmentation of critical voices is unfortunate: not only does the currency of critique become banalized, but we confront increasing signs of internecine strife. We begin to confront "culture wars." Wexler proposes that the analytic tools born of Marxist and Freudian theory offer the resources for integration. Others will surely take issue with this proposal; Wexler would welcome the dialogue. For as I know him, the central challenge for Wexler is that of moving toward the kind of mutual understanding that would further the ideals common to all; his commitment is, after all, to "a transformative hermeneutic." If Marx and Freud succeed in furthering these pursuits, so much the better.

Finally, this restored work enters an intellectual context in which a social constructionist epistemology is in the ascent. As the lessons of the sociology of knowledge and the history of science have become commonplace, as literary theory has moved toward the study of cultural signification, as studies of the rhetoric of science have eclipsed the philosophy of science, as historians have acquired the power to relativize the exigent cultural categories, as anthropologists have grieved over the limits of western scholars to do other than reinstantiate their own ideologies, as the marginalized dissidents have mastered the craft of deconstructing authoritative texts, and as the pragmatics of discourse has come to replace semantics and syntactics, so have we increasingly come to appreciate the extent to which all propositions about the real and the good are lodged within, and derive their legitimacy from, social process. Within this context, Wexler's volume will again act as a voice of conscience. Where, it asks, does a social constructionist epistemology stand politically? How does it not conduce toward a flaccid relativism? Is the movement prepared to reduce to discourse all that we commonly take to be domination, exploitation, injustice, or human suffering? These questions have not yet been adequately treated within constructionist circles, and Wexler's volume demands the necessary dialogue.

There is finally a sense in which the positive thrust of *Critical Social Psychology* works in productive synchrony with significant movements in social constructionism. In the latter chapters of the volume, Wexler lays the groundwork for a fully socialized conception of the self—a conception that places human subjectivity into the stream of history and culture. The attempt to revise individual action in terms of more inter-dependent, systemic, dynamic, and holistic processes is one that is also common to many constructionist conversations. If we abandon the individual as the font of meaning and of action, holds the constructionist, then we must generate conceptual resources that will enable us to appreciate the profoundly interconnected character of all human action. In effect, the message of the present work now speaks to a dialogue at the cutting edge, and its sophisticated arguments, inventive insights, and passionate engagement are resources to be treasured.

Kenneth J. Gergen
Swathmore College

Series editors'
introduction

While we have much to say in regard to our excitement about Peter Lang's republication of Philip Wexler's *Critical Social Psychology,* we will restrain our predispositions to verbosity. Be sure that in another venue we will elaborate on our reactions to Wexler's ideas, their historical consequence, and their relationship to emerging themes in a variety of psychological and other scholarly disciplines. Echoing our passion about the importance of Wexler's work, William Pinar, William Reynolds, Patrick Slattery, and Peter Taubman write in another volume of Lang's *Counterpoints* series, (*Understanding Curriculum,* 1995) that Philip Wexler is "quite possibly the most sophisticated theoretician on the Left in the contemporary [curriculum] field." Accolades aside, *Critical Social Psychology* is back in print with a preface by Kenneth Gergen and a new introduction by Wexler. This reprinting assures that the book will be available to students of social psychology, curriculum theory, cultural studies, and social theory well into the twenty-first century, and that it will gain the widespread recognition it deserves.

Significantly ahead of his time, Wexler recognized well-before the 1980s that Nietzsche's exposure of the mythological nature of modernist science's conception of reality as a well-founded rational order had forever changed the rules of the intellectual conversation. Unable to operate any longer in a naturalized science that issued objective descriptions of a cause-effect life world, Wexler focused on social psychology's tendency to confuse "reality" with the reflection of its own theoretical constructions. Seeing through social psychology's representation of ubiquitous rule-governed and predictable human behavior, he recognized and delineated the political implications of such scientific practice. Thus, Wexler divulged the historical, social, and political production of the discipline's "natural" categories. Knowing that there is nothing wrong with identifying conceptual patterns as long as we understand that they are social constructions, Wexler balanced a critical concern with human experience and suffering with a new paradigmatic discomfort and an unproblematized notion of reality.

Dialectical enough to understand modernist social psychology's disposition to regard knowledge as discrete and fixed, Wexler pushed a process-oriented epistemology that appreciated the discipline's etymology, actuality, and potentiality. Wexler's refusal to accept modernism's time/space decontextualization of its own practices allowed him to see social psychology's possibility, its potential as a practice of freedom. A reading or (re-reading) of *Critical Social Psychology* helps focus our attention on the embedded monocultural and class-biased dynamics of modernist social psychology replete with its normalization and regulation of what it has perceived as disorder. In this context, the author well-understood the depth of the social penetration of the psychological and the implications of such a relationship to the future of the discipline.

For those interested in Wexler's work in the late 1980s and 1990s, *Critical Social Psychology* provides an excellent opportunity to understand the genesis of his present intellectual concerns. Embedded in this book are the preliminary rumblings of his subsequent efforts to act on the insights provided by the critique of modernist science and social/psychological theory. Analysis of *Critical Social Psychology* uncovers the etymology of Wexler's concern with a socially informed spirituality and the possibilities it holds for critical discourses. Indeed, the roots of the future of critical theory reside here. We hope that the republication of this important work will inform all critical scholars as much as it has us.

Joe L. Kincheloe
Penn State University

Shirley R. Steinberg
Adelphi University

Introduction
to the second edition

I am grateful to my colleagues who have made possible this new publication of *Critical Social Psychology*. My hope, as I believe it is theirs, that social understanding is not simply an analytical practice, but an existential and redemptive one, has not been at all diminished in the years since the book first appeared.

Now, as then, social analysis is always grasped as a "creative hermeneutic." It belongs within a process of historical and personal unfolding in which making sense socially of events and experiences contributes to the enhancement and transfiguration of individual lives and to the transformation of the collective situations structuring those lives. Social analysis that enables these individual and collective changes is inherently critical, and not positive or indifferently analytical—as if that were possible. "Critical" means pushing common sense aside and not accepting the easiest symbolic organization of everyday life as the only or best one. Our nostrum that "what you see is what you get" is not true. A better proverb would be "there is more than meets the eye."

This quest for the "more," for the passing beyond the soporific veil of cultural Maya, to exercise an intellectual decoding capacity in order to change our lives, and in so doing, the worlds in which they are lived, is what critical social analysis means. We are doing this work not simply because of its intrinsic reward, the "pleasure of the text" of social interpretation or because it is our "job." Rather, the more profound reason is that we are trying to save our lives. Even now, under the cloud of polyvocal nihilism and anti-intellectualism, we believe in the power of reason and systemic understanding to make a difference. And, we believe that we can become "more" than what and who we appear to be in the eye of the uncritical everyday cultural mirror in which we see ourselves and others in the world.

Critical Social Psychology

I wrote *Critical Social Psychology* in an angry temper. Angry with American academic social science, and particularly social psychology, for offering a false and deceitful promise of critical reason and systematic understanding. False and deceitful because its rhetoric and practice of science implies piercing everyday interpretive practice to deliver something beyond, something more powerful and practically efficacious. Instead, I found sly reinforcement and affirmation of everyday culture, only recoded in a fancier, more prestigious language of the modern scientific discourse that we still are taught to believe in our hearts is the true and only knowledge.

The effect of this scientific recoding of uncritical culture is to induce a premature comfort, an almost magical sense of getting the right result by performing the correct ritual. In that way, it displaces other, less familiar, more unsettling understandings that are more distant from everyday meanings, but that may lead to more personally transfigurative and collectively transformative results. Social psychology, which is intended to enlighten understanding of precisely this relation between the individual and the collective works exactly in this way, I argued. It appears rhetorically to be different and analytically superordinate to prevailing everyday culture, while merely offering a translated reflection—a deflective mirroring that miscues away from critical analysis. Social psychology works within the main, dominant culture, protecting it from radical scrutiny by reflective recoding. It is in this sense that it is an "ideology," discursive blockage, containment, or set of interpretive practices that produce ignorance of the dynamics of organized social life and the subjective experiences and interpersonal relations that occur within it.

Describing how this false lead—which is a prematurely, ritually comforting, discursive cultural function of social psychology in producing social ignorance rather than enlightenment—actually works is one interest of this book. A second interest is to provide an alternative: an interpretation that does not reinforce and affirm the hegemonic culture by sticking close to its assumptions and commitments and encoding them in the rhetoric and ritual of science. Instead, illumination of individual and social relational processes is provided by juxtaposing what is different—even strange—and certainly not immediately obvious within ordinary culturally organized perception.

In the American culture, with all its seeming internal differences, and indeed, generally in modern culture, it is the individual and the particular that we take as natural. The collective, the social structure, and the general appear to us—if they appear at all—as abstract fictions, strange to the mass-produced popular ear, unnatural, intangible foreign constructions. Even in social science, there is a long history of distrusting terms that represent collective rather than individual processes. A social structural approach has not come naturally or easily, even to professional specialists in social understanding. And, of all the social structural approaches available, Marxism, and the eclectic critical social theories nourished by it, have been the least culturally assimilable, the strangest and most different—at least so far. Part of its interpretive value is in this difference and distance from ordinary sense-making strategies.

The "alternative" to a social psychology that rises and falls within the fortunes of liberalism in mass culture is a Marxism modified by Frankfurt School-style critical theory and elements of a non-dogmatic, historicized Freudianism. The alternative to scientifically recoded liberalism is a socially structural approach to understanding individual, interpersonal, and collective processes. Marxism is the base, construed not as a political economy, but, following Lukacs' lead (1971), as a general theory of social relations. Alienation, exploitation, and commodification are social structured interactional processes. But, the social structural alternative presented here is not simply the assertion that these general processes of capitalist societies are useful ways of thinking about how our lives are organized and experienced. These processes, too, follow one of the insistent subtextual methodological practices of our study of real life social psychology that supersedes the critique of academic social psychology as a cultural practice within a wider regime of liberalism. That practice is to contextualize (Toulmin, 1990).

Context

To contextualize means to relate the operation of the general to the particular, to see social practice, social relations, and mass and academic discourses within their settings—within their wider and contiguous situations. At once, it includes the personal or subjective moment in cognitive abstraction, the wider cultural locus and meaning of academic explanation, and the socially organized structuring of collective life in relation to the subjective and the culture. In turn, contextualizing or nesting that structure in its dynamic stream that we call history.

History, too, can be placed in the still more ambitious gambit of a transcendental context, like the cosmic structural survivals of primordial myths and rituals that Eliade (1957) finds in the equivalence between the collective archaic sacred and the real. And, in return, contextualizing is a recursive process, represented in a movement back from even such cosmic, archaic social structures to the unspoken, but, ineffectual, unconscious aspect of individual subjectivity (Jung, 1976).

Contextualizing Marx's theory of social relations means showing how these general processes are realized in particular social situations—historically changing relations among organizational and institutional processes and collectivities that alter their composition, function, and relation. A general Marxist social psychology is at once an historically variable account of what have been the most salient collectivities—social classes—and of what have been the most salient institutional sites of social relations—economic production. In that sense, the "alternative" is at once a general and particular one, an historically contextualized analysis of social classes and economic production and of how alienation, exploitation, and commodification work specifically in changing class and production contexts.

The book emphasizes social class and economic production as social structuring processes that have been significantly ignored, both in the general culture of liberalism and in the academic culture of social psychology. But, a contextual approach to social structural dynamics follows particular historical events, even more than fixed abstract theoretical categories. It was already clear more than a decade ago that if we look toward social movements as instances of the enactment of historical social structures, not only is economic production formative for subjectivity and social relations, but so too is consumption, and all that is not work. Indeed, the analysis of "intimacy" is a way to bring in all of the creative non-work aspects of collective life that are down-played by ordinary commodity consumption.

Social class, as production-structured, invidiously, unequally differentiated forms of life, is now even less discursively salient than it was when the book was first written. The need to talk the language of social classes and to use such terms as references for empirical study has intensified, and not diminished, with the deeper forgetting of such a language and such an analytic access to socially organized difference, enrichment, and suffering.

Nonetheless, as the discussion of social movements as the basis for a truly alternative, socially effective social psychology indicates, its is not class movements which were then, and are now, the most explicit leading edge of collective movements for social structural reorganization. Rather, radical feminism, African American critique and movement, gay theory and practice, and the now less-politicized importance of insanity as dissidence represent the collective dynamisms contained within the present social, historical, and subjective context.

The third element of a critical social psychology is to show specifically and contextually how the concepts of academic social psychology—concepts which simultaneously draw out of mass culture and feedback to help shape it—are interwoven with that culture, and with the class and production, gender, race, sexual, and mental health dynamics that constitute historical social structures and movements. Concepts of self, interaction and intimacy that not only become important in discourses which present themselves as explanatory, but also in the everyday social interpretive practices of ordinary people, are problematized, they are analyzed as historically changing elements of culture, as collective representations that play social roles as they simultaneously operate in the sense-making activities of everyday life.

Along with the bifurcation of liberalism into an even less social language of individual, economic market-thinking and a nostalgia-driven idealization of nuclear-familialism and fundamentalist, but establishmentarian, religions, these social psychological concepts for bridging understanding of the individual-collective relation begin to dissipate and dissolve back into the potentiating pool of unarticulated cultural resources. That is what it meant to say that the "crisis" of social psychology was part of the general crisis. In fact, as I suggested, the so-called "crisis in social psychology" has itself faded, without yet surrendering its claims to either academic legitimacy or to operative influence on popular consciousness. How residual these concepts will remain, and whether they will retain effectivity in consciousness and in mass interpretive practice or be superseded by new and different languages, with different commitments, was the question raised by *Critical Social Psychology*.

We already see part of the answer, in the tripartite division of market individualist regulation of productive spheres, ascendant claims to subjectivity in non-work life by rigid traditionalist territorializing of both the most transcendent and most subjective contexts, in religion and family, and in dissident pressure for voices to rationalize the identity politics of gender, race, and sexuality. Each of these socially structured dynamic movements legitimates its practical understandings in more systematic terms as "theories" of cosmology of self, society, and their relation. The challenge of a critical social psychology now is to not simply join the rationalizing chorus of what becomes familiar and taken naturally.

Instead, the critical response is to "make strange" what appears easy and natural to common sense. How shall we estrange critical social analysis from the present without losing our own contexts and commitments? In addition to methodologically principled subtext of contextualizing, I suggest a second heuristic rule of creative, transformative hermeneutical practice revision.

Revision

Revision is not simply editing, or recanting, or even a creative, cross-generational method of differentiating one's own identity from precursors, as Bloom argues (1982). Revision, following Scholem's (1971) Kabbalistic account, is a process of commentary on revelation, and incessant renewal within the traditional frame of what is already given and accepted as true. Such revision reconciles the apparent contradictions of revelation or collective insight, traditions of knowledge, and permanent revolution in thinking. Revision complements context as a methodological practice of creative, transformative hermeneutics.

Some types of revision underline continuity, showing differences to be amplifications and elaborations of what was already said or done. Other revisions uncover denied, repressed, or forgotten narratives, paradigms, concepts, and events. Still, the third and most dramatic revisions, appear to reverse course—only to remain true to basic commitments, hopes, and visions of the future.

A new critical social psychology, more than a decade after publication of the first version, could offer revisions of each type, and in so doing, provide an outline for work in a changed context, one that is both continuous and discontinuous with the context of the earlier production.

per 1°,

Continuity

The deep fault lines of the initial situation remain the same: the fracturing of corporate liberal capitalism and its consequences for social understanding, organized collective life, and subjective consciousness and mode of living. The dissolution of the liberal containment described as a analytical displacement or compartment within a broader cultural regime as "social psychology" and its "crisis" has continued to the point of clarifying the polarities contained by the unstable cultural defenses of liberalism. The splitting apart best exemplified in the division between subject and object has settled into *naturalness*. But liberalism itself has taken new forms, extruding subjectivity to its barely included margins, while effectively miniaturizing objectivism so as to redefine the meaning of even an already successfully privatized self.

This new shade of liberalism has taken the market to the heart of the subject. The new corporatism, which I have described in education, for example, (Wexler, 1993, 1994), redefines the self as objective high performance of measurable multidimensional skills. The early corporate liberal pseudo-*gemeinschaft* of managed consent through social interactional "fellowship" survives, but only as an instrumental, second-order technique subsumed by the hegemonic definition of self as organizationally-relevant individual, benchmarked, best-practice high performance.

Postindustrialism completes the managerialization of the self, wearing the production-defined cloaks of flexibility and autonomy. (Harvey, 1989; Casey, 1995). Consciousness, as reflection even (" critical reflectivity"), becomes an element of professionalized practice. In that way, it surrenders the possibility of distance and estrangement required for critical social analysis and for individual and collective transformative hermeneutics.

In this sociocultural regime, there is increasingly less need to translate economic relations of the market into more vague and opaque theories of social interaction. Who needs equity theory when the social can no longer be imagined as being anything different or other that the market itself? This marketization of social relation is accomplished, ironically, precisely within the apparatus of social production, which objectivized market languages deny as causally relevant.

The subjectivity polarity of liberalism is collectivized, just as its objective aspect has been subjectivized in the reflective, life-style engineered, high performing, benchmark-managed self. This subjectivization is more subtle, and more harmful to the project of a critical social analysis, or what I am calling a "transformative hermeneutic." It presents itself not as an obscured polarity of the classic subject-object splitting within liberalism, but as oppositional and critical. Indeed, it is critical; critical of the relative exclusion of women, people of color, homosexuals, and everyone who can be readily branded as "different," from participation in the mainline institutional apparatus.

This call for inclusion can become critical and transformative, as we saw in the earlier review of the social movements that have become most socially salient. But in its modality, in the way that it challenges European white male heterosexist professional middle class hegemony, these still fragmented social movements can work against their own interests by legitimating acceptance of particularity as a substitute for more general oppression and suffering. Hard-won respect for cultural difference can operate as a "by-off" for a more general, more radical critique of the organized, patterned social structures that produce sexist, racist, and heterosexist forms of social exclusion.

This identity politics, that I had hoped would transcend sterile old left Marxist analyses by bringing in culture and subjectivity, is itself continually vulnerable to becoming liberalism's internal, useable "other."

As I argued earlier, politically, without coalescence, and analytically, without reference to the social whole, late liberalism's fragmentation and switch-coded polarization of objectivism and subjectivism makes culturally-represented claims for equality into the false signifier of social structure—again, but in a new way, producing social ignorance. Unintentionally, the effect is to block a wider and deeper perception of the existence and transformability of the systemic structure. The particularism and cultural identity pluralization that postindustrial's culture of postmodernity has introduced under the signs of multiplicity and diversity becomes all that remains, and is permitted, of images of socially patterned structured. This strategic danger is only underlined by superordinate codes of decontextualization and detotalization.

These super-codes proclaim that there are only the particular and the segregated multiplicities of diversity and pluralism. As a reaction against the totalitarian, murderous state and its intellectual representations, such anti-narratology is inevitable and unequivocally necessary. But, without recontextualizing these reactions against totalitarian genocides in our times, we surrender also the desire for meaningful coherence, for a critical hermeneutic of social structure, and the political imagination and strategic thinking needed even to envision, no less actualize, a more profound and pervasive change in the organization of collective and individual life—and in their interrelation, as a theory and practice of a new critical social psychology.

Denial

What the postmodern academic inclination and identity politics have done is to always remind to position discourse, to ask who is speaking and from where. But the answer, however, is limited by horizons of social understanding and culturally available categories of analysis. Freud taught us well that forgetting is no accident. And what has been forgotten in the positioning of discourse, as a practice of contextualization, is precisely what I tried to remind in the earlier *Critical Social Psychology:* the social regime, as an aggregated collective active, dynamic structure, repeatedly induces (repetition is no accident either, in Freud's architectonic critical hermeneutic of the bourgeois self) forgetting and repression of all signs of social class as an organizing, practical, and analytical category that connects collective structure and individual life form. In the current pluralization of social analytic discourse (Lemert, 1995), there is a creative and powerful articulation of feminist and racial theory.

But where is the "voice" of different social classes? Who now speaks of a working class, or even a proletarian social analysis? And this during a time of empirically incontrovertible social polarization by occupational location, of economic immiseration, of reduction in the size of the managerial, professional, "new" middle class. Of course, some of this socio-economic suffering is patterned by race and by gender. But, that pattern, too, is nested within employment chances, in property ownership, and in the economic, and not only the cultural and psychic aspects of an organized social inequality.

We have stopped talking about class structure. It comes to appear as if inequality is a transhistorical, unalterable, constant fact of social life, or a question of discrimination in cultural preferences. Or, perhaps, as in the emergent political ideologies which coincide with the workplace marketization of subjectivity, inequality is patterned only by individual attributes—in a new, better-supervised, psychometric social darwinism.

Along with social class, human labor, organized as social production, has disappeared from discourse. The "new" ethnographies of identity politics are not about work, and postmdoernism has little to say about its twin, postindustrialism. Yet, the organization of work, particularly in its postindustrial transformation, continues to shape the dynamics of personal life, of what we still call "the self," or subjectivity, as Casey (1995) persuasively argues. Hers is a lonely voice, not denying either postmodernism or postindustrialism, and trying to demonstrate how collective and individual are mutually constituted at work, in organized social production.

The continuing and deepening denial and forgetting of social labor and production as a structuring principle in social life denies too the continuing, critical social analytical value of the concepts of alienation, exploitation, and commodification as relational generalizations from the production process. A still deeper denial undergirded by a loss of social, public confidence, is reflected not only the current silence about class and production, but in the denial of the very idea of social structuring itself.

Affirmative and critical cultures of individualism and particularism alike operate to reinforce the postmodern ideology of diffusion and implosion that fits so well new market liberalism's deep denial of class, production, and structure. And with that, liberalism finally succeeds in transcending the polar dualisms of object and subject, of collective and individual. One pole, the objective social, continues to be discursively dissolved, and lost from the memory reserve of cultural resources used to understand and change the social context of individual life.

Reversal

To counteract the growing impoverishment of cultural resources that can be used in social analysis, reminders about what is socially forgotten and denied are not going to suffice. We need a wider scope, and an even longer historical collective memory. This search for analytically useable cultural resources is not an expansionary, colonizing quest. The implosive churning of postmodernism throws up new and forgotten languages and cosmologies, both by its idealization of particularist cultural identities and by its warranting of eclecticism, sectarianism, and an aesthetic valuation of extant forms of irrationality.

Those are our new resources. The new languages and artifacts of a "post" postmodern effort to reconstitute shattered meaningfulness in everyday life appear in a wide array of social practices, cultural beliefs, and rituals. This new culture emerges in new forms of subjectivity that academic analysts categorized dismissively as "new age." But, if the culture of the "new age" is easily reterritorialized to the commodity world, it brings the vitality of a sincere, if apparently naive, quest as a counterforce to the addictive fetishism of declining modernity that postmodernism uses as its cultural engine. More than that, the creation of a new age culture itself draws, postmodern-like, eclectically and often with distortion, on core, premodern cultures that the rise of industrialism and modernity have suppressed for almost half a millennium.

I have tried to show how these new and forgotten cultural resources can be reconstituted, and redirected, in an altered, present context (Wexler, 1996). But, this path represents a radical recontextualization, that seems, at first glance, to be a reversal of earlier commitments and strategies. Yet, these seeming reversals redeem and recover, I think, deeper hopes and concerns about collective and individual life. Religion, for example, was ordinarily thought of in the Marxist, Critical Theory tradition as the paradigm for alienation. But, I argue that religious thinking has historically often served to counter alienation, and that in the suppressed, but clear and powerful, voices of dissident elements within the core civilizational religions—especially in gnosticism and mysticism—there are critical hermeneutic resources for theoretical and practical transformation that contravene alienation.

This reconstitutive path takes cultural artifacts and processes as active and creative, and not simply as a field for the enactment of culturally contained, social structurally produced contradictions. The seeming reversal in the relation between religion and alienation, for example, is accomplished by respecting our principle of contextualizing, and shows what I believe is a productive mode of revision as reversal. The aim is the same: to transcend alienation and to create the plentitude of existence that Fromm (1994) called the "dealienated" state. The recontextualization of critical, transformational social analysis to religious discourse only works if culture is now seen non-reductively.

My allusion to Sorokin's (1957) theory of sociocultural change may be taken as an endorsement of idealism, unless it is understood as an application of Weber's historical sociology, where causal priorities shift along with configurational and contextual changes. Belief and value organize collective action and social mobilization, and that recognition is not a denial, but a specification of the contextual force of social production and social classes in historical social action. A new critical social psychology works from an expanded analytical lexicon, and with a more refined and contextualized understanding of the interplay between what is often referred to as social structure, culture, and subjectivity.

The reach to new age belief and practice as a reserve of critical social analysis and transformative action and beyond that, to elements of core religious traditions, is testimony not only to historical, sociocultural change, but of the effort to shape critical analytical strategies to match the force of hegemonic social regimes.

The causal, temporal sequencing of the relation between subjectivity and culture and social structure also changes historically. Weber's (1946) "transformation from within" gives analytical strength to the historical experience of new left and feminist politics of personal transformation as a significant part of a collective path of social transformation. This reversal, too, between the subjective and the structural, takes account of the evidence of social investment in new age strategies of personal transformation, in a variety of individuated, but widely shared, social practices for changing subjectivity. These practices aim to undo the apparent social stasis of postmodernity and to counter the "mechanical petrification" of new market corporatist self objectivization. Like religious theories against alienation and analyses of cultural change which try to go beyond a critique of capitalism to a broader, civilizational understanding of our current naturalized social and personal limitations, interest in new age forms of practical methods for enhancing subjective capacities are part of the continuing, but revised, project of a critical social psychology.

Beyond

I concluded *Critical Social Psychology* with this observation: "In this society, the desire for wholeness is considered a thought disorder, a symptom of madness. That is why the current irrationality can only be reversed by a mobilization and transformation of the whole."

In his essay on the structural replication of religious dualism in culture, Eliade alluded to the possibilities for resolving the persistent appearance of polarities or sociocultural dualisms which have their archaic origins in religious myth and ritual. He wrote (1969: 175):

> Finally, it is important to note that the mediation between the
> contraries also presents a great variety of solutions. In certain
> cases the conflict is resolved in a union which produces a 'third
> term," while in others the polarities seem to coexist
> paradoxically. . .Or they are transcended, i.e., radically abolished

or rendered unreal, incomprehensible, or meaningless. This variety of solutions to the problems raised by the mediation between the contraries. . merits a special investigation.

The earlier critical social psychology explored the dualisms of a corporate liberal capitalist structure. It was an attempt to describe how academic social psychology—as an institutionally differentiated but disseminating cultural sector—dealt with socially structured contradictions or dualisms. That solution was through displaced analytical strategies of cultural containment. What the continuing dissolution of corporate (and now postindustrial) liberalism, and its postmodern culture now raises for us are possibilities of new, holistic solutions to their contradictions.

I cannot say whether the practical aspects of such solutions, in various new age, particularly ecological, movements, can "return to the whole" in novel and humanly progressive ways, or will turn out to be still another disappointing turn in a long humanly destructive century.

What we do know, is that our abilities to explicate the collective-individual relation, to do a critical social psychology, are enhanced and expanded by the recent developments of sociocultural movement, and the analytical reversals and insights which they make possible. Still, the practical and analytical efficacy of these shifts depends on our ability to appropriate them for the imagination and actualization of our furthest hopes and dreams—for an integrated, holistic, personal, and social revolutionary redemption.

Philip Wexler
November, 1995
Newcastle, Australia

References

Bloom, H. 1982. *Agon: Towards a Theory of Revisionism.* New York, Oxford University Press.

Casey, C. 1995. *Work, Self and Society.* London and New York: Routledge.

Eliade, M. 2957. *The Sacred and the Profane: The Nature of Religion.* San Diego, New York, and London: Harcourt Brace.

Fromm, E. 1994. *The Art of Being.* New York: Continuum.

Harvey, D. 1989. *The Condition of Postmodernity.* Chicago: Blackwell.

Jung, C. G. 1976. *The Portable Jung.* Joseph Campbell, ed. New York and London: Penguin.

Lemert, C. 1995. *After the Crisis.* Boulder, CO: Westview.

Lukacs, G. 1971. *History and Class Consciousness: Studies in Marxist Dialectics.* Cambridge, MA: MIT Press.

Scholem, G. 1971. *The Messianic Idea in Judaism.* New York: Schocken Books.

Sorokin, P. 1957. *Social and Cultural Dynamics.* Boston: Porter Sargent.

Toulmin, S. 1990. *Cosmopolis: The Hidden Agenda of Modernity.* Chicago: University of Chicago Press.

Weber, M. 1946. *From Max Weber: Essays in Sociology.* New York: Oxford University Press.

Wexler, P. 1993/4. "Educational Corporatism and its Counterposes." *Arena Journal,* no. 2.

Wexler, P. L996, in press. *Resacralization: Social Theory, Religion and Education.* New York: St. Martin's Press.

1
Introduction

The current revitalization of social theory has had little effect on social psychology. One aim of this book is to reduce the continuing isolation of academic social psychology from the critical perspective that has developed in other social sciences. This intellectual insularity of social psychology has scarcely diminished in the decade since Serge Moscovici (1972, p. 63) wrote:

> Despite its technical achievements, social psychology has become an isolated and secondary science . . . the gap that has been created between our discipline and other social sciences . . . has led us into a situation of ignorant expertise. The questions we ask are most often very restricted; and if it happens that important problems are taken up, we manage to transform them again into minor questions.

A reassessment of social psychology is not simply a response to more general theoretical developments. Among academic social psychologists there is an uncertainty and pessimism about the future of social psychology. It is almost commonplace to acknowledge the existence of a crisis in social psychology. But social psychologists have not linked the theoretic crisis with a larger crisis.

The critique and reorientation (Larsen, 1980; Archibald, 1978; Gergen, 1973) of social psychology has grown primarily from an experienced loss of confidence among some professionals: they feel that theories of human interaction cannot effectively describe, explain or ameliorate the suffering of individuals in society. They also sense the growing discrepancy between the provincialism of social psychology and the recent renaissance of social theory.

The most important source of the crisis of social psychology, the wider social crisis, is least evident to critics. Current questioning of

1

social psychology occurs at a time of academic retrenchment and intellectual repression, world-wide economic crisis, and the unanticipated intensification of mass individual suffering in the capitalist nations. Contrasted with the preceding period of relative affluence, academic expansion and the development of dissent, the current suffering is experienced as especially intolerable and senseless. In such a period, sciences of human interaction, which intend to explain individual action and social environment, yet ignore the contemporary sociohistorical conditions, must seem inaccurate. The abstraction of human interaction from the concrete sociohistorical situation has been the central blindspot of social psychology; the critics, very often, manifest the same blindspot.

The critique presented here aims to break through the denial of the social which typifies social psychology. It is guided by the tradition of critical theory which examines scientific productions in their social context. The aim of such an analysis is not reductionist, but emancipatory. Social psychology should offer insight into experience that goes beyond formalizing commonsense understandings. It should provide the cognitive power to aid in the alleviation of collective suffering. Critical theory stresses that knowledge can contribute to emancipation and enlightenment – to critical, rational action, based on a self and social awareness.

But, critical theory also stresses that knowledge, including academic knowledge, can function to prevent the development of such an enabling awareness. It can reinforce aspects of social life that impede the development of human capacities. In the United States, in particular, academic social science now operates as part of what Marcuse (1968) called, in another context, the 'affirmative culture'. For though it demonstrates connections among abstracted representations of contemporary phenomena, it fails to explore deeper tendencies, already contained within the present, which, if not suppressed, could lead to the realization of an alternative and more humane future. Academic social science is a system of collective representations that makes us content with the present, portraying it as natural and inevitable. It systematically excludes consideration of structured incipient changes and disjunctions, and thus performs the role of affirmation and legitimation.

To locate such theory in social history and social context is to create a practice for extricating social psychology from its currently affirmative role. Science need not serve the cultural dynamic of suppression and societal maintenance. The social contextualization of knowledge offers

2

an explanation for the partialness and irrelevance of the prevailing social psychologies. Its aim is to describe how theories become incomplete and distorted representations of social and personal reality. By describing the distortions of theory through an analysis of its social role, a path toward the development of alternative explanations can be cleared.

PROGRAM FOR A CRITICAL SOCIAL PSYCHOLOGY

Critique of knowledge, conventional critique and critical foundations

In the first part of the book, I introduce the tradition of critical social theory as one approach which helps extricate us from the limiting and affirmative character of prevailing social psychologies. The critique of knowledge is a characteristic theoretical practice of critical theory. It aims to demystify the scientific naturalization of socially specific, historically situated, partial explanation (Held, 1980; Krueger and Silvert, 1975). The critique of knowledge is a basic kind of remembering, a reminder that theories are socially, historically and humanly constructed.

Critique of knowledge must be contrasted with the critiques that have arisen at the centre and at the margins of social psychology. The first, the conventional critique, which has received the most attention, is narrowly methodological. The second, the dissenting critique, displays a commitment to a radical alternative in social psychology, but lacks the theoretical base which could produce such an alternative. Knowledge critique displays the fashion by which social psychology affirms the present social order and blockades the future against a socially transformative social psychology. The problem is then to develop an alternative explanation, which is both true to the social present and which better enables us to change rather than affirm current social arrangements.

To move toward this goal, in the second part of the book I review exemplary alternative approaches to social psychology, which have arisen outside the conventional borders of the academic disciplines. They constitute the foundation of a critical approach to social psychology. The central concerns of these alternative viewpoints include precisely what is denied in popular affirmative culture, and whose denial is reinforced by the theoretical operations of conventional social psychology.

Denial of important social psychological processes is not the result of scientific dishonesty, or of bad faith. Systematic denial occurs

3

because social psychology remains within the limits of the dominant culture. Its denials parallel that which is denied in the wider culture. Resistance to the development and diffusion of alternative, critical social psychologies is not simply a matter of status entrenchment and academic competition. The logic behind the resistance is that the challenge of critical social psychologies is also a challenge to culturally patterned defenses, and to the silences upon which individual identities are built. Critical social psychologies represent both a theoretical alternative and an assault – on a culture and a psychology which sustain beliefs and selves necessary to the preservation of the social present. The alternative social psychologies are challenging and unsettling (when they are not discounted as 'unscientific') to those who have made their peace in social hopelessness.

An alternative social psychology

Conventional social psychology systematically denies the role of repression and its representation in the unconscious and the way in which constructed social meanings constitute the formation of individual identity and social interaction. But the most important and pervasive denial is the elimination of the structure of social relations from social psychological theory. The alternatives from outside social psychology address these problems, and an alternative social psychology should seek to overcome the omissions of the conventional discipline.

When social psychology includes the social, it does so in an abstract, general way. The relevance of historically specified social formations to social psychological understanding is ignored. The sociohistorical formation of capitalism is not seen as central to the definition and constitution of social psychological processes. Instead of treating the social as a general category, or as an added background variable, I try to show that what are usually abstracted as general social psychological processes are integral aspects of the specific dynamics of capitalism. In opposition to theories which dissolve social specificity in an abstracted 'society', or reify aspects of historically specific social relations or of limited social groups as universal social psychological processes, I argue that many of the questions of conventional academic social psychology can be subsumed as aspects of the production and reproduction of social relations.

This social production vantage point leads beyond theoretical

4

translation to a consideration of several neglected social psychological processes. For example, the apparently philosophical and polemical category of alienation entails a theory, not only of social structure, but of social interaction and self-processes. The traditional Marxist economic category of exploitation provides a basis for describing interactional processes ordinarily excluded in social psychology. The production of labor power, its continuous reproduction and differentiation in the social division of labor, replaces the vacuous concept of 'society' as a description of what is social about social psychology. A critical social psychology moves from these specific sorts of regulative concepts in contrast to the reified and sociohistorically abstracted operations of conventional social psychology.

This social production viewpoint is not a result of deductive theoretical imperialism. Explanation of human interrelation from within sociohistorical life, rather than explanation by sociohistorical denial or abstraction, is also the result of living within and struggling to change the concrete organization and experience of everyday life. Desire for alternative theory develops out of the experience of current limits on both understanding and action. When actions and thought that approach these limits of conventionality are not successfully suppressed, then experienced existence can provide the impetus for the generation of new meanings and theories.

Restoring social context: analysis

In the third part of the book, I return to concrete activities of everyday life. I describe experiences at the limits of conventionality, ordinary frustrations, ambivalencies and contradictions which require more adequate meanings. These disjunctions of everyday life are the unstable midpoint between denial, hopelessness and complacency, on the one hand, and a vision of a different form of life on the other. Observed and experienced suffering, constraint and ambivalence are the ultimate existential bases of the search for more satisfying explanations.

I focus on three categories used by ordinary people and social psychologists: interaction, self and intimacy. I then reinterpret each of them from the vantage point of a theory of social production. The categories are themselves central aspects of the culture of liberal capitalism. Rather than take them for granted, and simply translate them into scientific language, I try to show how they operate as symbolic expres-

5

sions of the social relations of capitalism. The aim is to go beyond the routinization of everyday understandings, to dissolve the categories, and to reveal the social processes out of which they are constructed.

The first category is social interaction. I describe how a specific type of exchange, an only apparent exchange of equivalents, has been falsely generalized as a model for all human interrelation. Rather than accept the imagery of fair exchange at face value, critical social psychology analyzes how unequal exchanges occur and how they are culturally hidden. Exchange as exploitation, rather than as social interaction, becomes the starting-point for analyzing processes of human interrelation. The second category, the self, functions as a symbolic reification of social processes. I reintegrate the self-processes as part of the social construction of labour-power, a more general social division of labor and socially patterned contradictions in the changing organization of social production.

The third general category is intimacy. Instead of viewing intimacy as an exceptional case of social interaction, I explore its cultural compartmentalization and how that maintains, rather than questions, the exchange view of social interaction. In examining the meaning of intimacy, I describe how its compartmentalized specialness operates as a necessary and illusory aspect of capitalist social relations. In opposition to theories which try to construct social psychological laws based on the correlations of individual attributes, critical social psychology explains the dynamics of interpersonal intimacy by placing both the category and its enactment in relation to the operation of the social whole.

The uses of theory

In the last chapter, I return to the social context of social psychological theories. Theory has administrative uses. Social psychology is used to contain the social actions and relations which threaten existing cultural categories, personal formations, and social arrangements. By rationalizing commonsense concepts and ordinary practices that are part of the reproduction of the current social formation, social psychology contributes in a general way to its cultural legitimation. It adds the prestige of science to the existing social structure and to the social relational processes that sustain it. By refusing to question the central premises of the categories that make sense of the present, by remaining inside conventional limits, social psychology is affirmative. It naturalizes and helps continue the operation of the prevailing social organisation.

There is, however, an alternative possibility for social psychology. It could articulate ways that the interpersonal processes which sustain the social structure can be transformed to react back upon the context in which they are produced. It could develop new interpersonal processes which would change the social order.

But conventional social psychology works for social control and containment. In its most blatant form, social psychology is used as an interpretive device that facilitates management. It provides a scientific rationale and methods that helps contain the subjective aspects of social relations within boundries which conform to needs of the re-production of alienated labor power. It serves this function, often without intention, in its theoretical constructions of sanity. The theory of sanity is the culture of the psychiatric administrative apparatus. It polices all violations of selfhood that interfere with the social division and constitution of labor. Whenever individual identity promises to expand or to reinterpret itself in ways that impede the social work of commodity production, the psychiatric apparatus may be brought in, as a social last resport, to keep recalcitrant subjectivity in place or out of sight.

The older model, the conservative model of sanity, is the medical model. The newer model, the liberal social psychological model, is insanity as labelled deviance. Popular prejudices are scientifically legitimated as deviance. The liberalizing, pluralistic possibilities of scientific interpretation are rerouted through social psychology. In contrast to the medical control apparatus, liberal social psychologies proffer the tyranny of popular prejudice as a democratic regulator. The social construction and labeling of deviance manages human relations by keeping dissent close to public opinion and away from the social totality in which the stigmatized borders of the social division of labor are maintained.

Social psychology also rationalizes and contains broader spheres of social interaction. It not only ultimately protects the subjectivity of alienated, hierarchial labor, but also constrains interaction that stands outside of production. Social psychological theories become widely diffused through popular translations as guide-to-living manuals, which have in part, replaced religious cultural prescriptions. Instruction in self and other management rationalizes and contains human interrelation within instrumentalized social interaction. The social psychology of interpersonal management is expressed in the manuals of one-upmanship. The ideology of relationship-as-exchange is systematized and then returned to everyday life through the filter of neutral-sounding psychologies. Similarly, wandering, contradictory subjectivity is kept on track by an ideology of proper selfhood and psychiatric policing. The false appearance of equivalent exchange that sustains generalized exploitation is covered by a notion of enlightened interpersonal management. Thought and action that cannot fit these molds is acknowledged as a breakage in socially necessary consensus. Interaction labeling theories of deviance simultaneously remove the medical veil from sin and reduce the causes of socially produced stigmatization to matters of public opinion and common culture. Through each path, social psychologies, abstracted from the process of the social production of stratified, alienated labor power, affirm and systematize existing modes of cultural defense and social control.

There are aspects of human relations which less directly threaten commodity production and cannot be easily subsumed either as interpersonal management or as deviance, but yet resist narrowly coded tracking and instrumentalization. These are consigned to peripheral, residual categories of private life as intimacy and sexuality. Social psychology helps block the potentially disruptive reconnection of the affective domain to the public world of work by accepting this cultural category. It makes sense of intimacy and sexuality by solidifying the categories as the products of combinations of individual characteristics rather than as severed aspects of the totality of social relations. By individualizing and socially partializing explanations, current work in academic social psychology recreates the socially affirmative role of the categories of social interaction, self and intimacy.

The first aim of critical social psychology is to show how the production of social psychology is related to the social context. The current role it plays in that context is legitimating the prevailing and, I believe, disabling tendencies in contemporary social life. The second aim of a critical social psychology is to assist in the rethinking of social life. The purpose of this rethinking is to go beyond a demonstration of how social psychology contributes to societal maintenance toward the development of an alternative theory. The aims of critique and alternative theory are part of a social project. Commitment to objective neutrality does not prevent social and cultural incorporation, as I have suggested in discussing conventional social psychology. On the contrary, intellectual autonomy requires social vision and practical means for its actualization. A social psychology that is not affirmative offers the promise of a change-oriented counter theory and a counter practice.

Part One
Critique

2
The internal critique of social psychology

Social psychology has been the boom area of psychology in the twentieth century. In the 1920s, only a handful of books in the area existed — notably those of Freud (1924) and McDougall (1908). But by the 1970s, social and personality psychology was the largest specialty of affiliation of the American Psychological Association — one-quarter of academic psychologists are social psychologists.

Despite the boom, an internal critique of social psychology arose in the 1970s. One should really speak of two critiques, one from the center and one from the periphery. The former, the conventional critique, is mounted by prestigious researchers in social psychology and limits itself to methodological and conceptual repair (e.g., McGuire, 1973; Harré and Secord, 1972; Gergen, 1973). The latter, the dissenting critique, aims at a radical transformation of social psychology (e.g., Archibald, 1978; Armistead, 1974; Larsen, 1980). Both critiques fall short. I sketch each here and indicate the reasons for their failure. I'll begin with a brief discussion of my orienting point of view, which anticipates the extended discussion of knowledge critique in the next chapter.

Point of view

The most remarkable aspect of social psychologists' analyses of their self-proclaimed professional paradigmatic crisis is how asocial they are. Social and cultural analysts, on the other hand, are habituated to monolithic structural analyses of the class character of academic paradigms, to the direct correspondence between hidden social interest and false universalizing concepts and theories. My view is that scientific cultures can play both historically progressive and reactionary roles, and more importantly, that the relation between an academic paradigm, a broader culture and social structure is itself historically variable.

Social psychologists tend to offer methodological pluralism (Rosnow, 1981) as an antidote to a socially rooted problem. Social analysts provide either general cultural parallelisms between academic and popular culture, or institutional network analyses of the infra-structure of knowledge-production. But, the historical development of American social psychology especially suggests an historically specific and changing social function of social psychology.

In its earliest phase, social psychology was part of the emerging social sciences. In the language of scientized Pragmatism and later Progressivism, social psychology was an expansive and creative cultural expression, heralding the possibilities of the emergent corporate liberal social order. It was during this period that general social psychological theories, particularly of the social character of the self, were developed (Karpf, 1932). With the establishment of corporate liberal capitalist social forms in the United States, social psychology became more routinized, delimited, and directly utilized as a technical force of military and industrial production (Cina, 1981; Franks, 1975).

Social psychology still plays both of these social roles. It remains part of the general legitimation of the liberal cultural hegemony and serves also as a technical force of military and industrial production. It now plays an additional social role, a role which develops with the changing crisis character of corporate liberal capitalism, and the more recent instability of its liberal hegemonic culture. The new role of social psychology is the rationalization and justification, by the im-primatur of institutional sciences, of popular methods of containment. Ideology is no simple representation of the interest of the ruling class. Rather, ruling class effectiveness depends on the constructive rather than reflective character of ideology. During a period of fiscal, social and cultural crisis, ideology is the successful occlusion, the cultural blockage from view and understanding of the social structural tendencies and contradictions which are the identifiable source of personal conflict and suffering. Among the ideological methods of denying social contradictions, one of the most important is the con-struction of everyday methods to avoid facing what people believe they cannot change.

Social psychology increasingly serves to shore up these methods of social denial. It is not a high culture of intellectual creations, not a practical culture of immediate technical production. It is a diffuse

14

culture of ideological containment. It is the reinforcing scientized restatement of commonsense methods of systematic social ignorance and denial. Academic social psychology disclaims any connection to commonsense culture by its own continuous denial of biases, institutional separation, and the self-advertisement of its cognitive products as a type of knowledge more privileged and valuable than mere common sense.

The ironies of social psychology are: it really is common sense (abstracted, recoded, fragmented historically and class specific common sense); it now increasingly functions as an occluding strategy, a weapon of social ignorance, a defense against the potential popular grasping of the relation between everyday individual life and collective social organization — it blocks the development of a critical social psychology; and finally, despite its insistence on participating only in the discourse of the eighteenth century, it becomes so transparently ideological, so distorted and insularizing a representation of social life, so rhetorical in its mode of argumentation, that it calls forth ideology-critiques as the only suitable intellectual response.

This view — that social psychology subverts both science and social psychology — is hardly a popular one among social psychologists. For while they hold the academic positions and access to the means of communication, they cannot help but believe their own mystifications. They must deny that their own work is a contribution to social ignorance and illiteracy. But, in the brief moment of honest intelligence, some social psychologists glimpse the reasons for a tension produced by the task of intellectually containing the social contradictions of a dissolving, conflict-ridden, historically transient hegemony of corporate liberalism and its cultural defenders. Even among the rearguard of social psychologists, some desert, equivocate, compromise, or flee behind the currently emergent ideologies of the new right. Those who try to hold the liberal center launch the criticism of social psychology from within.

The conventional critique

Social psychologists are trying to undo in thought the demands of their cultural task. That current task is to commoditize and legitimate social ignorance as science. The commodification of social ignorance entails naturalizing and universalizing what is socially and historically specific. It includes the reification of dynamic social relations either as individual attributes or as fixed role requirements. It means separating intra-individual processes from collective social tendencies and, above all, it means finding ways to empty the particular character of social life into an abstracted and homogeneous, static concept of the social as society.

At the same time that social psychology joins advertising and mass-media entertainment in the cultural work of social ignorance production, social psychologists true to the ideals of truth and science increasingly recognize the distortions and limitations of their academic work. Caught in the contradiction between the ideological and truth-oriented demands of their professional roles, the most courageous social psychologists have sought a way out by an internal professional critique and reform of social psychology. Their self-criticisms range from procedural changes in research methods, to the use of more social concepts, the study of more relevant social issues, the commitment to values as an explicit part of research and even to allowing the historical relativity of theory and research in the field. Each of these critiques penetrates in thought one deeper aspect of the cultural package of mystification. To reform social psychology, but not to abandon it, is a possibility only from a vantage point which itself remains ignorant of the cultural task of social psychology. The calls for reform vary. Each internal critique sets up a false dichotomy, a bifurcation which substitutes for the deeper and less easily resolvable dichotomy of contemporary social psychology: cultural mystification and scientific truth. The crisis in social psychology is itself the expression of an effort to contain this more fundamental contradiction within social psychology.

What do the reform critics call for in their internal critique of social psychology? Most popular is procedural reform, the diversification of research methods, and the reduction of reliance on laboratory experiments. In a typical example, Rosnow (1981) writes:

> The time is ripe to *liberate* [emphasis added] social psychology
> from the mind-set of an outmoded or exaggerated paradigm and
> reduce our dependence on the quick-fix of using synchronic
> methods to try to answer all questions at every level of human
> activity . . . it must begin to pursue a methodological and
> theoretical pluralism.

An even more sweeping methodological indictment of social psychological research argues that it uses not simply too few techniques, or

16

neglects social change, but that it is modeled on an erroneous and outmoded form of thought. Against linear positivism, it is asserted that social psychology needs to become more dialectical. According to Leon Rappaport (1977, p. 679), 'it must be a social psychology grounded upon dialectical rather than positivistic principles.' The pluralists and dialecticians both separate the question of method from the substantive content of social psychological theory, to say nothing of its cultural history and current uses. The pluralists want to adopt more conventional methods of social science, like field studies, surveys and abstracted quantitative longitudinal macrostructural analysis. The dialecticians abstract dialectics as a logic from any social materialist dialectics which does indeed include a theory of social relations and social change. The substantive contradiction within the activity of social psychologist — between occluding the social and commitment to explanatory social psychology — is avoided by accepting instrumental procedure rather than content as the source of the current irrationality and dissatisfaction within the discipline.

A second mode of cognitive reform within social psychology is the assertion about content: accentuate the social. Ivan Steiner (1974, pp. 94, 98) wrote, in an observation recalling my earlier hypothesis, about the historically shifting social function of the theoretic culture of social psychology:

> By the late 1950s, social psychology had turned inward. It had
> largely renounced its concern for larger social systems, and had
> centered its attention on internal states and processes; dissonance,
> attributions. Whatever happened to the group, and why? . . .By
> the 1960s, social psychology had become much more individualistic.

The 'social' which is ordinarily called for has two typical characteristics. First, it is the most static aspect of traditional sociological functionalism, in which social roles, as a moment in an alienated division of social labor, are posited as the most fundamental units of a social analysis. Second, the social as opposed to the individual is considered solely a question of norms and values. This characteristic interpretation of the social includes a view that social psychologists should study norms and values. But, it also refers to the 'value-relevance, committed view of the job,' as Ingleby (1974) wrote of social psychologists. Among radical critics of social psychology such as Resler and Walton (1974, pp. 261, 292), it is argued:

17

> The reconstruction of social psychology thus requires as a pre-
> condition the thorough examination of all the norms and values of
> the society in which we live . . . . The difficulties of radical
> psychological work should be apparent. Every challenge to every
> norm, every questioning of every value.

Sometimes, the assertion of the importance of the social is something other than a stereotypical return of an absent term, whose
absence is in no way repaired by the empty mode of its reinsertion.
Then, however, the 'socialing' of social psychology precludes a social
analysis by dichotomizing the category of social. For example, it is
argued that the social means more small groups studies, or even 'larger
social systems.' This injunction precisely ignores the interrelation of
aspects of the social, the analysis of social mediations and interconnections, as the social is bifurcated into the macro and the micro level.
  Similarly, the divide and conquer method of cultural hegemony
proceeds by posing dichotomies which both drop out the central
content as well as interconnections of aspects of the social. It occurs by
abstracting values and norms from behavior and from organized,
patterned, socio-economic relations and privileging them both causally
and morally. Even the most sophisticated and political of the internal
professional critics of social psychology, such as Moscovici, argue for
the priority of abstracted ideational elements of the social (1972,
p. 55): 'The central and exclusive object of social psychology should be
the study of all that pertains to ideology and communications from the
point of view of their structure, their genesis and their function.'
  Values and ideology are detached from social life and become the
social aspect of social psychology. The less analytic implications of the
value-behavioral or ideology-social structure dichotomies are the
appeals to reform social psychology through value commitment. A
recent critic of social psychology (Larsen, 1980, pp. 162-3) proclaims,
against the evidence of practical activity (in so doing, revealing the
critics' efforts to resolve the social contradiction of social psychology
solely in the realm of thought): 'An examination of the contemporary
state of social psychology suggests that the positivistic model has
thoroughly failed . . . psychology must move beyond the sterile
concepts of positivism, and incorporate a normative perspective.'
The emphasis on norms and values returns to the ideological commitment to individualism, to an asocial conception to which the liberal
cultural of social psychology contributes. The importance of a normative

18

psychology, in the service of humanistic values, is to restore, Larsen writes, 'the conscious role of the individual.' The social is a detoured return to individual choice.

The denial of the social is most effectively accomplished by the most well-known of the internal critiques, Gergen's 'Social psychology as history.' Gergen wants to replace the false universalization of social psychological concepts with an understanding of their historical specificity and social effects. He writes that (1973, pp. 315, 316):

> the observed regularities, and thus the major theoretical
> principles are firmly wedded to historical circumstances . . .
> the continued attempt to build general laws of social behavior
> seems misdirected. . . . In essence the study of social psychology is
> primarily an historical undertaking.

But Gergen's historicizing of social psychology means, not the study of historically patterned, changing social structures, but an emphasis on cultural and value changes. The abandonment of social psychology, or at least the claim to greater modesty, occurs at the cost of accepting the value-culture abstraction of social relations, and by accepting history as a realistic alternative to experimentalism and static social structuralism — but a history without discernible pattern. In the name of an historical view, both social structure, patterned social relations and historical patterns, conflicts and movements are displaced by a history-as-values-culture, flowing on beyond the grasp of intelligible theory. History is forced to join individualism as anarchic counterpoint to a very brief flirtation with a potentially serious treatment of the social aspect of social psychology.

The internal critical reformers of social psychology have neither added an alternative theory, nor recognized the specific social sources and historical contradictions of their work which are experienced as identity-tensions and intellectual dilemmas. The methodological critique remains within the bounds of social scientific instrumental pluralism or, when it challenges positivist science, ends up in a dialectic of contentless forms, and a preoccupation with the grounds of knowing. The attempt to include the social leads either to an acceptance of the reification of social activity in the concept of role and the static functionalism which is its persistent back-drop, or eventuates in the abstracted glorification of cultural values as synonomous with social. A values position discourages a structural or organizational analysis of the crisis in social psychology, and instead winds up as a series of exhortations to individual morality and free choice. Even becoming aware of the cultural bases and consequences of academic knowledge, and the historical specificity of psychological concerns, is accomplished at the cost of surrendering the project of developing a social psychological theory.

The dissenting critique

Outside, and at the margins of the academy, social psychologists have not served as the organic intellectuals of the dominant class. There is a tradition of dissent in social psychology (much of which lies outside traditional disciplinary boundaries and which will be reviewed in chapter 5), one which has been rediscovered as the persuasiveness of the ideology of liberal social psychology has faltered. Both the earlier and current dissenting social psychologists differ from the so-called mainstream not only in their social locations, but also in their understanding of the social meaning of their work, and of their own relation to it. Theory and research in social psychology is, for the dissenting social psychologists, a conscious part of a larger project and, often too, of a social practice. The dissenters have differed among themselves about: how closely connected theory is to social tendencies, the theoretical categories best able to capture historical social psychological realities, and the social role of the social psychologist. Dissenting social psychologists are not a homogeneous group. But, they have agreed on a awareness of the existence of a social totality, a patterned social structure, and about the oppressiveness and suffering caused by particular kinds of social organization. They have not been affirmers of the *status quo*, but social critics. For them, the understanding of the dynamics of individual life in relation to sociohistorical structures is a moment in a much larger project: human emancipation through conscious, theoretically informed, social transformation.

During the past several years, three major books have explicitly offered themselves as alternative social psychologies. Yet, each of them moves within the orbit of the internal critiques, while stretching by appeals to personal authenticity and Marxist theory, toward an alternative.

Armistead's critique

The earliest, Armistead's (1974) reader, describes the 'alienation' of the professional social psychologist. One reads it as a first step out from the liberal center of social psychology in Britain. One finds: the sense of the disconnection between the academic experiments and the real life needs and experience of the professional; the awareness of the irrelevance of conventional knowledge in the field, and the articulation of some reasons for that socially useful irrelevance – the ideology of psychology (Sedgwick, 1974, pp. 29-36); the insistence on the importance of values, and bringing one's own moral concerns to bear in social psychological work; the suspicion of positivist methodology and the application of symbolic interactionist and ethnomethodological approaches for challenging the official categories of meaning. Experiential relevance, values, morals and interpretation are the main elements of the first way out of the mainstream. While a number of the essays are described as 'Marxist-influenced' (the editor reminds the reader that 'Marxism has never had much of a social psychology') the most explicitly social, to say nothing of Marxist, essay indicates what a Marxist social psychology might mean (p. 289):

> In our period the contours of advanced societies are determined by
> their relationship to the world market – a capitalist market. Thus,
> a social psychology which ignores these relationships and their
> impact on the psyche of the individual cannot be regarded as
> social . . .[p. 291] It must therefore be critical of present bourgeois
> society, for many of the so-called psychological problems here are
> problems whose sources are structural and political.

In this, the best, I think, as well as the earliest of the recent dissenting social psychologies, the main effort is to establish the bourgeois ideological character of social psychology and to promote phenomenological, interpretive research – while Marxism is asserted as a background ideology. Even in its Marxist-structuralist aspects, the book seems an attempt at de-reification of social psychology, of asserting that social psychology is about real people living in a real society, about which these contributors care. But for all its good intentions, the anthology does not offer a critical theory of social psychology, or an analysis of the social conditions which limit (there are few hints in Ingleby) or make possible such a critical theory. In this sense, the book is valuable as the offering of a counter ideology to market, reified liberalism – it reasserts the liberal culture of humanist concern against a commodified and uncaring profession and its alienating cognitive products.

Critique

Archibald's critique

Archibald's (1978) *Social Psychology as Political Economy* quickly dispenses with the individualistic and voluntaristic ideology of contemporary academic social psychology. His positive alternative is for social psychologists to understand the existence of social structure, institutions and the operation of coercion in society. Individualistic-voluntarist assumptions are replaced by the recognition of the effects of inequity and the existence of 'coercive interaction.' While Archibald's review of research on exchange, cooperation and competition and description of socially patterned inequalities may be helpful to a social psychologist — and certainly provides an alternative to the standard text — his injunction to 'slay capitalism' does not contribute to the development of a critical *theory* of social psychology. Social psychology is returned to the concepts of mainstream sociology, and an appeal to end inequality and alienation.

Larsen's critique

The most recent of the counter social psychologies, Larsen's edited *Social Psychology: Crisis or Failure*, provides several staples of the crisis in the social psychology market: critiques of specific areas of research in conventional social psychology; metatheoretical epistemological critiques; and a final appeal for a more caring, humanistic social psychology based on a commitment to freedom and human development (1980, p. 162).

Each of these books is a contribution to the development of a critical social psychology. But, they share an abstracted enshrinement of procedure, intention and critique as principles; they lose the sense of the historical, collective and personal character of domination and the struggle to survive against it which is the existential basis of the conceptual critique at its firsthand most authentic best. The critiques bifurcate experience and critical principles cum moral encomiums, and leave out the reflexive theorizing of both personal suffering and collective oppression. Like the mainstream from whom they are trying to distance themselves, they empty social psychology of historically specific social content. In doing so, they discard the substantive general theory which is produced from specific content and which returns towards the social as a material transformative practice. The modern dissenters,, de-historicize, de-personalize, and what is especially relevant here, de-theorize both the critique and the construction of an alternative

22

social psychological understanding. Unlike their predecessors in critical social psychology (see chapter 5), they seem detached from any awareness of the contradictory character of social existence and the active place of social psychology as both a theoretical and a social practice. Resistance to ideological containment occurs through the development of theory and through practice.

I want to suggest two alternatives. First, a critique of social psychology which goes beyond asserting its cultural isomorphism, to an analysis of how cultural domination works, what the character of social science has been historically, what the modes of critique of knowledge might be and their application to a critique of social psychology. Second, an analysis which takes seriously, which does not deny the social production of daily life under the cover of values: a critique and an alternative.

To carry out these analyses, it is necessary, first to consider the tradition of knowledge-critique; and, second, to review some of the earlier work, from other disciplines, which constitutes the foundation of a critical social psychology.

3
Knowledge critique:
a general approach

To drive further the critique of social psychology, we must relate social psychology to its social context. The Frankfurt School theorists have been among the most important elaborators of ideology critique, and I begin by describing their treatment of the relations of knowledge and society and the nature of adequate critique. I then examine the fashion in which knowledge critique has been applied to the other social sciences in the past decade of developing social crisis. In the next chapter, I will apply knowledge critique to social psychology.

Critique of knowledge in the Frankfurt School tradition

Theory is a part of a wider culture. The relation between institutionally produced theory and the wider culture is continuously obscured by theorists' insistence on their own cultural autonomy. On the other hand, the relationship between theory and culture is not one of auto-matic homologous correspondence. Academic theories are not always simple representations of cultural beliefs and values. Nor is the mysti-fying oppressiveness of culture – its ideological aspect, the generalization of the particular view and interests of the ruling class as universal – always representational. The way that ideology works is to obscure scientific knowledge changes, along with the historical ascendance, descent and relations of ruling and subordinate classes. The conceptual character of the work performed by the intellectuals organic to that class also changes historically. In our times, what we increasingly observe is that the ideological function of culture requires more than the simple generalization of stock ideas as truth. Ideology now works harder and becomes a constructed solution to social contradictions which threaten to make themselves thoroughly and irrefutably obvious and transparent.

The theoretic culture then does not only generalize extant belief, but rethinks, reorganizes, selects and streamlines from among everyday solutions the most plausible and rational methods of blocking awareness of the fractured and irreconcilable character of social life. Ideological work of this kind calls for increased responsibility of the organic intellectuals of the decadent class — not the least of which is to deny that their work has anything to so with the cultural task of producing and maintaining a specific set of social and organizational conditions (which in turn make it possible to do the very work which they assert is socially detached).

A few social psychologists, like Kenneth Gergen, for example, move toward acknowledging a place for theoretic culture within a wider cultural system. But even for him, culture remains largely socially deracinated, rather than a fundamental aspect of the social apparatus used in constructing methods for the production of knowledge and ignorance. The majority of social psychologists accept the foregrounding ideology of the work of pruning and purifying everyday strategies of contradiction-containment: the claim that science has little to do with the wider culture and that whatever it may have to do with the society in which it is produced has no bearing on the content and meaning of its conceptual products. Against such a traditional view of detached social knowledge, the Frankfurt School argued for a critical, social understanding of theory in and against culture and society.

The work of the Frankfurt School suggests both a general and specific analysis of methods or modes by which culture operates within a structure of domination. Their descriptions of the ways that cultural domination works clarifies, I think, the particular social role of contemporary social psychology. It is this social role and not the recalcitrance of technical procedures or the lack of forgotten concepts, which makes a totally conceptual solution an unlikely resolution of the current crisis in social psychology. A first step out of the crisis is through the understanding and overcoming of cultural domination.

Reification and domination

First, the general perspective. By assigning academic theoretic knowledge a place above and beyond social relations, traditional theory recapitulates the affirmative and alienating cultural role of religion. It becomes a congealed object, a frozen authority glossing over the human

25

labor, imagination and hope contained in the history of its production. The sad irony of the reifying neutralization of knowledge is the extent to which the power of knowledge as an expression and means of human realization becomes another fetishized thing, an addition to a simultaneously de-naturalized and de-socialized environment. Knowledge use becomes another site for alienated labor. The aim of critique is to redeem creative history and human vision from the reified forms produced in alienated social relations. The failure to realize historic human hopes is not simply, as critical social psychologists like Archibald believe (1978, p. 12), the result of coercion by the powerful. Social emancipation is inhibited by the internalized self-restraint and self-deformation of the powerless and the oppressed.

Domination is self-limitation and it is in the accomplishment of this voluntary servitude that the operation of culture is important. For example, as high culture (or as high professional science), cultural forms encapsulate experienced frustration and transform the desire to change the world into a sublimated, high status enclave called 'culture.' This high culture works to sublimate dissatisfaction and imagined alternatives within a privileged but compartmentalized realm above and beyond everyday life. Thought is separated from action and the capacity to articulate dissatisfaction with the social *status quo* is transformed into a realm which is abstracted, socially detached and not immediately threatening — the domain of truth, beauty, goodness, of high culture.

Cultural domination also works by routinizing and making thoroughly mundane as well as by isolating, elevating and sublimating the cultural potential for social criticism. In a culture of instrumentalization, all questions are recoded as questions of means, adaptation, procedure and technique. The capacity to ask 'what for', to imagine ends and goals rather than calculate means, is diminished. Horkheimer, Adorno, Marcuse, and, to a lesser extent, Habermas have described these cultural processes of domination as: sublimation, instrumental routinization, repetitive repression and the separation of critical thought from action.

Modes of cultural domination

For Marcuse, cultural domination occurs through sublimation. Bourgeois culture displaces unmet needs and unrealized desires into a transcendent 'culture.' 'By affirmative culture,' writes Marcuse (1968, p. 68), is meant:

26

That culture of the bourgeois epoch which led in the course of its own development to the segregation from civilization of the mental and spiritual world as an independent realm of value that is also considered superior to civilization.

Art, philosophy and morality 'surrender the earth to bourgeois society and make its ideas unreal by finding satisfaction in heaven and the soul.' The possibility of socially produced suffering reacting upon the social-material world is short-circuited and frozen in the abstract idealization of the high culture. They function to affirm what exists by making these wordly concrete deprivations into abstract, cultural ideals. Affirmative culture pacifies desires. The affirmative, compartmentalizing culture is not, however, totally suppressive. For it preserves, even if only as ideals, hopes and visions which may become the basis for critical thought and transformative social action.

The forms of cultural expression and domination change historically. As the marketplace of individuals is replaced by a bureaucratized administrative apparatus, high culture is increasingly accompanied by the diffusion and power of mass culture. Mass culture does not produce cultural domination by transcendence, compartmentalization and sublimation of social, individually felt deprivation. Instead, it works by a repetitive deadening of the individual, through eradication of difference and by the recycling of the hope for something different into the sameness of its hopeless and routinizing message. Mass culture, the deceptive final phase of Enlightenment culture, according to Horkheimer and Adorno (1972), does not promise transcendant spirituality, but entertainment and amusement.

But, it is a false promise. The internal structure and thematic content of this culture become the media of deceptive difference. In the guise of entertainment, fun and freedom, the commodity form of everyday social relations, the deep hopelessness of real individual powerlessness and the impossibility of transformation of the conditions of existence appear as the real, constant and deeper message of mass culture. Its familiar, but unadvertised deeper form is the narrative of limited individual choice, the passive consumption of differences which have been leveled into standardized and buyable products. The hope for something different is displaced into the commodity rather than sublimated in spirituality and abstraction. Mass culture teaches alienated division of labor, powerlessness of employees and commodification of the human interrelations of social production, as the real true story beneath the romance of entertainment, escape and individual happiness. This culture dominates not by separation but by assimilation, repression, denial and resale of its social forms as cultural escapes. The enduring message of the culture industry is repetition, imitation, timelessness, standardization and interchangeability of parts. It is the cultural expression of the administered whole which it represents.

If the form of mass culture is the hidden return of a social form of labor power, from which it promises relief, then its thematic message is social stability. It tells the story of aroused desire which must be denied, of the 'rhythm of the iron system', of the 'immutability of circumstance' and the futility of resistance. In a society of employees and customers, advertising becomes the typical cultural form: imitation, incantation, sameness. Differences are diminished and stigmatized, while the individual is reminded of the commodity-character of his/her individuality. As Horkheimer and Adorno wrote (1972, pp. 150, 153, 167):

> Anyone who goes cold and hungry, even if his prospects were once good, is branded. He is an outsider; and apart from certain capital crimes, the most mortal of sins is to be an outsider. . . . Life in the late capitalist era is a constant initiation rite. Everyone must show that he wholly identifies himself with the power which is belaboring him.
>
> The most intimate reactions of human beings have been so thoroughly reified that the idea of anything specific to themselves now persists only as an abstract notion: personality scarcely signifies anything more than shining white teeth and freedom from body odor and emotions.

For the Frankfurt School, each promise of freedom is turned back, through the operation of culture, to another element in social domination. The transcendent spirituality of bourgeois high culture offers a momentary glimpse of freedom only to prevent its actual, practical realization. The democratization of culture occurs only as part of the mass production of the culture industry. The freedom of not laboring, which entertainment signifies, becomes an occasion to reinforce the structure of the commodity world. Finally, science and technology also function as sites of cultural domination.

Horkheimer, Adorno and Marcuse all describe the instrumentalization of reason — the triumph of technique over substance, of adaptive over reflexive thought, of means over ends. Habermas attempts to

account for the reduction of substantive critical thinking to instrumental thought, and for the role which science and technology have
come to play in the process of cultural domination. Where once science
questioned the dogma of traditional authority, it now functions as a
meaning system that obviates any questions that go beyond instrumental adaptation. In a state-managed capitalism, according to
Habermas (1970), both politics and science are absorbed into administration. Science is incorporated within military and industrial
production and ceases to offer a detached vantage-point from which to
evaluate the rationality of social production. In Habermas's language,
an institutional, normative framework which is directed toward
practical activity and interaction, is absorbed within the production-
apparatus. Science functions both as production resource and background ideology. The way that science and technology serve cultural
domination is to rule out of court questions about ends, and views of
knowledge as reflexive and emancipatory. Cultural domination operates
by constricting the definition of the possible. The possibility of critical
evaluative thought is denied by the 'technocratic consciousness' (p.
105):

> It is a singular achievement of this ideology to detach society's
> self-understanding from the frame of reference of communicative
> action and from the concepts of symbolic interaction and replace
> it with a scientific model. Accordingly, the culturally defined self-
> understanding of a social life world is replaced by the self-reification
> of men under categories of purposive-rational and adaptive behavior.

In each of these modes of cultural domination, collective self-
understanding, social knowledge and their potential use for social and
self-realization are suppressed. High culture turns away from the truth
of everyday this-wordly suffering. Mass culture subverts the search for
alternatives into the redundant messages of the administered corporate
world. Technocratic consciousness, as scientific technology, becomes
the judge of social rationality and promptly rules as irrational second-
class knowledge all that is not immediate or evidently means-oriented.
This technocratic consciousness stigmatizes — with its historical
parvenu power of legitimation — as unscientific and therefore inadmis-
sible, value-laden and ideological all discourse that is socially critical.
Ideology as social denial and the production of ignorance are accomplished through these largely unintended cultural defenses.

These general patterns of ideology are recapitulated within each

29

domain of culture. High culture, mass culture and scientific culture all now include as constitutive ideological processes: compartmentalizing sublimation, repetitive repression and silent denial. If social psychology now functions as a legitimating, selective reprocessor and packager of the methods of cultural contradiction containment, it does so through exactly such patterned and identifiable modes of constructed cultural domination. The less effective each method of social ignorance, the greater the appeal of the ideological professional practitioners to the superordinating ideologies, like science and professionalism. The specific critique of social psychology as a series of ideological processes, can itself be contained by appeal to such superordinate legitimations. The demonstration of the transparency of social psychology as increasingly ideological is now possible because these superordinate ideological legitimations are themselves under question and that questioning is part of the wider crisis of liberal culture − and the social infrastructure which sustains it. Social psychology is not merely a cultural domain. It is also a part of a larger social formation.

Knowledge critique, social science, and corporate liberalism

Despite the intensity and pervasiveness of the discussions and analyses of the 'crisis in social psychology,' critical analysis of social psychology remains detached even from recent critical analyses of the other social sciences. There is a continuing, though sometimes thin and lonely, tradition of interpreting social science culturally and in relation to social structure. The cultural analyses generally suggest a parallelism between wider cultural trends and the changing content of paradigms in social science. Gouldner (1970, p. 139), for example, describes Parsonian structural functionalism as the theoretical reflection of an historical cultural conflict:

> Parsons' combination of functionalism and voluntarism was a reflection within the idiom of technical social theory, of the continuing conflict in bourgeois culture between utility and morality or natural rights, and it was an effort to confront and resolve this cultural conflict on the theoretical level.
> In the 1930s, the economic system had broken down. It could no longer produce the massive daily gratifications that helped to hold middle-class society together and foster commitment to its values. If the society was to be held together and its cultural patterns

maintained – as Parsons clearly wished – one was constrained to look for *non*-economic sources of social integration. In the time-worn manner of the conservative, Parsons looked to individual moral commitment to cement society (p. 141).

Schwendinger and Schwendinger (1974, p. 3) echo the view that the concepts of social science have reflected the culture. In their view, American social science has generally reflected the culture of corporate liberalism:

> And perhaps more profoundly, the outstanding intellectual contribution of academic sociologists has been the further development and refinement of corporate liberalism. The major trends in American sociology, therefore, will be regarded as *one aspect* of the complex social processes generating and regenerating liberalism. Many of the very basic categories and analytic strategies produced by American sociologists have emerged as an inherent part of the liberal ideology.

The cultural critique of social science is, however, a generally recent development. A critical social theory – one which links the development of knowledge to social structure and critically analyzes the social meaning of such relations – has never really been very popular in the United States. Where theories of the social whole have developed, they have emphasized social evolution or social integration rather than social domination – to say nothing of including academic social science as a moment of the process of domination. Veblen (1918) stood virtually alone until the mid-twentieth century in analyzing the role of culture in the process of social hierarchization and domination, and the inclusion of institutional knowledge production in the social relations of a business society. Mills's (1943) analysis of the contextually determined limitations and distortions of American social science was an exception to a surprising lack of sociological self-criticism among social scientists.

After the Second World War, the earlier tendency to justify social detachment became more deeply rooted under the banner of value-neutrality. Even a socially tamed reinterpretation of the critique of knowledge as the purely intellectualized academic sociology of knowledge gained few adherents. During the 1950s, Merton (1957) attempted to explain this lack of interest. He argued that the sociology of knowledge was 'European,' while the American interest more democratically favored the study of public opinion and mass communication as the central analytic issue of the relation between belief and social context.

The challenge to an apparently neutral, well-supported and institutionally respectable social science does not come from within the pragmatic liberal social sciences. The crisis of sociology developed during the 1960s as part of the much wider cultural crisis of the liberal society. The Southeast Asian War, the Black movement, and the immediate frustrations of students with bureaucratic academic supermarkets (Altbach *et al.*, 1971) fused to form a significant cultural opposition. It was the activists' challenge to the social organization of the university and its claim to neutral, socially disinterested knowledge that first called into question claims of the prosperous social sciences (Ridgeway, 1968; Smith, 1974; Wexler, 1976). During such a time, Mannheim's description of the social origins of the critique of knowledge is accurate. A knowledge crisis, even for Mannheim, is not a matter of a failure to develop methodological pluralism, or attend to individual values and choice. The critique of knowledge begins during a social crisis (1936, p. 64):

> Only in a world in upheaval, in which fundamental new values
> are being created and old ones destroyed, can intellectual conflict
> go so far that antagonists will seek to annihilate not merely the
> specific beliefs and attitudes of one another, but also the intellectual
> foundation upon which these beliefs and attitudes rest.

The social crises of the 1960s were followed by a variety of sociological works on social science as ideology (Blackburn, 1973). But, the critique of knowledge went beyond the demonstration of cognitive and conceptual parallels and reflections between the wider culture and social science. It included also sociohistorical studies of the development of social science. From these studies (Eakins, 1966; McVey, 1975; Silva and Slaughter, 1981) emerged a detailed description of how the rise and the success of the academic social sciences was financially, organizationally, and personally integrated with a transition in the composition and mode of class rule. Social meliorism became the conscious, self-interest program of the emergent corporate leaders, who joined forces with conservative labor leaders, altruistic social reformers and significantly, the newly formed social science associations. Silva and Slaughter document the thesis that the professionalized social science of the German trained new PhDs, who replaced the old guard upper-class New England reformers as the arbiters of social science knowledge, were supported by and, in turn, lent intellectual expertise to the goals and interests of the new corporate leaders. Through interlocking networks of the groups which Silva and Slaughter identify as: 'political economic resource holders, university managers and leaders in the emerging professional associations of the new social sciences,' during the Progressive era (1865-1910), social knowledge was produced, if not always directly to order, than at least to aid the cultural legitimating and more circumscribed technical production tasks of the new corporate liberalism. They describe the new American Economic Association (1981, chapter 5, p. 2):

> As economists were more routinely called to expert service and initiated in the politics of power, they refined their notion of constituency. Although using the rhetoric of objective science and the public welfare, their clientele was the Progressive wing of corporate capital and other professionals . . . . Claiming to be impartial and scientific arbiters of social questions, they used the ideology of expertise in the interests of social control and developed pragmatic, technical mechanisms to consolidate and finance control – colonial fiscal policy, federal industrial relations commissions, the income tax. Thus, social science experts became advocates for the existing order, hegemonic intellectuals serving the emerging, national corporate elite.

Describing the organizational mediations of the professional expert social scientists and the corporate leaders, organizations like the National Civic Federations, they continue:

> Such ideological construction was inherently abstract, being somewhat removed from the day-to-day processes of political economic production. Unquestionably important in its own right, manufacturing ideas justifying the power of the emerging corporate center was only half of what the discipline leaders had to offer in exchange for a patron's support. The other half was the skill to rationalize production, to make the emerging order technically more efficient.

Despite the continuation of some critical work begun during the previous period, social science has again returned to the business as usual of cultural legitimation and ancillary of technical production. The operation of academic social science as an element in cultural domination is now so profound, and so much taken for granted, that there is scarcely any need to assert more general legitimating principles such as value-neutrality. Instead, the dual social function of social science now bifurcates: into the general cultural theory of the new center-right, on the one hand, and suppliers of measurement technique for managerial administration, on the other. The current division between cultural generalists and administrative specialists relegates social concepts to the role of symbolic cultural affirmation and practical social science knowledge to administrative implementation. The cultural conditions which make it possible to perceive the need for a critique of knowledge and the development of a practically aimed transformative theory are dissipated in this bifurcation of the social functions of social science.

The result of the losses of the intellectual liberal center of social science (manifested in, for example, the rightward conversions of liberal American social scientists such as Daniel Bell, Irving Kristol, Seymour Lipset, and Amitai Etzioni), during precisely the period in which the US and other western capitalist nations find themselves in an economic and social crisis, different, but no less significant than the crisis of the 1960s, is that the crisis (Castells, 1980) and the role which social science plays within it has become less accessible to academic consciousness. Now the pursuit of critical social analysis and the critique of knowledge particularly are made to appear as intellectually unwarranted. Critical intellectual activity is de-legitimated and its younger generation of practitioners purged from American universities (Parenti, 1980). When the younger generation of critics are not totally excluded, they are consigned to the margins. Acceptance of an ever smaller number of academic critics fits the star system, expressing the very stratification of knowledge against which the critical analysis is directed. Despite these severe constraints, critique does continue within the academy and outside of it — a critique aimed at revealing the role which contemporary social science knowledge plays in the wider processes of cultural domination and social stabilization.

The crack in the liberal consensus that occurred during the 1960s made possible several types of critiques of knowledge which have been practiced among a minority of social scientists in North America and England — critiques of knowledge which have barely found expression within social psychology.

The critiques were focused at different distances from the most concrete aspects of everyday social production and reproduction and they addressed different aspects of the role of social science in cultural domination. A first type demonstrates the continuity between social science concepts and popular ideologies. Gouldner's (1970) discussions of 'background assumptions' are an example of an effort to reassimilate social science into the more general symbolic universe of culture from which it pretended to disconnect itself by using the procedural trappings of natural science. A second type shows the common structural position and organizational interlocking among social scientists and corporate leaders. The cultural analysis is embedded in a description of the social infrastructure within which social scientists work to produce knowledge. A third type recognizes that the hegemonic role of social science knowledge is realized in the concrete contexts of ordinary, everyday and professional activities as well as academic settings. The relationship between corporate capital, general cultural belief and the form and content of professional knowledge has been examined, for example, in studies of engineering (Noble, 1977), law and medicine (Larson, 1977) and education (Franklin, 1974).

Critiques which combine these types of analyses of the social production and function of social science and the general critical theory analysis of cultural domination indicate the empirical and theoretical shape of a critique of social psychology which has scarcely begun.

4

Knowledge critique: social psychology

Even the most social of current critiques of social psychology remain at the first level of knowledge critique. They describe correspondences between a wider culture and general social psychological paradigms. Such critiques, however, do not ordinarily explore parallels between popular and theoretic culture for specific concepts and they scant description of historical cultural and paradigmatic changes. There is even less work using the second type of critique, the social institutional analysis of the production of knowledge. The third aspect of knowledge critique, analysis of the everyday uses of theoretic culture, goes unnoticed by critics and the defenders of social psychology alike.

Neglect of a knowledge critique of social psychology and the unequal attention paid to each type of critique has a particular historical importance. For while social psychology has several concurrent social functions, it also has, I suggest, gone through several successive phases, each corresponding to a period in the development of liberal corporate capitalism. During each period, paradigmatic concepts expressed historically specific efforts to resolve the most pressing social contradictions of the period. My view is that social psychology is a compromise in thought of contradictory social tendencies which fuel the social dynamic of the times. In social psychology, the attempt to resolve contradictions conceptually has served, successively: the interests of forging a new hegemonic ideology for the ascendant corporate class; of resolving, at a more practical and specific level, issues of industrial and military control and productivity; and of maintaining the categories of everyday interpretation through the imposition of reified, smoothed-over and seemingly consistent concepts upon a system of everyday meanings and behaviors which the developing contradictions of the whole threaten to tear apart.

In this chapter, I offer some brief examples of several types of knowledge critiques of social psychology. I outline a broad cultural critique, describe an example of a rare social institutional analysis and begin developing a specific analysis of the most recent and ignored role of social psychology as everyday cultural domination.

Cultural critique of social psychology

Soffer (1978), in her analysis of the origins of social science in England, provides a typical example of a general cultural analysis. She allies the early British social psychology of McDougall and Trotter with an elitist solution to the culturally perceived conflict between instinctual theory and the rational and moral action seen as socially necessary (p. 244): 'The social psychologists' answer was that the elite, unlike other men, would understand human nature well enough to recognize and discipline their own irrational impulses.' In England, in Soffer's view, among the new social sciences that developed before the First World War, social psychology expressed the revisionist reaction, the intellectualization in the new social science language of the fear of democracy (1978, p. 217). Unlike

> the economists, psychologists and political scientists [who] were
> encouraged in their reforming activities by their reading of
> evolution, the social psychologists found a bleak confirmation of the
> a priori fears about inescapable instinctual compulsions . . . . These
> fears led [them] to urge that the rational few must control the
> mindless many for their own good . . . . An elitist social psycho-
> logy came into being.

Development of the wider theoretical bases of a social psychology in continental Europe belongs less to an evident culture of elitism. Rather, its deeper roots are, I think, part of a general cultural reaction against the possessive, rationalistic individualism identified with utilitarianism. Durkheim and Freud are among the most unclaimed important theoretical forebears of social psychology.

Durkheim and succeeding generations of structural-functionalists have insisted on analysis which asserts the importance of social rules constituting desire and regulating exchange. Durkheim (1954) recognized, for example, the social character of the self — at least, its constitution in collective ritual. His social analysis of the self meant that inculcation of collective moral beliefs required new national institutions, like schools to replace the older religious mechanical solidarity. The lack of social self-regulation through attachment to rules unleashes boundless individual desires, an anomie that is the source of individual pathologies. For Durkheim (1951) the self is no neutral mechanism of market calculation; it is desire encoded in collective morality, and necessarily regulated by norms or rules that specify it. In this sociological reaction against utilitarianism, private calculating hedonism as the social psychology of early capitalism is replaced by the moral self. Social rules become more important as constitutive of the self as a necessary antidote to the socially anarchic market self. This is the first socialization of the monad pushed from organicism into the marketplace. As a theoretical culture, it locates the determination of normal and pathological selves in the effectiveness of collective morality.

Freud also develops a social psychology in reaction against rationalistic marketplace individualism, a social psychology which represents the culture of an ascendant class: the ideals of a post-utilitarian, bourgeois self.

He describes the conflicts of this bourgeois self. He catalogues, but without naming, the private costs of capital accumulation. In his analysis of the bourgeois self, Freud described the personalized dilemmas that result from production and class contradictions, but he described them in the language of morality. Freud, who saw both the public good and private harm of internal self-regulation, like Durkheim, reacts against the pseudo-rationality of possessive individualism to exalt morality as the core self process. Internalization is morality (Freud, 1957, p. 17): 'The extent to which cultural rules have been internalized — to express it popularly and unpsychologically: the moral level of the members.'

Jacoby's (1975) defense of Freud is that unlike his successors, he did not dissolve the tensions between the individual and the collective into a fully incorporated, accommodated social self. But, despite this and more recent French psychoanalytic and Marxist defenses of Freud (Turkle, 1980, pp. 150-83) as dialectical iconoclast and founder of the subversive method of psychoanalysis, a Freudian social psychology remains within the cultural orbit of the bourgeois self. Freud's theory, which Jacoby praises for its realistic retention of the tension between individual and society, dehistoricizes that tension. According to Adorno (1968, p. 62), Freud 'should not be reproached for having neglected the concrete social dimension, but for being all too untroubled by the social origin of this abstractness, the rigidity of the unconscious.' Marcuse's (1962, p. 33) disagreement with Freud's ahistorical social psychology centers on the hypothesis of necessary 'repressive regimentation.' In Marcuse's view, such repression 'is the consequence of a specific organization of scarcity, and of a specific existential attitude enforced by this organization.' He epitomizes this critical historical view of social repression by the concept 'surplus repression' (p. 34):

> the specific historical institutions of the reality principle and the
> specific interests of domination introduce *additional* controls
> over and above those indispensable for civilized human association.
> These additional controls arising from the specific institutions of
> domination are what we denote as *surplus-repression*.

Freud's social psychology denigrates belief in the possibility of fundamental social change as naive (Freud, 1949). It omits analysis of the bases of the ego and its mechanisms of defense in the social relations of production in favor of universalizing abstraction and ascribing variation in individual functioning to the family. Freud rationalized familism as the false signifier of capital accumulation.

The theory of the self-society relation as an aspect of a broader cultural formation is more evident and better displayed in early American social psychology.

In America, during the same period, the perception of a conflict between individual need and social order was resolved – in theory – as a model of natural and voluntary conformity to social needs through processes of social influence. The early American social psychologists consciously opposed the received Social Darwinism and the *laissez-faire* ideal of social relations.

As Karpf (1932, p. 214) observed: 'Also, traditional psychological and social theory with its individualistic emphasis and its association with *laissez-faire* doctrine had little to offer that seemed relevant. *Laissez-faire* doctrine and traditional individualism were alike intolerable as a refuge.' Co-operation and adjustment were heralded as necessary to social progress, and if the corporate liberal theorists of the Progressive era were later to try to construct institutionally – through educational reform (Spring, 1972) – a social method for the production of co-operative individual adjustment to collective need, the social psychologists constructed the theoretical foundation for the social compromises of the Progressive period.

In one of the few social histories of American social psychology,

Franks (1975) argues for a general correspondence between the wider culture and the concepts of an emergent social psychology. He describes this wider culture (pp. 37-8):

> A new liberalism was beginning to emerge that was more in line with the contemporary social reality, and the statist assumptions of the progressives. This new or reconstructed liberalism . . . . Social psychology can only be viewed as an aspect of this emerging liberal pragmatic social science.

While Franks argues that early American social psychology was a theoretic expression of an elitist culture, through conceptual emphasis on leadership, exceptional individuals and social control of 'the mob,' my view is that this social psychology is the constructed expression of a culturally displaced effort to resolve historical socio-cultural contradictions.

The central contradiction of the period was, I believe, that even during the first decades of the twentieth century, managerial forms and the organization of work were increasingly socialized, while the form of ownership remained private. Progressivism was a social movement in which continuous attempts were made to moderate the social costs of American capitalism, while also streamlining its effectiveness, in part by inhibiting incipient tendencies toward collectivization. Early twentieth-century American social psychology acknowledges and contains the contradiction that Cooley calls individualism and socialism. He wrote (1902, p. 50):

> I do not see that life presents two distinct and opposing tendencies that can properly be called individualism and socialism, any more than there are two distinct and opposing entities, society and the individual, to embody these tendencies.

But the solution to the simultaneous need for individual freedom and collective social betterment — which would not require the reorganization of society — was that the individual became conforming in the natural interactive process of personal development.

Social psychology preserved the individual and theorized an historically altered social character — the corporate self — as the discovery of a universal human process. The implication of the concept of the social self, observed Baldwin (1913, p. 129), is that, 'it thus reverses the point of view of historical individualism, and gives collectivism its *point d'appui* in the process of mental development itself.' Certainly the theorists of the social self spoke of the interactive formation of the individual, a far cry from the instinct psychologists. Cooley wrote (pp. 29-30) of 'human nature.' 'Man does not have it at birth; he cannot acquire it except through fellowship, and it decays in isolation.' The new sociality of the corporate state was described in the language reminiscent of Christian ideals — not conformity to interpersonal demands as an aspect of the changing character of social production, but a natural process of 'fellowship.' Baldwin wrote (1913, p. 97):

> Everything he learns is copied, reproduced, assimilated from his fellows; and what all of them, including him — all the social fellows — do and think because they have been through the same course of copying, reproducing, assimilating, that he has.

The possessive aspect of the self, however formed, was, nevertheless, still emphasized by some of the early social psychologists, like James, who according to Karpf (1932, p. 252) 'point[s] out, first and foremost, that thinking is always personal; i.e., it is an expression of a personal mind and belongs to a personal self, so that every thought is, as he says, "owned".' The continuation of the individualist emphasis in social psychology is expressed later and again by Floyd Allport, who insists (1924, p. 4): 'Social psychology must not be placed in contradistinction to the psychology of the individual, whose behavior it studies in relation to the environment comprised by his fellows.'

The more social view of Cooley, Mead and Ross, while it did not assert the possessive or central character of the individual, socialized the self only by naturalizing and de-historicizing it. The self became theoretically social through a constructive process of admitting the social as a category and restricting its meaning. The social is reduced to: the 'mental' (a precursor of the society-as-value-and-culture view manifested so often in the internal critique); interaction in face-to-face groups; or, the 'organic,' i.e. abstract, indefinite and causally pluralistic. E. A. Ross, one of the earliest socially oriented social psychologists, wrote (1908, pp. 2-3): 'Social psychology deals only with uniformities due to *social* causes, i.e. to mental contacts or mental interactions.'

Within this 'social' view, the self is neither a pleasure machine calculator, collective conscience, nor necessary moral solution to instinctual disorder. It is, rather, a compromise between private will and co-operative social communication. It is internalization, not of the villains of external civilization nor of personal attachment to the ritualized effervescence of the collective morality. The self is rather 'a looking glass,' a reenactment of the perception of others (Cooley, in Gergen, 1971, p. 41):

> ashamed to seem evasive in the presence of a straightforward man,
> cowardly in the presence of a brave one, gross in the eyes of a
> refined one, and so on. We always imagine, and in imagining share
> the judgments of the other mind.

The resolution of the contradiction between the everyday of social communication that the new corporatism demanded, and the continuing lack of self-directive power that the continuing capitalism implied, is expressed, in theory, as sociability. (The 'social fellows,' as Baldwin wrote.) Any connection between the changing social organization of production and changing labor power is obscured by a theoretical emphasis on perception and mind. A socialized subjectivity is detached from the social relations of production in which that socialization occurs. In this social psychology, the self is not sublimated. But the theory of the social constitution of the self represses knowledge of organized social production, especially economic production, and insists instead on the fragility of social interaction and the perceptual, symbolic determination of social relations.

The abstraction of the self from social production also characterizes the cultural denial of production, and is represented in a concept of the social which not only emphasizes 'mind,' but the immediate rather than wider social milieu. That is one reason that Cooley's concept of the primary group is so important. Cooley (1909, p. 310) on the primary face-to-face group:

> They are only in part moulded by special traditions, and, in
> larger degree, express a universal nature. The religion or government
> of other civilizations may seem alien to us, but the children of the
> family group wear the common life, and with them we can always
> make ourselves at home.

The abstraction and de-structuring of the socially specific into an 'organic whole' is the way that the social is simultaneously admitted and denied. Socialization as the social formation of the self in fellowship and family individualizes the resolution of contradictory social tendencies as natural child development. The major cultural accomplishment of early social psychology, especially symbolic interactionism, is that it presented a picture of the world-as-social at precisely the time that both the new social sciences were becoming organizationally established (Silva and Slaughter, 1981) and the production demands of socialized production stimulated active social reform toward the creation of co-operative, adjusted students and workers. Previous *laissez-faire* theory could only deal with the social by repressing it. The overcoming of the repression of the social succeeded only, in Marcuse's terms, in a 'sublimation' of the unspoken concreteness of social structure into the organic, plural, mental, and undifferentiated transcendental concept of the 'social.' Social psychology became an affirmative theoretic culture of corporate liberal capitalism.

American sociological social psychology later extended the self-model developed during this early period, in a theory based on inter-personal tenuousness, perceptual negotiation, and a preserved sphere of private will. By mid-century, the self is viewed as even more fragile. It is seen as in a process of continuous reconstruction. Private will realizes itself through choices of how to manage an appearance of self (Rose, 1962). Self-appearance (Stone, 1962) and self-presentation (Goffman, 1959) substitute for the self. Mind is replaced by less universal, more easily disassembled and repackaged social rules, which are the regulatory conventions of the social interaction. Ethnomethodo-logy, like Freudianism and Durkheimian structural functionalism, reasserts morality. However, it is morality at a cool, cognitive distance. Morality is now read as the constitutive, but flexible, rule of everyday life. Social interaction requires competence rather than commitment. Interaction is intersubjective work to be accomplished (Garfinkel, 1967; Turner, 1974; Psathas, 1979). Assertions of historically patterned and structured social relations are dismissed. For ethnomethodology, social structure is a reification (Douglas, 1970).

From this perspective, the failure to place subjectivity within a context that transcends conventional social rules is no failure at all. It almost seems that for ethnomethodology and modern symbolic inter-actionism, ideology as false consciousness has finally ended. But, in fact, private ownership of the means by which people produce their lives, the strategies of effective domination by which capital is main-tained, and the continuing effects of this social form on the organiza-tion of personal energies has not ended (Zeitlin, 1980). Along with the repression of social production, as a material practice, the denial of collective structure becomes paradigmatically enshrined in sociological social psychology.

Psychological social psychology shows the same pattern of historical and structural denial. Despite Gergen's (1973) landmark appeal for historical awareness among psychologists, contemporary psychological social psychology, like symbolic interactionism, has moved even further away from an historical and social understanding of self and interaction. The research emphasis on small groups, and Kurt Lewin's (1951) liberal practical group psychology have given way to the study of less socially structured patterns of interaction and attribution (Harvey, Ickes and Kidd, 1978). Recall Steiner's (1974, pp. 94, 98) complaint:

> By the late 1950s social psychology had turned inward. It had largely renounced or postponed its concern for larger social systems, and had centered its attention on internal states and processes; dissonance, attitudes, attributions. Whatever happened to the group, and why? . . . By the 1960s social psychology had become much more individualistic.

Social critique

While as yet there is no empirical research on social psychology that compares with Silva and Slaughter's (1981) study of other social sciences. I nevertheless want to suggest the hypothesis that in its second phase social psychology offers not a general theory of human nature, society and the character of human association. It does not provide a praise of *gemeinschaft*, fellowship, and social control for telic evolutionary betterment. It provides technique — first to aid in the industrial production apparatus by sorting and facilitating 'morale,' and then in providing the interactional means by which the military accomplishments of psychological warfare can be best achieved. It studies group dynamics, attitudes, and values, leadership and decision-making. Its role as cultural foundation for the hegemony of an ascendant class in a new social order gives way to its role in rationalizing and maximizing production efficiency and offering instruction in the control and manipulation of the 'enemy' — and also, people on the 'home front.'

Such a transformation of social psychology from a generalized theory of cultural legitimation to a specific technical force of production has been only marginally documented. We now know, of course, how psychology aggrandized itself during the First World War and about the subsequent flourishing of the testing industry (Samelson, 1977; Kamin, 1974). Baritz (1960) has traced the adaptation of psychology in industry, from the early Taylorism, through personnel

44

selection and counselling, to the infamous Hawthorne experiments at Western Electric.

There is, however, increasing evidence to support the contention that the mass development of the social psychological profession, at least in the United States, was less a product of industrial scientific management than the creation of the military. Cartwright (1979), who is a friendly critic of social psychology, but also a long-time inside dopester, asserted in his Katz-Newcomb lecture (1979, p. 84):

> There can be little doubt that the most important single influence on the development of social psychology up to the present came *from outside the system itself* [emphasis added]. I am referring, of course to the Second World War and the political upheaval in Europe that preceded it. It is difficult for anyone who did not experience it to appreciate the magnitude of the impact of the war upon American social psychology . . . . When the war was over, the field was incomparably different from what it had been just three or four years before.

In a recent analysis of previously classified documents, Carol Cina (1981, p. 166) observed: 'It was there that I found the reason for social psychology's rosy future: the socio-psychological study of populations was the social scientific centerpiece of psychological warfare strategy.' Cina documents not simply the funding patterns of military influence on theory and research in social psychology. The crux of her argument is that the national military actually organized social psychology through a series of contracting-out arrangements, as well as by the direct establishment of research institutes and the support and control of professional organizations. After an examination of Office of Strategic Services (OSS) and Office of Naval Research (ONR) documents which indicate the importance of social psychology for the development of techniques of psychological warfare, Cina (1981, pp. 261-71) provides a content analysis of types of published research and their relation to military funding. In funding, in interpersonal networks, in group formation, in choice of research topics, and in organizational dynamics, Cina argues persuasively that the US military built American social psychology, which, in turn, as Moscovici suggests has had a lasting impact also on work in European social psychology (Moscovici, 1972). An organizationally routinized social psychology moves, according to Cina (1981), from the psychological warfare model to counterinsurgency research. In the extreme case, the infrastructure of

45

international scholarship is imperialism.

Less critical analysts of social psychology have also begun to acknowledge the possibilities of a social critique of social psychology. Dorwin Cartwright, for example, noted (1979, p. 85):

> The entire conceptual framework of social psychology including all of the unexamined assumptions about its proper subject matter and acceptable methods of research and most of its empirical findings are therefore largely the product of a single generation of people who were trained by a relatively small group of teachers with a common background and a rather homogeneous point of view. And due to the social conditions of the time in which they entered the field, they are predominately white, male, middle-class Americans.

A dean of American social psychologists offers a mild sociology of knowledge perspective on the development of the field. It may be true that social psychology is, as Cartwright argues, the product of a relatively socially homogeneous group, who share a common culture, class and gender location, but a social critique of social psychology can no more be reduced to these immediate causes than can the social determination of individual behavior be analyzed as the result of 'social influences' and the dynamics of face-to-face groups.

Even a move to a social analysis of social psychological knowledge, one which goes beyond cultural reflectionism, and mentions 'class,' repeats the model of social psychological reasoning essential to the production of social ignorance: denial of the whole. I suggest, instead, that an analysis of the crisis in social psychology begins with the view that theories, concepts, and methods of research are scientized, localized, and functionally specialized aspects of a changing social totality. The crisis in social psychology is a moment in the crisis of that whole.

Domination critique of social psychology

The establishment of a general legitimating culture and the streamlining of industrial and military production leaves only the sphere of everyday life unattended and unpredictable. The importance of the sphere of everyday interaction and interpretation becomes even greater as more and wider aspects of personal energy are harnessed to an increasingly marketized organization of everyday life. Abstract systems of belief are devalued as no longer adequate to the level of interaction regulation which is necessary to maintain production levels and profits.

Under these new conditions, social psychology plays a social role that is analytically intermediate between that of cultural legitimation and technical force of production. As interaction regulator, its newly important role, unlike mass advertising (Ewen, 1976), is not to create new needs but to insure ignorance about the social formation. Social psychology, in this view, becomes the legitimating (by its appropriation of the 'science' label) processor of everyday methods of self-delusion. In advanced stages of cultural domination, the population makes internal war against itself. Social psychology naturalizes the domination of self-delusion as scientific knowledge. No longer the cultural buttress of an optimistic emergent corporate liberalism or simply its military and industrial cultural workhorse, social psychology now functions to contain the polarizing contradictions of the cultural and social formation of an internally rent social class — it culturally protects liberalism in decline. The sublimation, repression and denial which the Frankfurt school described as working through high, mass, and scientific cultures, now all operate increasingly within the scientific domains. In the academic division of labor, social psychology deals most immediately, in abstracted language of course, with everyday issues of self and other management. Cultural domination simultaneously comes down to earth and is scientized. It is given the culturally generalized stamp of respectable, scientific truth.

The specific theoretic culture of social psychology can be described as a series of methods for the occlusion of knowledge of the social formation and of the relation of the individual to that formation. Its cognitive, collective structure can be analyzed as a set of cultural defenses which operate at a variety of levels of abstraction. The importance of this cognitive structure is that it selectively reinforces popular methods of social ignorance production — a production which, when it fails, exposes the individual to the experience of autobiographically encoded social structural contradictions. Social psychology contributes to contradiction-containment particularly through its dissemination as popular psychology guides. It is a crucial moment in the reproductive cycle of mass false consciousness. Beyond the most evident questions of class, status and power, the real social issue in the so-called crisis in social psychology is the challenge to the larger system of cultural reproduction.

Critique

Social psychology as cultural domination takes at least three different forms. It functions as:

(1) *A general cultural defense mechanism.* At the most general level, social structural contradictions are contained by theories working as media of sublimation, repression, and denial.

(2) *A falsifier of the historically specific social present.* The very concepts which social psychology uses represent aspects of liberal culture which are undergoing dissolution.

(3) *An ideological language.* Social psychology provides a language of ideological, contradiction avoidance categories. While later chapters specify in detail how the categories of social interaction, self, and intimacy provide historically appropriate types of false consciousness, here I wish simply to gloss these levels of dominance.

(1) Cultural defense mechanism

Social psychology literally functions to sublimate, repress and deny contradictions.

Sublimation
For example, in the customary self-society dichotomization practiced in social psychology, suppressed and unrealized aspects of social relations are projected onto a reified screen of the self (or onto 'society' in psychological and sociological social psychology, respectively). This is the characteristic separation and elevation method, by which failures of social relations are hidden and the *status quo* affirmed.

Repression
The false promise of the difference which only returns as more of the same and so squashes the imaginative grasp for a real alternative is the method of mass culture. It accomplishes repression by the deadening repetition of the stereotype and the elision of any recognition of difference. It occurs in social psychology also, under the label of scientific generalization. The marketplace description becomes the metaphoric model for the study of private life, intimacy and sexuality. The extension of commodity relations into all life spheres is given advance theoretical notice by theories which model market relations as true — even where there might in fact remain private spaces of eros and play. Obversely, public life, mass violence and imperialism are portrayed through the lens of updated primary group models. The ranges

of potential difference are erased — at least in theory — and the imagination even of what already exists (perhaps only as a minor chord) is eliminated.

Denial

But denial, proud blindness, is always the best weapon of cultural defense. It works, as Habermas complains (1970, p. 8) by the omission of whole categories of life, like 'ethics as such,' and in the typical denials of the historically specific character of social relations which are reiterated in virtually every social psychology textbook (see Sampson, 1971; Archibald, 1978, for exceptions). Social integration appears as if it is taking place in a society without any organized pattern of social production. It is not simply, as old-line group psychologists like Steiner and Cartwright complain, that current work overemphasizes intra-individual cognitive processes. Rather, it is the total omission of structured social relations, in their historic and class specificity, which underlines systematic denial of the concretely social.

(2) Falsifier of the social present

A central hypothesis of this book is that three of the major categories in everyday sense-making and in social psychological theory represent containment of specific social contradictions. In addition to a genera-lized production of social ignorance (claiming science, imitating ritualis-tically the physics of a bygone era, buying what it can from the legitimation storehouse), social psychology constructs away the social future, and the structural roots of individual suffering in the very cate-gories it uses. I shall argue, in several succeeding chapters, that the concepts of interaction, self, and intimacy are each glosses of internal contradictions — and that further — the specific conceptual crisis in social psychology is that these concepts, aspects of the liberal culture, are dissolving in everyday life. Social psychology's task is to rationalize the commonsense basis of social psychology paradigms which are no longer believed by the participants. The everyday meaning of the 'liberal center not holding' is that these interpretive practices are currently bifurcating — a bifurcation which is specifically represented by cultural movements of the right and left. The interpretive mass base of social psychology is itself being eroded.

(3) An ideological language

This is the most familiar category of domination. Social psychology translates. The irony of social psychology texts directed toward 'social relevance ' is that they best exemplify the transcoding of the social into ideological, contradiction avoidance categories. A recent (Brigham and Wrightsman, 1977) issues-oriented text provides some common examples. After introducing an historically specific, concrete social event — Watergate — the authors observe (1977, p. viii): 'The question was asked again and again: How could intelligent, hardworking people have been drawn into this disastrous caper and its aftermath?' The answer is to study 'conformity and obedience.' What is particularly interesting in this example of social ignorance production is that a social macrostructural issue is introduced. Then the problem is framed within customary interpersonal level concepts. Next, small group, interpersonal-type experiments are reported. Finally, conclusions are drawn about the importance of the immediate determinants of behavior — rather than so-called 'vague' or 'glib' cultural, social, or historical explanations. In the Watergate example no questions of elite class rule, or even traditional parliamentary concepts like separation of powers, are discussed. Class analysis is not a category that can compete with the immediate specificity of obedience-conformity. The pattern of substitutions follows in every chapter.

Questions of social interdependence are phrased as a reduction of the social conditions of interdependence and reciprocity to unusual cases of so-called bystander or helping behavior. The situational reframing of social interdependence issues and questions of social fragmentation are experimentally explored as socially influenced matters of individual choice. In studies of aggression and violence, national and international questions soon become — by the mediating redefinition of social determination as learning (recall Baldwin and Cooley) — studies of the effects of television programs. The pairing, violence and aggression, despite the imitative learning studies, suggests instinctualism which is then ruled out in favor of the social-learning view. Similarly, questions of solidarity are discussed as problems in the study of interpersonal attraction. Social solidarity becomes liking which, in turn, becomes attractiveness, which is then largely putatively determined by physical appearance and trait similarity. Self-worth is in no way related to invidious social stratification.

This is only a brief hint of the kind of critical cultural analysis of social psychology texts and journal articles which needs to be done. Fitzgerald's (1979) analysis of history textbooks provides a worthwhile example of how such textual analyses might be accomplished. Mills's

(1943) analysis of social problem texts still stands as a model for future analyses of social psychological products.

The ideology of social psychology is not simple, and it is not a direct representation of cultural beliefs. It is rather, increasingly, a produced cultural defense against social knowledge. The extent and pervasiveness of the conceptually constructed defense require a series of cultural undoings through internal, textual knowledge critiques as the necessary complement to corporate liberal, social infrastructural research and critique. From the point of view of a systematic social critique and analysis of social psychology and its crisis, the negative, critical moment of the demystification of social psychology has just begun.

Part Two
Theory

5
Alternative viewpoints: foundations of a critical social psychology

I noted, in discussing the dissenting critique of social psychology, that not all social psychologists have served as organic intellectuals of the dominant class. Beyond the small group of radical critics within the field of social psychology are a number of other theorists who have worked on problems in social psychological theory. They have of course, been generally ignored by the powers-that-be in social psychology. The rediscovery and recovery of the work of these theorists is part of the cultural legacy of the 1960s, and part of the foundation for the incipient dissenting critique. To carry this critique further, I intend to review their accomplishments and their failings.

My overview of these alternative viewpoints on social psychology is brief and selective. My aim is not to be encyclopedic, but to outline the historical moves, in the domain of social psychological theory, toward the articulation of a critical analysis of social interaction. I think that each of these theories has offered conceptual illumination and has had practical results. But each of them falls short of a critical theory of social psychology adequate to the present historical conjuncture. I see these alternative viewpoints as a bridge between the conventional social psychologies of the liberal hegemony and the critical theory and social alternative toward which history now presses us.

Marxists and Freudians

The culture of liberalism was at its most transparent period in the 1960s. Cultural critics and intellectual renegades again looked beneath the surface of the most immediate aspects of everyday life toward its material substratum in psyche and social relations. An important model for the 1960s was the work of the critical Marxists of the 1920s and

1930s. They had attempted to account for the failure of proletarian revolutions in western capitalist nations in which objective economic conditions pointed to revolution. The critical Marxists' demonstration that mass immiseration, intensification of the rate of exploitation and even economic polarization were insufficient conditions for socialist revolution proved tragically true. The attempt to take ideology seriously as an historic material force and to recognize that ideology is humanly embedded in personal formations and everyday relations, above and beyond its ideational aspect, led Marxists to a search among the so-called bourgeois theories (Anderson, 1976) for an alternative explanation and counter practice.

As Horkheimer wrote (in a view opposed to Archibald's equation of Marxist social psychology with coercive interaction) (1972, p. 57): 'All this already means that naked coercion *cannot* [emphasis added] by itself explain why the subject classes have borne the yoke so long.' At just about the same time, Wilhelm Reich was writing (1972, p. 56): 'The problem is not that the ruling class disseminates and defends its ideology; the problem is why the masses accept it.' Horkheimer articulated the practical contradiction between material conditions, on the one hand, and class consciousness and collective action, on the other. This contradiction was the basis of theoretical work directed to grasping and transcending the contradiction in practice (Horkheimer, 1972, p. 60):

> Rather when great masses of people have, against their interests,
> held fast to their mode of production, a great role has been played
> by a crippling fear of moving out of the old world of beliefs and
> ideas which had taken such deep hold on the individual psyche.

The failure of theoretically predicted social changes to occur became for the Frankfurt School the question of social domination, while Reich understood the same question as an issue of class consciousness. The theoretical departure of these theorists was to seek an explanation that was not at the level of ideas — but, instead, a materialistic explanation through ideology conceived as the organization of personal dynamics. Freudian theory became for them, at that time, one way of articulating the historically specific concretization of ideology.

The inhibition of rational collective action that they tried to explain was an early sign of the failure to maintain a liberal capitalist social order. The rise of Fascism was the second socially given problematic of the theorists; the degenerative moment of the failure of class

56

consciousness at the personal level. Historic events and the effort to master and change them in practical as well as theoretical life is what led to the early efforts at constructing a critical social psychology.

Reich

For Reich, the reconciliation of dialectical materialism and psycho-analysis was an act of theoretical concretion rather than abstract synthesis. It was a theoretical moment of developing in practice mass class consciousness. For Reich, social psychology is a practical necessity asserted against the abstract, idealist tendency within Marxism. The materialist antidote to idealist economism is a concrete material social psychological theory of practice. In his 1934 pamphlet, 'What is Class Consciousness?,' Reich describes both the role of a social psychology in furthering a socialist revolution and in combating the rise of Fascism. Against the abstract theoretical projections of the Communist party theorists, 'the subjective idealists,' who chastised and finally expelled him, Reich poses the centrality of everyday life (1972, p. 309): 'The revolution can only develop out of the contradiction of life as lived today, not out of debates.' Through the analysis of everyday life, it would be possible (1972, p. 288) 'to create the subjective preconditions for a social revolution.'

This second socially given problematic, Fascism, also had to be dealt with at the concrete level, which, for Reich (1970, p. 47) meant 'psychic reality . . . one of the best illustrations of an ideology that had become a material force.' He criticized the 'high politics' of the left (1972, p. 353): 'They see the personal and the political as opposite poles instead of recognizing the dialectical relationship between them.' Against the view of ideology as ideas and practice as theoretical debate, Reich urged that social mobilization against Fascism required an under-standing of its appeal at the non-cognitive level (1972, p. 284): 'While we presented the masses with superb historical analyses and economic treatises on the contradictions of imperialism, Hitler stirred the deepest roots of their emotional being.'

The feeling and the freedom necessary to develop class consciousness and fight against Fascism are blocked, not by ideas, but by the cultural aspect of capitalist domination — its repression of instinctual social expression in sexuality and by its restriction of trust, feeling, and sexuality to the family. Sexual repression, Reich believed, was the primal repression which inhibited and deformed all the other kinds of the 'will to freedom.'

Theory

Sexual repression, the blockage of free personal development and the bourgeois family that he called 'the factory in which the state's structure and ideology are molded' (1970, p. 30) eventuate in the production of the authoritarian character structure. The effort to compensate for sexual inhibition gives rise to metaphysical thinking of racist-fascist ideology. Sexual economy of the personal formation is the mediating substructure of articulated ideologies of domination, such as Fascism. Fascist ideology rests on a Fascist character authoritarianism, which is produced by the authoritarian family's sexual inhibition, and patriarchalism (1970, pp. 53, 60):

> In the figure of the father the authoritarian state has its representative in every family, so that the family becomes its most important instrument of power . . . the authoritarian family . . . represents the foremost and most essential source of reproduction of every kind of reactionary thinking; it is a factory where reactionary ideology and reactionary structures are produced.

Reich's sexual economic materialist was both a source and result of his practice in the sex clinics of the sexpol movement in Germany (1972, pp. xi-xxvii). Sexual materialism which developed for Reich as the social psychological theory of a revolutionary social practice directed toward class consciousness and against Fascism, ultimately became materialistic only in a biological sense. The theoretical underpinnings of Reich's social theory later became its foreground. A critical social psychology ended up a reductionist biological theory of human behavior.

Frankfurt social psychology

Horkheimer shares Reich's historical and critical application of the psychoanalytic emphasis on repression, character, and the family. But, in his classic essay, 'Authority and the Family', Horkheimer displays the less monolithic, unilinear character of the Frankfurt School's Marxist-Freudian social psychology. Like Reich, the theoretical development of a social psychological understanding is a result of attempts to explain two overriding social facts — the lack of a mass socialist movement among the oppressed, despite proper objective economic conditions, and the rise of Fascism. The theory develops to counter the perceived inadequacies of 'vulgar,' 'economistic' and 'orthodox' Marxist analyses and as an adaptation of Freudian theory to explain the workings of ideology at the concrete, personal level. As with Reich, the family is a key mediating institution in the production of individual dynamics needed for the reproduction of the oppressive social order. According to Horkheimer, the bourgeois family is the central training ground for the authority oriented character who upholds the bourgeois society. The family inculcates the habit of obedience, 'the impulse of submission,' the guilt, and the cognitive parallels of conventional factitious, rather than theoretical, thinking and a general lack of any independence of thought. Identification with the powerful father − paternal education − leads to the 'deep sense of inferiority that afflicts most men,' and their willingness to blindly follow leaders. The group psychology of submission is not a timeless, natural process of the social psychology of society (Freud, 1922). It is an historically specific dynamic of capitalistic domination, accomplished through the social psychology of the bourgeois family. For Horkheimer (1972, p. 107): 'growing up in the restricted family is a first-rate schooling in the authority behavior specific to this society.'

Horkheimer's theory of the family is more than a theory of microcosmic reproduction of functionally suited characterologies through the social psychological work of 'cultural institutions' like family, school, or church. The family contains also a negative moment, an autonomous counter principle against the patriarchal authoritarianism spawned by capitalism and which, in turn, helps reproduce its human, but dehumanized, reproducers. The counter principle, which the family keeps alive *at the same time* that it trains for heartless, fearful submission − the psychological base of ideological individualism − is the principle of 'maternal and sisterly love' (1972, p. 118): 'Because it still fosters human relations which are determined by the woman, the present-day family is a source of strength to resist the total dehumanization of the world and contains an element of antiauthoritarianism.' Within the unjust order, driven by fear and the bad conscience of the patriarchally cowed sons, the family nevertheless contains, not simply as a vestige of mother-right, but also as a collective social form, the possibility for an alternative in social relationships. Horkheimer foreshadowed the communitarian alternative which the family promises, when he wrote (1972, p. 124):

there can arise a new community of spouses and children, and it will not, in bourgeois fashion, form a closed community over

59

against other families of the same type. . . . Children will not be raised as future heirs and will therefore not be regarded, in the old way, as 'one's own'.

The Nazi genocide, from which Horkheimer, Adorno, Marcuse and other associates of the Frankfurt institute fled eventually to the United States, surely turned their thinking away from the subjective and institutional social psychological conditions necessary for the development of class-conscious mass movements for socialism toward the study of the cultural and socio-psychological conditions of the barbarism of Fascism. They continued their earlier study of the relation between family and authority, with Adorno codirecting (Held, 1980, pp. 141-2) the empirical study of prejudice, anti-semitism, character structure, and the family which social psychologists know as *The Authoritarian Personality* (1964).

During the post-war period, 'totalitarianism' replaced Fascism as the social problematic of the critical theory of culture and social psychology. The bourgeois family was no longer portrayed as the educator of authority oriented character, nor as containing the alternative resistant moments of sisterly love and communalism. Rather, the analytic route through the family as the social psychological site of reproduction and change, and as the domain which a cultural Marxism could draw from and reformulate, was replaced by an assertion of the characterological value of the family as a bulwark against totalitarianism.

The Freudian approach to ego development through identification with parents, which Horkheimer earlier described as the socially and individually regressive 'bad conscience' of the bourgeois family is seen by Horkheimer and Adorno during the post-war period, as the social psychological method which prevents easy identification with surrogate, mass leaders. The family ego is insurance against the more diffuse fatherless ego upon which totalitarianism feeds. The bourgeois family is seen as the historically progressive basis of training in the production of the personal formations which are resistant rather than submissive (Frankfurt Institute, 1956, p. 141):

human beings who learned through the other's example an attitude of independence, a joy in the free dispositions and inner discipline . . . .Where the family was adequate to its tasks, they gained a conscience, a capacity to love, and consistency. This was productive and progressive. In contrast to this, the historical decay of the family contributes still further to the danger of totalitarian domination, produced by those same economic tendencies which are destroying the family.

Freud's *Group Psychology and the Analysis of the Ego* (1960) is now rehistorized and seen not as a naturalizing reification of the social psychology of authoritarianism, but the opposite. The lack of family authority leads to the identification with mass leaders. Social authoritarianism is not the continuation of family authoritarianism, but only the realization of its absence. Frankfurt Institute (1956, p. 43):

> it is much more valid to regard the Third Reich as an exaggerated substitute for the no longer existing authority of the family, then representing the continuation of such an authority. . . . Hitler and the modern dictatorship are in fact the product of a fatherless society.

The application of Reich's Marxist-Freudianism led to a biological psychology. The application of the social psychology of the Frankfurt School to the study of the family as a central social psychological moment of social domination, led to a social psychological, qualified, historical defense of the family.

In addition to the development of a social psychology as a response to the historically changing conditions and concerns of cultural domination, the Frankfurt School also offered a general theoretical statement on the question of a critical social psychology. Typically, Adorno's position is contradictory. A theory that articulates a society characterized by contradictions becomes a concealment if it denies those contradictions in the medium of concepts. Adorno recognizes the need and value of a social psychology (1967, p. 68): 'To be able to come to terms with Fascism it was, therefore, considered necessary to complete social theory by psychology, and particularly by analytically oriented social psychology.' A social psychology is necessary to describe the relations between the inner and the outer, the individual monad and the social whole and to avoid the ideologies of both psychologism and objectivist sociology.

But, individualistic psychology, as a theory and as a therapeutic practice, is of course a false consciousness. As a theory, it ignores the way in which objective social conditions affect the life of the individual, the way in which the social contradictions of the whole are represented, though not mirrored, in the inner life of the individual. 'All varieties of psychologism that take the individual as their starting point are ideological' (1967, p. 77). Indeed, the individual only becomes possible under particular objective conditions. The irony of psychological individualism is that it best flourishes as an ideology where true individuality is least possible. 'The fewer the individuals, the more the individualism' (1966, p. 46). As a practice, psychology further buries consciousness of the whole. It teaches a therapy of individual adaptation to an irrational society, a systematic denial of the 'societal madness.' Psychotherapy, by encouraging social adjustment, makes the patient really sick. Psychoanalysis helps rationalize a society of minimal choices and so stunting the imagination of freedom, performs the 'long-standing practice' of substituting conformity for self-realization.

Objectivist sociology, on the other hand, 'disregards the subject.' It focuses on the statistical description of social factual end-products and ignores the constitutive process of social production. When it tries to append the 'subjective factor,' by taking account of people's opinions, it slips into a psychologistic understanding of action, ignoring social determination.

The individual is, for Adorno, ultimately socially determined, even in his/her lack of historical individuality. But so too is the character of the relation between the individual and the social whole. The current character of that relation is a severed connection — a socially determined lack of the capacity of the individual to grasp the nature of her or his relation to the totality. Because of the opacity of the contradictory social whole to a subject who is himself trapped by a non-mirrored representation of these contradictions, the pretense of harmony between the individual and the society is a kind of social psychological false consciousness. This false consciousness, this harmonizing ideology, is the ironic result of an effort to transcend the bifurcated ideologies of psychologism and objectivism.

It is for this reason that Adorno criticizes attempts, such as Parsons (1955), to formulate a theoretical social psychology. If the historical social reality is the unconscious separation of the contradiction ridden monad from the contradictory and irrational societal totality upon which she/he is dependent, any attempt at 'conceptual unification,' any methodological discussion of merger, misses the point of the critical theory of society. Socially antagonistic contradictions cannot be resolved in theory. In this sense, the construction of a social psychology denies both the current historical conjuncture of individual alienation and affirms, as some kind of intellectual matter, the separation of theory and practice. Adorno opposes the reification of both the individual and the social. (For an elaboration, see Jacoby, 1975.) The possibility of a critical social psychology depends on, as does the family, the rationality of the social whole (1956, p. 145). 'There can be no emancipation of the family without the emancipation of the whole.' Otherwise, even Freud's psychology (Adorno, 1967, p. 68) 'the only one seriously to go into the subjective conditions of objective irrationality, becomes another technique of domination.' It trains, concludes Adorno (1968, p. 97): 'those it encourages to champion their drives to become useful members of the destructive whole.'

Everything depends on the whole, but the concreteness of the whole recedes before its development into an irrational, barbaric and administered society. Social psychology, by refusing to become a unified theory, by refusing to become an explanatory social psychology registers its protest against de-differentiating social domination. For Adorno, the 'destructive whole' loses its internal contradiction, the negative moment that is a first step toward an alternative future.

Cultural revolution: the rediscovery of a dissenting social psychology

The cultural revolution of the 1960s renewed interest in the Frankfurt School, Reich, and in critical cultural Marxism (Howard and Klare, 1972). This phenomenon may be understood in terms of Anderson's (1976) thesis — that there is a correlation between practical social failures and interests among Marxists in superstructural theories — or as an effort to anticipate and bolster a social movement in progress. There are, of course, various attempts to explain the cultural revolution which occurred in the western capitalist nations during the 1960s, as well as attempts to explain the relation between the character of the social movements and the development of particular types of social theory. Brown (1973), for example, sees historical parallels between the 1920s and the 1960s cultural, subjective, and totalizing critical social theories develop when there is a break — such as deep and visible social disruption of social routines that rationalized social action becomes 'dereified', open to view. During such periods, awareness of the 'total character' of domination calls forth efforts to explain the cultural and subjective psychological moments of domination and to include them as goals for change and liberation. During this time, much of the earlier Frankfurt work was translated into English, Reich was read again, and the slogan of everyday life became the popular antidote to the perceived economism of the old left. Theoretically this was a period of mass reeducation among radical students and younger academic intellectuals. The best known voice of the second generation of the Frankfurt School was disowned, both politically and theoretically, by the German student movement (Krueger, 1976). Marcuse, of course, became a hero of the new left, and his rereading of Freud was used as a philosophical rationale for a hippie, rather than more directly political counterculture. *No new critical theory of social psychology developed* as part of cultural and political movements of the period.

What did occur, however, was a revaluation, a refinement, and re-statement of the earlier traditions of Marxist-Freudianism and critical theory. The Marx-Freud tradition reappeared, in Germany, where it had always been strongest, while in the United States, critical social psychology, as articulated theory, remained restricted to commentaries and footnotes on the work of theorists of the earlier period. At the same time, the Black Movement and Feminism, while developing practical psychologies, particularly of small group process, did not yet offer a theoretical alternative to the variants of the Marx-Freud traditions.

Despite their common bases in class politics and analyses, both Reich and the Frankfurt School had shifted their ground. Reich pro-pounded an orgone energy theory of human behavior. The Frankfurt School, which distinguished itself from the mechanical Marxist analyses of the period by an insistence on the contradictory character of social events, true to their historicism, now abandoned a dialectical theory as the contradictions of history were flattened and absorbed in the one dimensional administrative apparatus of the new totalitarian barbarism. While the Frankfurt School insisted that the social psychology of such a period must theoretically recapitulate the fractured character of social existence by refusing to combine sociology and psychology, they nevertheless offer outlines of a social psychology which emphasizes the psycho-social dynamics of incorporation and resistance to the bureaucratic machine (Breines, 1972).

The historically ironic abandonment of contradiction as a central theoretical category leads to the absence of a social psychology related to the processes of social production and class conflict. The concept of social production appears in Frankfurt theory. But its course is a movement from the early descriptions of exploitation and class conflict to an increasingly vague allusion to the irrational or administered society, and then finally, to the 'destructive whole.' What Adorno

64

wrote in his critique of psychology (1967, p. 78) becomes finally true for his own social psychology. 'Psychology, on the other hand, looks to the individual's interests, but after an equally isolated *abstract* fashion. Ignoring *the social process of production* . . . [emphasis added] .'

The appeal to the whole, despite its value, may be an avoidance of the arduous task of specifying: the precise historical social forces and relations, the mode of production; the internal contradictions of that mode of production; and finally, the concrete, lived relations of self and other production and reproduction within an historically specific mode of social production. Adorno recognizes the task. He even warns against theories of individual social relation as simple reflections or correspondences. But the concept of the 'whole,' for all its necessary theoretical power, particularly in a period of obscured fragmentation, may function not only as a theoretical avoidance of the social psychology of social production, but may be a means of avoiding class identification, and the concrete conflicts which it entails.

Social psychology which takes the position of the abstract whole is an historically appropriate rhetoric for dissatisfaction that has not yet found its basis in historical social classes and concrete social relations of production. The social psychology which remains only at the level of the irrational whole, is as Breines (1972) noted, a 'prospectively revolutionary theory.' It is a theory of pre-class consciousness responding to a systems failure of cultural reproduction. It is precisely the emblem of the conceptual unification which Adorno disdains — but at a higher and more opaque level of abstraction. The theory is resonant in part *because* it conceals and mystifies concrete class and production relations. Ironically, in its abstraction, Frankfurt School critical social psychology plays the dialectical, but largely sublimating and disempowering role of an affirmative culture.

Michael Schneider

Among the recent critical social psychologists of the post-1960s cultural revolution generation, Michael Schneider (1975) returns the Freud-Marx synthesis to the question of social class and social production. He reverses the tendency of alternative social psychology to revert to biologism, familism, or mysticism.

Schneider repudiates both what he calls the 'vulgar Russian Marxism' (1975, p. 3) and the bourgeois ideological aspects of psychoanalytic theory in order (1975, p. xi): 'to derive Freud's phenomenological description of the "bourgeois psyche" from the very laws of the economic movement of bourgeois society.' His central argument is that exchange relations based upon the production of abstract labor displace the possibility of the expression of concrete sensuous activity in use value or concrete labor. Repression is created because of the prevalence of abstract over concrete labor, of exchange over use values and relations. The organization of capitalist social relations 'reflects back' (1975, p. 127) according to Schneider, on instinctual and need structures of the individual.

Schneider retains the depth psychology concept of character structure in order to describe the effects of capitalist accumulation on the individual character and pathology. The reification, or as Marx (1967, p. 71) described it, the fetishism of commodities – the conversion of concrete social relations of production into abstracted, quantitative measures of exchange value – has a dual individual consequence. Reification represses immediate concrete satisfactions, which Schneider refers to as 'instinctual,' while at the same time inducing, at the individual level, the 'capital-psychosis' of greed and insatiability. The desire for abstract accumulation and the repression of concrete gratification in relations of abstract exchange produces the typical 'anal-compulsive character' of classic capitalism. Schneider here retains Freud's character types, the emphasis on an instinctual structure, and the use of the mechanisms of ego defense, central to which is repression. The dynamic of this instinctual, defense character is produced not by the particularity of the small group, for example, the bourgeois family, but by the structuring principles of the general social organization of collective social production.

For Schneider, the very basis of the social relations of capitalist production is pathological. Following Lukács's generalization of the process of reification (Lukács, 1971, p. 83), 'the central structuring principle of capitalist society in all its aspects,' Schneider asserts reification as the fundamental source of individual 'mental illness.' The parallelism of Marxist and Freudian concepts between the repression of the concrete and sensuous in the abstract labor embodied and prized in reified social relations, becomes apparent when he describes psychological symptomatology of the return of the repressed use value and concrete labor (1975, p. 147).

Every symptom – according to Freud – is a compromise between an instinctual wish of the 'id' and the moral interjection of the ego, that is, superego. The 'return of the repressed' in the symptom therefore has the same meaning as the 'return' of the repressed sensuous — concrete natural-economic 'use-form' of the libido.

The id becomes almost synonymous with use value and concrete labor, while the ego-superego is the abstract labor of exchange value. Reification is the distorted regulation of the relation between types of labor and exchange, on the one hand, and the ego and the id, on the other. Symptomatology is a subversive, progressive moment against the social production of the thoroughly reified and pathological subject of capitalist society. Therefore, Schneider asserts (1975, p. 62): 'Freud's dynamic model of neurosis — regarded in this way — is a disguised political model, the model of an impeded revolution.'

The attempt to translate the dynamics of capitalist relations of production into individual character and pathology is then concretized by a specific analysis of the actual conditions of the labor process and its class differential effects on the lives of workers. Schneider's analysis indicated a willingness to: specify the meaning of the whole at the level of social organization; describe the dynamics of the individual in relation to a central category of Marxist social theory that has been systematically neglected by previous critical social psychologies — labor; and finally, describe the relation between personal life and the operation of a societal institution *other than the family.*

The other central aspect of Schneider's important effort is the discussion of production and consumption as determinants of the various forms of psychological pathologies characteristic of capitalist social formations. Despite the importance of an analysis of individual existence within the spheres of production and consumption, and the value of the empirical studies from industrial social science research which Schneider amasses, his effort is sometimes hampered by an apparent need to justify both Freudianism and Marxism — not only as valid, but also as parallel and corresponding systems. For example (1975, p. 172), 'Fear of castration is certainly not a primal, so to speak, "biological" fear, but rather the *reflex* [emphasis added] of that social "castration".' The social relations of production are the source of the typical forms of so-called mental illness. The reification, the excessive division of labor, and the class differentiated degrees of powerlessness are the social basis of the activation of various forms of defense mechanisms and formation of pathological symptoms, like schizophrenia. Consumption, on the other hand, feeds the 'commodity psychosis' and becomes the exemplar for the typical behavior of drug

67

euphorias and escapes. Production creates individual deformations and suffering, while consumption is based on phantasmagorical marketed delusions of wish fulfillment and escape from the drudgery of labor. The de-differentiation of abstract labor is supplemented by the de-differentiation of dreams and illusions, and their addictive absorption into the commodity.

In a manner reminiscent of Reich, Schneider calls for a political psychological practice (1975, p. 260): 'All purely economic strategies are necessarily shortsighted in view of the historically new level of psychic mass impoverishment.' Mental illness replaces sexuality as a central site for the organization of political resistance and social emancipation. Mental illness is impeded class consciousness, the reassertion of the concrete repressed against the abstract degradation of reified and repressive work relations. Mental illness, as resistance to capitalist relations of production, has to be recognized and transformed as a 'subjective instrument of politicization' (1975, p. 258). The commodity society contains internal contradictions and the seeds of its own surpassing in the dissolution of the bourgeois character structure.

Schneider gives content to a critical description of the social whole. Society is organized according to historical principles of social production, which have destructive effects on individual functioning. The individual is both the deformed and the transcending moment of the social contradiction between the reproduction of capitalist social relations of production and consumption, and the alternative social possibilities contained within them. With Schneider, and the modern school of German Marxist-Freudianism, the dissenting tradition in social psychology is renewed.

Assessing the Marxist-Freudian tradition

The Marxist-Freudians go well beyond the internal critiques (described in chapter 2) which remain far removed from either a social structural or depth psychological analysis. Questions of values, methodology, and individual commitment still prevail. The dissolution of the liberal culture of social psychology is slowed by the internal academic critics' encapsulation within the conventional social paradigms of structural functionalism, the free market model of economics, or the subjectivizing perspectives of phenomenology, symbolic interaction and ethnomethodology. In this latter view, there is no social structure (Douglas,

1970). Despite the facile homologies, the mirroring of social processes at the microscopic level, despite the absence of a description of the social psychology of social interaction – of the mediating processes between the social matrix and the intro-individual dynamics, the Marxist-Freudians, on the other hand, do provide a critical model of the relation between social structure and the functioning of the individual.

However, the Marxist-Freudians remain at the periphery of American and English criticism of social psychology. This peripheral place, despite the accomplishments of the Marxist-Freudians, is, in part, justified (though they have probably been ignored by liberal social psychologists for different reasons). A critical social psychology should include a description and analysis of precisely that intermediate level of social processes which the Marxist-Freudians omit: how are the reproduction and transformation of social relations and the individual life processes which constitute them accomplished in social interaction? A critical social psychology is an attempt to include that mediating process. Schneider makes a beginning toward social psychology with the application of the concept of reification and the mediating dynamic between capitalist work and consumption relations and individual processes. But, he remains within the orbit of social structure and personality theorists, leaving the dynamic interactive terrain of social psychology relatively unexplored. Yet, Marxist-Freudianism goes beyond the liberal critics' appeal to morality, the biologism of Reich, and the Frankfurt School's drift toward an irrational, dehistoricized and socially emptied holism.

The return of Marxism

One effect of the failed cultural revolution of the 1960s was the legitimation of academic Marxism. The new Marxism of the academy was, for the most part, disconnected from any wider social and political movements. The intellectual form of this work involved specifying the 'scientific' structuralism of Althusser (1969, 1970, 1971) and the assimilation of Marxist concepts to the culture of positivist methodology (Burawoy, 1978; Wright, 1979). The earlier critical and cultural Marxist theory which appeared with the onset of the cultural and social movements was increasingly displaced by the revival and reformulation of the so-called 'orthodox' political economy. Questions of culture and psychology, while still of some interest to isolated pockets of academic Marxists gave way to neo-Marxist economics (Schwartz, 1977), theories of the state (Wright, 1979), and empirical analyses of class structure (Zeitlin, 1980). At least in the United States, the theory of the old left became the brand of Marxism that was academically acceptable.

Schneider's work in Germany can be seen in retrospect as a balancing between the critical Marxist interest in the subjective — usually defined as depth psychology — and the positivist and structuralist Marxist return to political economy. This rationalization and displacement of a critical social psychology as an important moment of the cultural revolution was reinforced by the general rightward tendency of the capitalist nations, beginning with what Mandel (1978) has called the 'second slump' of the mid-1970s. The bifurcation of a critical theory of social psychology into a diffuse psycho-cultural, existential critique, on one hand, and a Marxist political economy, on the other, is expressed in the difference between Deleuze and Guattari's *Anti-Oedipus* and Lucien Seve's *Man in Marxist Theory*. Analytical theory divides between metaphoric theoretical play and the earnest work of expanding political economy to psychology.

Deleuze and Guattari

Capitalism is the name of the machine that stands behind the Oedipal family, which terrorizes and falsely codes desire. The dialectic of the capitalist machine is its tendency towards schizophrenia, its scrambling of the insane normality of the familied ego. In the post-Laingian world of self-becoming through the destruction of the encoding and territorializing messages of Oedipus' anti-desire, the schizophrenic is the subjective vanguard of the reclamation of subjectivity, without which there is no revolutionary politics. The dialectic of capital is the tendency to unleash and de-territorialize desire, but yet to recode and contain it — the work of the interiorized family and the external state. The schizophrenic lives at the point of this contradiction (1977, p. 35):

> The schizophrenic deliberately seeks out the very limit of capitalism:
> he is its inherent tendency brought to fulfillment, its surplus
> product, its proletariat, and its exterminating angel. He scrambles
> all the codes and is the transmitter of the decoded flows of desire.

The conventional depth psychology 'libido' is now encoded and decoded 'desire.' Territorialization and de-territorialization are the processes of social and individual structuring and regulation, which serve as a generalized description for institutional, socially regulative, and intra-individual processes (1977, p. 258): 'One sometimes has the impression that the flows of capital would willingly dispatch themselves to the moon if the capitalist state were not there to bring them back to earth.' The destruction of the superego within a social linguistic, libidinal energy field of contradictory tendencies is a step toward the activity of the 'subject group' (1977, p. 348): 'a group whose libidinal investments are themselves revolutionary; it causes desire to penetrate into the social field.' The task of 'schizo-analysis' is the disintegration of the normal ego. As in Laing (1959) and Cooper (1971), the break-down is the inhibition and social labeling of the potential breakthrough to the flows knotted by the personal, familial, the conventional and bureaucratically political. Like Reich, the precondition of the social transformation is revolutionary subjectivity. Like Schneider, the schizo-analysis is only a preface to the emergence of a collective political subject. Deleuze and Guattari, like Henry Miller, believe that death − of the conventional self − is the first requirement of life. Against the subjective-existentialist liberation on the field of capitalism, their aim, as Foucault writes (Deleuze and Guattari, 1977, p. xiv) in his introduction, is 'the tracking down of all varieties of fascism, from the enormous ones that surround and crush us to the petty ones that constitute the tyrannical bitterness of our everyday lives.' The social problematics of dissenting social psychology are pursued, even in this poetic medium that begins and passes out of the breakthrough of madness: class consciousness, collective action and fascism.

Lucien Seve

Seve's Marxist psychology is not created in an encounter with either Freud or existentialism. His hero is not the schizophrenic, but the political activist as 'militant.' Class consciousness can be recouped not by the politicization of the deformed subjectivity of madness, but by the realization of 'pride in one's work.' Seve develops a Marxist theory of personality. Seve's theory of personality, of the concrete individual, is that the contradictions of capitalist labor are the basis of the individual dynamic. His general view, it seems to me, is that the personal formation is itself a productive apparatus. Like the economy, the individual has several 'sectors'; Sector I includes the activities which develop capacities, while Sector II uses and applies the capacities (which we might think of as the self-capital, although Seve does not use this term). His 'humanistic' interest is the 'full-flowering' of human

71

capacities. It is presumably that interest which he combines with the generalization of traditional Marxist categories of labor and capital to form his Marxist psychology.

The dynamic of personality development and arrestation is the relation between abstract activity, as in wage labor, and concrete activity as personal activity, directly related to individual needs. The medium of the contradiction between abstract and concrete labor needs is use-time. 'The development of the personality,' writes Seve (1978, p. 359) 'depends on permanently maintaining a high rate of organic composition of use-time' (the relation between time used in the production of capacities and time used in the use and application of capacities — Sector I and Sector II). For individual development to occur, there has to be a correspondence between the level of capacities and the structure of use-time. Alienation, then, is the containment of personal development in a social formation which requires as a condition of its reproduction the continuous transformation of concrete needs and capacities into abstract, commodity labor. Concrete capacities are not necessarily developed.

On the contrary, the tendency of capitalist society is for an underemployment of capacities and an atrophy of concrete use-time needed to develop Sector I. Pride in work is asserted as one of the contradictory counter-tendencies to the tendency of the falling rate of profit. The militant life and pride in work are the specific activities which counter the abstractive absorption of needs and capacities in the alienated social labor of the commodity exchange society. In sum, what Seve is proposing is that, with minor qualification, the laws of personal development can be derived from Marx's theory of capitalism. It is a psychology of activities, capacities, abstract and concrete uses of time, and correspondence between sectors of the personality. In my view, it is Marx's theory of alienation restated in the political economy of Marx's later work.

Seve is very helpful in his critiques of the various types of individual-society dichotomies of the American culture-personality school (1978, pp. 231-86). He modestly acknowledges that his work is an essay directed at theoretical foundations, and not yet a fully developed Marxist psychology. The irony of Seve's long essay, however, is that he quotes Marx's sixth thesis on Feuerbach — 'But the human essence is no abstraction inherent in each individual. In its reality it is the ensemble of social relations' — only then to argue against a Marxist *social* psychology (1978, p. 275): 'the psychology of personality differs no less radically from the *psychosocial sciences* [emphasis added] in that it studies the living system of social relations between acts *in the form of the concrete individual.*' He appears to identify the possibility of a social psychology with the dichotomizations and abstractions of the bourgeois theorists whom he criticizes (1978, p. 248): 'social psychology tends to short-circuit the analysis of infrastructures, the real basis of the ensemble of social relations and the social forms of behavior and consciousness.' The science of personality, on the other hand, rests on the possibility of elaborating (1978, p. 272): 'the theory of the relations and processes within which a concrete personality is produced.'

However, a description of the system of capitalism not only as an ensemble of social relations, but also as a set of relational interactional processes which make possible the production and reproduction of both the concrete individual and the structure of social relations is absent from Seve's theory. It leads Seve to the direct correspondence between the laws of social dynamics and the development of the personality which he is at pains to avoid. Political economy becomes, generally, with important exceptions like his analysis of alienation in the language of labor (1978, pp. 362-3), an abstract calculus for a personality dynamic which is abstracted from the immediate social interactional processes of its production. Without a developed social psychology, the theory of personality remains a suggestive, but historically abstract (except, of course, that capitalism is an historical social formation) analogy between the dynamics of capitalism and the 'flourishing' and 'stuntedness' of the personality.

Seve may (Shames, 1980) attempt a 'scientific humanism', but this most political economic of recent critical psychologies loses its desired concreteness in the absence of an infrastructure of social psychological processes. Describing that infrastructure is obviously no easy task. The historically conditioned difficulty of developing a critical social psychology was adumbrated by Adorno when he wrote (1967, p. 77):

> He is, in the strict sense, a monad, representing the whole and its contradictions, without, however, being at any time conscious of the whole. But as such a contradictory microcosm he does not constantly and continuously communicate with the whole, and does not derive directly from the experience of the whole.

The absence of a critical social psychology is the theoretical aspect of this historical social limitation: unconsciousness of the character of

73

immediate social relational processes, and their connection to the life of the individual, on the one hand, and the totality of the socially organized forces and relations of production on the other. The lack of individual development of the character of socially required abstract labor and the lack of developed awareness of the social relations of self-formation are the result of the very infrastructural processes which conventional social psychology denies by its abstract objectivism.

Limitations of the alternative viewpoints and the future of critical social psychology

Each of these contributions toward a critical social psychology expresses not simple limits of conceptualization, but the constraining practical historical conditions of social life, the cultural milieu, class structure, production relations and collectively patterned contradictions within which social psychology is produced. The individualistic organization of social psychological work in the United States described by Lubek (1980, pp. 129-57) rewards the most elaborated and obscuring aspects of social psychology as an ideology of late liberal individualism. The critics of social psychology, themselves caught within the production and reproduction of socialized individualism in their own daily lives, try to challenge the perceived boundaries of the cultural perimeters of the culture of social psychology. They attack with counter methodologies, value assertions, and, at times, knowledge critiques. Whether the critique can transcend the hegemonic limits of the background assumptions and infrastructural institutional support for conventional social psychology and move toward an alternative social psychology remains to be seen. This, like the critique and emancipation of the family, in the Frankfurt Analysis, depends on the social future.

The social whole is no longer mysteriously indecipherable. The debate over social psychology increasingly reveals not simply the representational ideological character of social psychology. The construction of ideological work, as contradiction containment, and as particular intellectual methods for the production of social ignorance, is being made evident by: the loss of professional confidence within the so-called mainstream; the diffusion of critical social science, even in its positivist versions, within the academy; and the wider economic and cultural crisis of liberal capitalism. As the crisis comes to demand tighter cultural controls in the face of the inability of the system to deliver instrumental rewards (Habermas, 1975), social psychology moves up front. The legitimation, commodification, and diffusion of the popular methods of social sublimation, repression, and denial, become simultaneously a more precarious and socially necessary task to those whose interests are knowingly and unconsciously bound to the *status quo*. Under pressure of its new social role, conventional social psychology unintentionally reveals its cognitive methods, its interpretive ideological practices.

At the same time, an oppositional tendency, an alternate tradition ordinarily excluded from the largest centers of academic knowledge production, finds its way into academic discussion. The alternate discourses collect and gather as adherents alienated individual social psychologists, some from among established professionals whose commitment to truth is strained by the increasingly ideological role of social psychology; some from among the ever growing ranks of the young unemployed and underemployed academically trained social psychologists; and some from among the critical sociologists, social theorists and analysts of culture who recognize the role of social psychology as producer and packager of the ideological aspects of the normative system which only experts can now satisfactorily provide.

Residual lives and thoughts of the aborted cultural revolution of the 1960s have, for at least a decade now, found expression in academic theory and research. There is a critical sociology (Connerton, 1976), anthropology (Hymes, 1972), economics (Schwartz, 1977). The social psychological concerns of activists in the social and cultural movements are now just beginning to be expressed in the dimension in which they were first experienced and articulated, but for which no proper intellectual discourse seemed available: social psychology. With the simultaneous self-depreciation of conventional social psychology and its increasingly evident social importance, a space for a critical social psychology begins to appear more likely.

The long-run trend in the decline of American intellectual isolationism, which began with the Second World War, has added a third historical inducement to a critical social psychology: the availability in English of the dissenting traditions of social psychology among German and French theorists. The renewed Anglo-American interest in continental theory has included a heavy dose of structuralism — Marxist and otherwise. But, it has also included the translation of the works of the Marxist-Freudians, the existential Marxist psychiatrists, and the

75

applications of structuralist Marxism to psychological questions.

Within this conjuncture that includes: contradictory social and cultural tendencies; defections from the mainstream; a crisis literature in the discipline of social psychology; and the renewed interest and availability of continental theories — I shall try to offer an outline of an alternative critical social psychology.

6
Dimensions of a critical social psychology: production, lived experience and class

Introduction

The methodological dispute in social psychology (Parker, 1981), between the norms of positivism, on the one side, and interpretive, existential, psychoanalytical and dialectical approaches, on the other, is not simply a ritualistic displacement of substantive issues. By insisting on an immediate correspondence between thought and routinized observation, positivism works to delegitimate all attempts to theorize socio-historical tendencies and contradictions in advance of their historical resolution. As an overarching methodological regime, the ideological role of positivism is to confine theory to the rearguard of history, and to dismiss as 'speculation,' all attempts to articulate the social present before it becomes managed and measured. My intention here is to violate that regime.

The need for a critical social psychology, now no less than before, is a response to social conditions that are perceived as problematic, threatening and undesirable. The twin classical problematic of the alternative social psychologies has been class consciousness and Fascism. Within this general social problematic, each theorist has had particular goals: sexual freedom, critical thought and aesthetic capacity; the removal of the conditions which induce developmental 'stuntedness'; the realization of the possibilities of individual social autonomy; reduction of the repression of the concrete sensuous experience by the abstraction of exchange value and wage-labor; the transformation of socially reproductive neurosis into the freeing schizoid flow of psychosis; the disintegration of the normal ego; the emergence of a collective subject.

The current movement toward a critical social psychology occurs during a period when the expansion of high, academic critical theory continues, but now within a context characterized by what Stuart Hall (1981, p. 113) referred to as the 'great moving right show,' and an even more general social transformation that is widely acknowledged as a socio-economic crisis (Castells, 1980). One characteristic of the present situation is that economic explanations, particularly from the theorists of the right (Gilder, 1981), and debates about the financing of public institutions, such as schools (Bernbaum, 1979; Wexler, Whitson and Moskowitz, 1981), seem to have supplanted the cultural and psychological public issues of just a few years ago.

Feminist, gay and anti-psychiatric movements still resist the reduction of politics to an individualistic new economics of old free market images. In the meanwhile, the relation between cultural hegemonic processes, social crisis, political conflict, and the social psychology of the participants sinks deeper into unconsciousness. The liberal culture to which psychological argument was integral is now increasingly represented in fights against the ascendance of anti-liberal elements within the ruling class by the more traditional, 'rational,' arguments of economic efficiency and constitutional legality. Under these conditions the task of the critical social psychologist becomes even more difficult. The advance of liberal social psychology in introducing the discourse of social science as an acceptable popular language has itself now to be protected. This means that commonsense knowledge and everyday discourse become less reliable sources of critical theory. The critical social psychologist has to reach up, as it were, toward articulated theoretical traditions, while simultaneously digging down beneath the unarticulated surface in order to grasp theoretical changes in popular social psychology. The task of a newer critical social psychology is to redeem and articulate the increasingly repressed social psychological dynamics that make possible the reproduction of the current organization of social life.

DIMENSIONS OF A CRITICAL SOCIAL PSYCHOLOGY

A critical social psychology must operate in three dimensions. I will adumbrate the three dimensions here before discussing them in detail in the remainder of the chapter. (1) *The sociopsychologic of capitalism.* The general tendency laws which Marx derived must be seen as a theory of mediations which apply to all social relations in capitalism. (2) *Lived experience.* A specific description of the historically specific contradictions of the formation and disintegration of the particular mediating or relational process for a given society must be worked out. (3) *Class Analysis.* The surface social psychology of a given class must be understood in relation to that class.

The sociopsychologic of capitalism

At the most general level, a theoretical and critical social psychology is based on the view that Marx's theory of the social relations of capitalism is a social psychological theory. It contains a theory not only of the structured totality, or of the internal dynamic of the individual, or an assumption that one may be superimposed on the other. Marx's theory (of which Archibald, Schneider, and Seve all include at least one aspect) is that a capitalist social formation is made possible by the relational processes of alienation, commodification and exploitation of human labor power. I suggest that these social relational aspects of production can be generalized. They describe general interactional processes which provide a matrix for understanding social psychology that is omitted by the prevailing paradigms.

Reigning academic social psychology is a partial and ideological statement of the relational processes which connect the life of the individual with the operation of the social whole. Concepts that are currently used to describe the individual-collective relation are based on a very limited, historically specific understanding of the social whole. For example, concepts like 'helping behavior,' 'interpersonal attraction,' or 'socialization' are social psychological descriptions. But their assumptions about how societies work are often simple, undifferentiated and counterfactual. Even where the tacit social theories of conventional social psychology are partly right, they still omit a significant range of social psychological processes. Archibald (1978) tries to correct the omission by arguing that individualistic voluntarism should be supplemented by an analysis of coercive power in social interaction. The reproduction of society, however, is not usually accomplished either by individual choice in a rational market or through coercive conformity. The need is for a social psychology to avoid the bifurcation of choice and coercion and instead to describe the dynamics of the social relational processes.

The first dimension of a critical social psychology therefore dispenses with the vacuous abstraction 'society,' and begins with a theory of society which leads to an examination of relational processes virtually excluded from any serious consideration in the conventional paradigms. This exclusion is culturally rational. If the current social role of those paradigms is to reinforce cultural blindspots, then a social theory which focuses on the silences and leads to a critical analysis represents a cultural threat as well as a scientific disagreement.

Historical analysis of the contradictions of lived experience

These general relational processes, the sociopsychologic of capitalism, are structuring tendencies. The second dimension of a critical social psychology aims to describe historically specific contradictions of relational processes in a particular society.

I have suggested that the current social role of conventional social psychology is to normalize and legitimate everyday cultural reifications. When, however, historical contradictions, that the reifications contain and obscure, polarize and reveal their contradictory internal constitution, popular and academic reified categories become less believable. Legitimation crises are then not the result of deficits of meaning, but expressions of perceptible polarizations and the inability of ordinary methods of cultural defenses to contain them. The current legitimation crisis and the crisis in social psychology are the result of such an increasing polarization.

In this particular historical and cultural period the cultural categories being exploded in everyday life and in social psychology are interaction, self, and intimacy. Interaction is a label that encompasses contradictory processes of equal exchange and exploitative interdependence. The self is a cultural representation of a process containing the simultaneous and contradictory exaltation and dissolution of the private ego. Intimacy is the term representing and containing the opposing development of a privatization and communality. Conventional social psychology, as a cultural construction, denies the contradictory constitution of its reified concepts. This denial is rooted in the deep affinity between its concepts and the culture of liberalism. With the polarizing transformation of corporate liberalism, as culture and social formation, social psychological concepts slowly become unglued, and falter in their affirmative role.

Class analysis

The third dimension of a critical social psychology is socially narrower and empirically less evident. I suggest that the social psychology of a particular social class contains clues for articulating a more general social psychology. Rather than deny the particular social bases of theoretical explanations, I try to explore the social psychology of a particular class as a key to the social psychology of the future – a future that is still structurally, relationally, and individually contained in collective and private undeveloped and unarticulated regions. The class that I am referring to is sometimes called the new class (Gouldner, 1979). The open and hidden life of this rising class includes its own social psychological self-awareness and its own particular psychological dynamics. I offer an impressionistic analysis of this social psychology as an additional spur to the articulation of a critical social psychology.

1 The sociopsychologic of capitalism

Marxist categories make better sense of the character of contemporary interactions than do the ultimately psychologically ideologizing and reductionist concepts of various versions of market or romantic individualism and conservative organicist social thories. A first step in developing a critical social psychology which draws from the Marxist tradition is to generalize these relational categories (Wexler, 1981a). I suggest that we generalize the categories of alienation, commodification (commodity fetishism) and exploitation; not as abstract social structures (society), or as personalized traits (the individual), but as interactional processes. The concepts of alienation, commodity fetishism, and exploitation all refer to an historically specific social organization and constitution of human labor. Specific social organizations have specific consequences for human labor. Each concept has, I think, been too narrowly interpreted. For each category, I indicate: the general implication for social psychological processes; how it constitutes a critique of a conventional social psychological theory, a specific and obviously non-economic application; and some questions for research suggested by the discussion.

Alienation

As Ollman observed in his treatise on Marx's theory of alienation

81

(1971, p. 170), 'For him all human relations in capitalism are part of the necessary conditions and results of what occurs in production and exchange and, and hence, a proper extension of their subject matter.' Alienation is the most widely cited and (mis)applied of Marx's concepts. It is a description and analysis of the social relational process by which the capitalist organization of the social division of labor and constitution of labor power as wage-labor fragments and diminishes human capacities. Despite its romantic and metaphysical overtones, Marx's description of a particular social organization of human productive activity as destructive remains compelling: human labor is a process of self-constituting and environmentally transformative activity. It is purposive, conscious and self-transformative activity. The particular social relations, however, in which this activity is placed in capitalist social organization diminish the possibility of realizing these potential capacities (cf. Seve's theory of human development). Marx speaks of alienation as a process of relational constitution of activity (Bottomore and Rubel, 1956, p. 170):

> The more the worker expends himself in work, the more powerful
> becomes the world of objects which he creates in face of himself,
> and the poorer he himself becomes in his inner life, the less he
> belongs to himself. It is just the same as in religion. The more of
> himself man attributes to God, the less he has left in himself. The
> worker puts his life into the object, and his life then belongs no
> longer to him, but to the object. The greater his activity, therefore,
> the less he possesses. What is embodied in the product of his labor
> is no longer his. The greater his product is, therefore, the more he
> himself is diminished. The *alienation* of the worker in his product
> means not only that his labour becomes an object, takes on its own
> existence, but that it exists outside him, independently, and alien to
> him, and that it stands opposed to him as an autonomous power.
> The life which he has given to the object sets itself against him as an
> alien and hostile force.

Ollman (1971, p. 135) notes: 'The whole has broken up into numerous parts whose interrelation in the whole can no longer be ascertained. This is the essence of alienation, whether the part under examination is man, his activity, his product or his ideas.'

Attempts to generalize Marx's theory of alienation usually result either in idealism or economism. The idealist error, common in conventional sociology, is treating alienation as a purely subjective state, a set of attributes, which may, of course, have objective correlates (Seeman, 1975). The effect is that alienation — as a social relation of capacity diminution through dispossessing fragmentation — is reduced to a multidimensional opinion. The economistic error is to identify the process of alienation entirely with the workplace, with economic production in the narrowest sense (Shepard, 1977). If instead we see alienation as a socially structured process of fragmentation, in which we each become and are reduced to a specialized and limiting en-actment of a social function, then we can begin to see its general applicability.

First, the alienation perspective provides the vantage-point for a critique of a conventional social psychological theory — role theory (Biddle, 1979). The concept of alienation turns the notion of role on its head. In role theory, specialization is taken as a neutral, trans-historical social necessity and not as a specific sociohistorical organiza-tion of human activity. Indeed, role theory studies the forms of alienated social being as social facts rather than as an historically produced and socially organized limitation on the expression and development of human capacities. Role theory is neither critical nor historical. Typically, after naturalizing an historically produced condition, it then introduces, as addenda, issues of strain, conflict, and non-performance of the role.

If instead, the partialization of human capacities and their norma-tively sanctioned freezing into social characters is understood as an historically contingent process, then the concept of alienation can be developed as part of a critical theory of interaction. For example, we need not restrict the concept of motivated social interaction to drives for cognitive consistency, maintenance of arousal levels, or social conformity. The concept of alienation suggests instead the importance of organismic resistance to the socially patterned partialization and atrophy of human capacities (Laddis, 1979). Garai has posited produc-tion as self-realization and social transformation, i.e., non-alienated activity as a fundamental need and drive. Eros summarizes an applica-tion of Garai's alienation theory to theoretical psychology (n.d., p. 367):

Now alienation conserves the particular system of social relations as if it were a natural constraint. Alienation excludes the possibility of satisfying the fundamental need in either a 'harmonizing' or in a 'contrasting' way. The fundamental need, while it remains unsatisfied, strives for satisfaction in a fictive way. The various forms of fictive satisfaction . . . which the ideology justifies. Garai then develops a theory of fictive satisfactions.

A less systematic application might be found in rethinking conventional interpersonal attraction theory in social psychology. This research usually explains interpersonal attraction in terms of value homogamies or of individualized traits such as physical attractiveness; or even more socially, in theories of complementary needs. For example, Huston and Levinger note in their review of interpersonal attraction research (1978, pp. 145, 146): 'More than two-thirds of the studies reviewed dealt with impressions and emotions, usually removed from their social context . . . we found no studies on the effect of power and wealth on sexual attractiveness.'

Yet, phenomenological descriptions of the earliest stages of love and intimacy are remarkably similar to Marx's descriptions of the expressions of the effects of alienated social relations in religion: of the social psychological efforts to overcome paralysing fragmentation and powerlessness by the idealization of a powerful, mysterious other, whose very completeness reflects the character of our felt inadequacies. Intense attraction can be understood as a manifestation of alienation and the effort to overcome it by valuing and glorifying not only what we do not have, but also what we have learned to believe is beyond our capacity to mutually create in ourselves. Following on this view, specific socially patterned self-devaluations could become the basis for predicting contextually variable kinds of interpersonal attraction behavior — not value homogamies or universal traits.

The way in which I've applied the concept of alienation to the intimacy literature shows how a Marxist concept can lead to alternative hypothesis generation — but hypothesis generation of a conventional sort. Let me try to go further, with an example that leads to a questioning of and an alternative to the larger conceptual frame of social psychology. Specifically, this example will show that what conventional social psychology conceives as autonomous self-formative processes can only be understood in relation to socioeconomic production processes.

Commodity fetishism

Marx wrote in a famous passage from Capital (1967, p. 72):

A commodity is therefore a mysterious thing, simply because in it the social character of men's labour appears to them as an objective

character stamped upon the product of that labour: because the
relation of the producers to the sum total of their own labour is
presented to them as a social relation, existing not between themselves, but between the products of their labour. . . . There is a
definite social relation between men that assumes, in their eyes, the
fantastic form of a relation between things. . . the mutual relations
of the producers, within which the social character of their labour
affirms itself, take the form of a social relation between the
products.

Powerlessness in the capitalist production process takes a specific
form: human beings are treated, and treat each other, as objects. The
orientation of energies toward the production of profitably exchange-
able objects or commodities penetrates the social organization and the
social perceptions of the producers themselves. Their interactional labor,
and its concretization in the material which they transform into socially
valued objects becomes, and is seen as, itself a commodity. The social
character of the production process may be so far obscured that the
sense of human agency is reversed: the products, things, are understood
as the source, rather than the effect, of human actions. Lukács (1971,
p. 83) posits this process as 'the central, structural problem of capitalist
society in all its aspects.' Human thinking, active capacities, and social
relations take on the form of commodities and relations among commodities. This central relational process of becoming and participating in
commodification is currently virtually ignored by conventional
paradigms in social psychology, as a fundamental social psychological
process. When commodity relations are a generalized mode of interaction in a society, then shared belief in abstract values is a less central
means of attaining social order and stability. The commodity fetish
concept provides the basis for a critique of theories of the self and of
value consensus and of socialization theories of social control.

Older forms of identity based on value internalization, as I argue in
chapter 8, appear to be replaced by self-definition through social
negotiation. This negotiation is, however, not an amorphous process
of symbolic exchange as it is often represented in symbolic interactionist
and ethnomethodological views. Rather, the negotiation of selfhood
occurs in structured social settings — organized in commodity terms.
Self-value is attained by the accumulation of institutional products of
all kinds (e.g., money, grades, orgasms). As organizational processes are
obscured in favor of organizational products, accumulation results in a

85

loss of individual capacities for self-directive planning and imagination, and contextually specific experiential discrimination – put otherwise, the dissolution of the self or ego. The commodification of the self (see chapter 8) is only the most general example of how self-processes are altered by the changing character of the social organization of production. The conventional concept of socialization as the crucial link between society and the individual is based on a particular, moral integration model of societal structure. If social order is maintained instead by the transformation and individualizing of social relational capacities through commodity production, then it is the process of abstracting, individualizing, and deflecting social relations which needs to be described. Commodification rather than socialization is the process by which the 'society-individual' dynamic can be described in capitalist societies.

The question raised by both the alienation and commodification concepts is whether these processes are in fact generalized across different institutional social sectors. Does the process of commodification occur differently in different social classes? The commodification of the self and the historical transformation in modes of social control are only indicative of the wide-range application of the concept of commodity fetishism.

Exploitation

Exploitation is a central Marxist economic concept. Exchange, especially the exchange of labor for wages, is only apparently equivalent. In fact, the appropriation of the surplus value of labor by employers, the exploitation of labor-power, is a necessary, if not central, component in the economy for the accumulation of capital. This inequality, exploitation, is socially obscured through ideology, and socially routinized. Hegemony means, at least in part, maintaining or mystifying that process of exploitation.

There are theories in conventional social psychology, such as equity theory, which borrow economic concepts. But equity theory, as I argue in chapter 7, portrays social interaction through the lens of individualistic market trading models of interaction which see exploitation as an unfair trade and not as a central socially produced and continuously obscured aspect of social interaction. Instead of accepting bourgeois economics as a model for social psychology, we can instead suggest that the Marxist economics concept of exploitation can be generalized. We can add to the economic conception of exploitation the assumptions that (a) labor, narrowly conceived, is not the only source of value in advanced capitalism. All kinds of activities can be understood as resources and exchange values; and (b) the structure of economic production and accumulation patterns is realized outside the most obvious spheres of economic production. Then, a central question becomes the study of the interactional implications of exploitation in other activities and through other currencies – of exploitation as a central structuring process of all social interaction.

The study of exploitation would include existing research on how linguistic exploitation and appropriation occur in social interaction. It would relate also a view of perception and affect not simply as individual qualities, but as a kind of social psychological production through interaction, an interaction structured by production and characterized by exploitation and its mystification. Precisely this kind of affective exploitation and cognitive mystification is described by family therapists and critical observers of family interaction dynamics (Napier and Whitaker, 1978). In the extreme case, we find the theft of the selfhood of the least powerful family members (Laing, 1959; Cooper, 1971). The various forms of exploitation are not ahistorical or universal processes. In advanced capitalism, for example, the self becomes a battleground. Its negotiation and exploitation become one arena for the enactment of the changing forms of an abiding contradiction of capitalism: the contradiction between social production and individual ownership or appropriation. Exploitation refers to the process of that appropriation – whatever its domain. It is that process which needs to be seen as problematic, no less theorized and researched in social psychology.

Each of these categories describe general, structuring tendencies of interaction. These processes can be thought of as dynamic relational building blocks or matrices within which more specific social psychological relational processes are defined. The socio-psychologic of capitalism only sets the stage.

2 Historical contradictions of lived experience

Though Marx's theory of production relations provides regulative concepts which are essential to a critical social psychology, the most distinctive and important aspect of a critical social psychology is the analysis of historical contradictions of lived experience. To stay at the level of general social relations is to fall into a sociological reductionism which severs theory from immediate needs and experience. As Reich noted, in criticizing German Marxism of the 1920s for the same sort of error, the consequences are disastrous at both the theoretical and practical levels. Only in the specific, historical analysis of particular mediating concepts and categories does a critical social psychology come into existence.

What concepts provide the focus for a critical social psychology? The concepts of conventional psychology, both in everyday and academic language, are abstract representations of specific and contradictory processes of interactional production. They are frozen representations of dynamic social relations. One task of critical analysis is to decompose these naturalized categories into the relational and contradictory processes of which they are the routinized resultant containments. Decomposition of natural everyday categories into relational processes follows Nicolaus's description of Marx's method of analyzing money (1973, p. 17):

> Marx does not 'discover' any new functions of money. His contribution is rather, to uncover the social, political, legal and other presuppositions of the stock definitions of money carried in political economy texts, that is, to treat value and money as social relations.

The relationship between critical social psychology and conventional social psychology is an important one. Despite its profoundly ideological character and limited focus, conventional social psychology does create concepts and collect knowledge that reflect historically lived experience. A critical psychology which ignores the conventional discipline scants its own possibilities. The return to Freud, though it has been of value to many theorists, often coincides with an avoidance of positivistic social psychology, which seems to offer no critical possibilities. The results of such an avoidance, I would argue, are fatal. By the same token, a critical social psychology cannot simply fuse, as Archibald (1978) attempts, the findings of conventional social psychology with Marxist concepts. An aim of critical analysis is to discover the social reality hidden by the ideological concepts of conventional social psychology.

Because I consider the analysis of specific categories of mediation to be the most important aspect of a critical social psychology, the next three chapters are each devoted to a specific concept of social

psychology: social interaction, self, and intimacy. My central contention is that *each category represents a phenomenon which is dissolving
in everyday life as society polarizes between right and left and liberal
hegemony breaks down.* The concepts and their history in social
psychology represent a changing contradiction containment.

Interaction

Exploitation is becoming more evident as the marketplace model of
exchanges becomes generalized. At the same time, the understanding
of exploitation leads to a social analysis that goes beyond the market
to the study of production. The evolution of social movements,
feminism for example, from concerns with distributional equity to
analyses of the social production of inequality (Saffioti, 1978) is an
historical instance of this change.

The 'end' of social interaction, a category whose cultural ascendance
is tied to the historic fortunes of corporate liberalism, is increasingly
evident in practical, everyday social life. The fix-it shop of liberal
society was the interaction of the encounter group, the sensitivity
training session, and various forms of methods for smoothing the flow
of social relating though empathy. Now, when popular and theoretic
culture give way to 'exchange' in everyday life, the encounter group is
being displaced by more technical means of interpersonal management
(Dwyer, 1978; Cohen, 1980). The latest social psychological methods
for converting labor power to newer production relations are part of
the economization of social psychology. Economization is commodifying, but also demystifying — when it leads to an analysis of production
and introduces the possibility of conscious, collective rationality as a
social mode of self-regulation. Practically, interaction now divides
between this possibility of collective, conscious social organization,
on the one hand, and cost accounting and technical interpersonal
management, on the other. Theoretically, the ideal of management
joins authority as conceptual pillars of the challenge to liberal social
psychology from the right.

The self

To call the self an ideology and a reification of contradictions means
to indicate current empirical tendencies toward self-centeredness, on
the one side, and self-decentering on the other — tendencies which
occur in concrete institutional contexts, such as work, family, and
school. My interpretation of this tendency is that the self represents

a personalized mode of appropriation and accumulation of the social relational processes that produce the person. If we used Marxist analogies, we might say that current self-dilemmas are an expression — in the sphere of the mediating social psychological processes — of the classic contradiction between the socialization of the forces of production and its contradiction with the privatizing relations of production.

Intimacy

Intimacy, close personal relationship, is a rule of defining public-private spaces. It is a summary abstraction of privatizing and socializing tendencies. The extension of intimacy as a general quality of relationships, one not limited to particular institutional or organizational definitions, was one of the changes that developed with the new corporate liberalism (Gadlin, 1977).

Technicization (Edwards, 1979) of organizational control systems and the intensification of Taylorist organization of the labor process (Braverman, 1974; Zimbalist, 1979) diminishes the importance of human relations skills. The diffuse generalization of human relations as interpersonal sensitivity, the early love-ins of the counterculture, the tendency to bring to the so-called public sphere the qualities associated with privatized, personal life, that tendency is itself now being displaced.

The category and mode of relation — intimacy — which contained both socializing and provatising processes is, I suggest, now dissolving back into its integral constituent, contradictory processes; socialization and privatization. Here too, as mass concept, mode of relation, and theoretic culture of social psychology, the right social reactionary tendency is now ascendant. This concept of intimacy contains, as a reified midpoint, two tendencies — the privatizing, familistic tendencies, on the one side, and the possibilities of bringing to the so-called public or social, the *gemeinschaft* aspects of the private, i.e., solidarity, on the other. The reversion to familism as the common sense of everyday life is currently triumphing (*New York Times*, October 1980). Both familism and religion are the new collective reifications of the social aspects of private life (*New York Times*, June 1980).

Social psychology discovers intimacy theory and research as the very category gives way to a new fundamentalism which claims for the family and for religion everything which is truly social. The development of a post-liberal capitalist conservatism is completed: management, family and religion.

3 The unspoken social psychology of the new class

The third component of a critical analysis is the interrelation of concepts to the class which has developed them. Here, I will try to analyze the class background of conventional, liberal social psychology by reading through a liberal conceptualization of that class — the new class theory. My attempt is impressionistic and metaphorical, but a necessary part of critical social psychology's anticipation of the future.

Every social psychology is an expression of an historic class, particularly of the intellectuals organic to that class (Gramsci, 1971). The liberal social psychology that now finds itself in the midst of a cultural and socioeconomic crisis and the dissenting social psychologies of the earlier and later period, all express in their problematics, concepts and theories, something specific to their own class experience. We recognize the ideals of corporate liberalism in the narrow, manipulative practices of instrumental bureaucratic experimentalism, which are undertaken to substantiate other people's opinions. In conventional social psychology's preoccupation with what the other guy is thinking, in the older group dynamics and the newer theories of invidious sorting by internal ostensible moral differences — the hyperindividualistic ideology of developmentalism (Sullivan, 1977), we can recognize the fearful employee class, the personnel of the corporate liberal state.

The critics and dissenters are also socially recognizable. The theory of cultural domination and disdain for the mass culture, as a theodicy of the exiled outsider, appears in a portrait of a totalizing, excluding, and murderous society. We recognize bourgeois exiles, witnesses to the barbarism of our century, who, educated before the reign of scientism, really did refuse to be quiet. We can identify also veterans of the revolution of 1968 and psychiatrists who, taking seriously the effort to free the mind from distorting repression, began to see themselves and their colleagues as mind police. For them nothing will do but making a clean sweep of it — expunging the interiorized family in the breakdown that is a breakthrough.

What is the social reason behind the recent effort for a critical social psychology, and what is the class history which it represents? Gouldner (1979) sees the beginning of an historic 'new class,' with a potential for social emancipation, due in part to its unprecedented symbolic power, training and informational technology. Gouldner sees this symbolic capital (following Bourdieu and Bernstein) as so powerful in part because he dissociates the new class from the deeper structural tendencies of both capitalism and the class psychology of the unconscious.

The symbolic power of the new class cannot be understood in abstraction from either its exterior or interior forces and relations of production. Accumulation of symbolic competence is only powerful in relation to the development of social relations in which that symbolic competence can be used. Symbolic competence, as commodified exchange value, may increase to levels which cannot be utilized because social relations of interaction are lagging behind, because they are adapted to earlier and lower levels in the organization of labor power.

The symbolic competence of private selves — a mass of partially associated producers — is a fragmented force of production. It outruns the social relations of production of interaction. In metaphoric terms, this can be seen as a matter of overproduction — at the individual symbolic labor level, or of underconsumption — at the system level. I see the inner traps of the early 1960s counterculture reported by psychologists like Laing (1959) and Cooper (1971) as vanguard expressions of this disjunctive contradiction between symbolic labor power production, and concretely rationalized and limited social relations of bureaucratic interactional production. Laing can at once be seen as both greedy petty bourgeois capitalist of the self and as the most vanguard social revolutionary. His was a proposal for the complete utilization of the excessive symbolic capacity of self labor power against the ordinary systematic repression and waste of this symbolic capital.

I suggest that the structural substratum of the ego is socially and historically specific. Now, *the unconscious is the substructure of the privatized aspects of modern symbolic labor power*. Freud's (1959) view of the unconscious as the storehouse of ideology, of what gets left behind, particularly repressed memories of childhood, is only part of the story. If the unconscious, as a productive process, encodes and transforms incomplete and unrealized repressed aspects of social relations, as Schneider (1975) argues, then it has not only an ideological moment but also a utopian one. The unconscious is not an ahistorical primary process. It is a storage of the ideological and utopian moments of the social present. This present is idiosyncratically coded according to personal history and stored as motivationally relevant memories, as beliefs, in language.

What is revealed in the crisis of symbolic ego greed typical of the new class are memories of both ideological and utopian moments from the social present – not just memories of the past. The unconscious also contains the subjective conditions of the future.

The social function of cultural methods of defense is to contain, sublimate, repress, and deny the relational processes contained beneath the everyday reifications. The unconscious notes the fragmented bricolage, the bits of news, the seepage and by-products of inefficient ordinary cultural containment. Crises, not any discursive incremental accumulation of symbolic or material resources but *breaks* at the individual and collective levels, are the essential mode of dereification and access to knowledge of internal constituents. Nicolaus (1973, p. 30) states this dialectical principle simply: 'Only when things suddenly crack and break apart does it become obvious that there was a dynamic within them all the time.'

Beneath the veneer of instrumental symbolic facility, the ideological moment of the new class, is indeed a memory of family romances (Freud, 1959, vol. 5, pp. 74-9). The family romance is a primitive story in the face of the historically changing ratio of cathected information between private and public spheres. The family is historically less important at fixing the precise content of the ideological storage because it is being continuously outweighed by the information-rich symbolic environment of modern collective forces of production. The authoritarian personality is now corporatized, defamilied, diffused, and yet functions within the same structural dynamic as the family scenario upon which it builds. It supplants familied authoritarianism by its more limited, but not less demanding, corporatized superego. This is the ideological moment of the unconscious.

The utopian moment of the unconscious is the memory of the future. It can only be constructed of fragments, strewn in the junk-shops and secondhand stores of emotionally meaningful language and imagery. It is locked in every reified cultural artifact, in every conversational gesture, in every contiguity or noticeable disjunction that we call inappropriate thought or action. For the anti-Oedipal dissenters of critical social psychology, the dissolution of the ego is a necessary, but not final, utopian moment in the 'schizophrenic charge of capitalism' (Deleuze and Guattari, 1977).

From a social relational perspective (which does not deny the unconscious aspects of labor power) the utopian moment is rational. It is the recoupage of the imagined or constructed social relations of interactional production in which the monadic self discovers its own unconscious self production. It redeems symbolic capacity — the very substructural source of its relational disjunction. It turns that symbolic capacity toward the articulation of inabilities of the social relational context to absorb its symbolic energy. The reflexivity of this activity is the creation of class consciousness at the level of the unconscious. This activity negates the individual's isolation, but it is still subject to containment, both from its own inner distortions and from the administrative apparatus of the psychiatric mind police.

The bifurcation contained in the fragments of the unconscious of this new class is between: the corporatized authoritarianism that builds on the residual memories and attachments of familism; and, the social rationality and courage to assemble the grounds of monadic crisis. Stepping outside this contradiction entails the delusional monism of the self in order to interrogate the social relations of its own symbolic production.

As the cultural milieu displaces specific human relations with advertised and caricatured corporatized representations (Ewen, 1976), the capacity for cognitive differentiation that the utopian moment requires is destroyed. The expansion of symbolic competence as an aspect of the labor power of the new class is accompanied by the proliferation of cultural stereotypes as redundant overloaders of unconscious storage (Klapp, 1978). Symbolic capacity is simultaneously developed and retarded. There is a contradiction in the substructural forces of self-production.

Class consciousness and the dangers of Fascism are still the socially given problematics of critical social psychology. Now, however, these themes are played out in an informationally rich corporate world that organizes, and simultaneously subverts, its own reproduction in the unconscious, and in the social relations of production. In the present conjuncture, symbolic accumulation and its occasional crises of underconsumption combines with stereotypical cultural content and socially mobilized repression to deplete the monadic resources of conceptual appropriation. This makes it less likely that social knowledge for rational collective action can be developed. The Enlightenment (Horkheimer and Adorno, 1972) does not end in myth but in ignorance.

Part Three
Analysis

7
The end of social interaction

As society becomes increasingly commodified, social interaction and the conditions which make it possible disappear. Social psychology, instead of developing theories which treat interaction in relation to specific social and historical conditions, creates a series of abstract and universal theories which reflect changing social conditions and which ideologically distort the nature of interaction under those conditions.

Both subjective trends and objective trends are evident in the history of social psychology. Social interaction is reduced to internal mental structures in cognitive attitude theory and ethnomethodology; later, with changing production relations, person and process disappear in equity and exchange theories. Theoretical construction becomes rather elaborate as subjectivity or society is fabricated from its opposite.

In analyzing equity theory, which reduces social interaction to exchange relations, I hope to show how theoretical construction in social psychology functions to occlude the social. A great part of the analysis of equity theory is therefore given over to a textual critique of equity theory in order to show how social psychology produces social ignorance.

Equity theory not only objectivizes social interaction, it objectivizes it falsely. It theorizes exchange without production, and exchange without exploitation. I try to restore the concepts of production and exploitation to bear on the problem of interaction and the theory of equity.

The end of interaction in theory, its reduction to exchange relationships, is tied to the crisis in corporate liberal capitalism, for which, I have argued, social psychology speaks. While equity theory functions ideologically to conceal this crisis by emptying interaction of any specific content, its contradictory contribution, in the form of an opaque and universal sounding theory, is the acknowledgment of the increasing commodification and organization of all human relationships as abstracted exchange values. The current social abstraction and economization of social psychology unintentionally brings to the surface of awareness the question of the relation between what is called social psychology and what is called economics. It does this by introducing the marketplace as a central metaphor. But, this also makes questions about the organization of social production and everyday social interaction sound less strange. Up until now the production of ignorance in social psychology, its occlusion of the social, has consistently ignored and repressed any mention of social production as even an aspect, no less theory, of social interaction.

One result of the separation in the academy between economics – which, of course, is almost never Marxist economics – and social psychology is the underdeveloped state of any Marxist or critical theory of social interaction. The theoretical situation has not changed much in the five years since Krueger (1976, p. 99) wrote of a materialist theory of interaction: 'Systematic research in these areas has hardly begun!' But this analysis, again only hints at a positive theory of interaction. Its accent is critical and methodological.

Social psychology, social interaction, and corporate liberalism

There are a variety of social psychologies of social interaction, both within psychology and in sociology. In the absence of a systematic content analysis, I want to suggest two overall themes: (1) Changes in theories of interaction express changes in the role of interaction in the periods of the rise, and dominance, and finally the crisis of corporate liberalism, and (2) social psychology obscures and ideologizes the problem of social interaction by either subjectivizing or objectivizing the phenomenon.

It is the rise of the large corporation in this century which brings the problem of social interaction to central attention. Problems in social coordination and human management engender social psychology as a research discipline. As corporate liberalism reaches dominance and then crisis, interaction begins to disappear as a social category, as it is increasingly commodified.

Marcuse (1964, p. 9) has graphically described this historic transformation of social relations:

The people recognize themselves in their commodities; they find
their soul in their automobile, hi-fi set, split-level home, kitchen
equipment. The *very mechanism* which ties the individual to his
society [emphasis added] is anchored in the new needs which it
has produced.

Similarly, Braverman observes (1974, p. 276): 'not only the material
and service needs but even the emotional patterns of life are channeled
through the market.' The extension of advertising (Ewen, 1976) simultaneously grasps and extends the interpretation of all aspects of human
association as market relations mediated through objectified abstractions of human social activity.

As the movement of corporate liberalism first brings interaction in
society to the foreground and then eventually destroys it, theories of
interaction in social psychology undergo historical shifts. During the
rise of corporate capitalism, psychological social psychology produces
work on group cohesion and sociological social psychology on social
integration. During the period of corporate liberal dominance when
psychology produces cognitive attitude theories, sociology develops
ethnomethodology, also concerned with cognitive rules. Finally, as
corporate liberalism breaks up, and as the regime it imposes on social
interaction destroys it, equity theory and exchange theories come to
describe social interaction. There is a final, methodological displacement, particularly in sociological social psychology, to multivariate
analysis which is the end of a theory of interaction.

Social psychology has always presented an ideological picture of
social interaction, but the ideological character of the discipline only
becomes evident with each retreat from the social regime of corporate
liberalism. As corporate liberalism arose, so did theories of group
cohesion and social integration. Both stressed the importance of social
interaction in society, as the corporation demanded increasing coordination and control over social interaction. Both theories were
ideological — they separated social interaction from the production
relations which structured it, and presented theoretical pictures which
naturalized and universalized the social interaction of a particular
historical epoch.

The ideological character of social psychology is becoming increasingly evident with every retreat from the social regime of corporate
liberalism. The epigrammatic social psychology of the period of
corporate dominance was interpersonal social psychology. There are

according to this mode (Bennis, 1973) certain individual dispositions or motives. But the individual traits are modified and shaped by inter-personal, or as they are commonly referred to, 'situational factors.' There are a number of different interpersonal processes, but they are generally characterized by a concern with the specific aspects of mutuality, interdependence, and dyadic adjustment. In a period such as the 1950s — the boom time of the social psychology industry — with the expansion of industrial management through human relations (Bendix, 1956) at the workplace, and the post-war glorification of familism (Baxandall, Gordon and Reverby, 1976), the social psychology of interpersonalism was a reliable guide for the everyday activities of white middle-class men. Social psychology was even then an ideology or systematic misrepresentation of social reality — for women (Sherman and Beck, 1979), minorities (Ladner, 1973), and the blue collar working class (Shostak and Gomberg, 1964).

The ideologization of social psychology intensifies and expands with the social transformations of the past thirty years. As an increasing part of everyday life has become commodified, and its concrete aspects converted into abstract values to be bought and sold on the market, the social psychology of interpersonalism has become an ever less accurate portrayal of the everyday lives of even the white, corporate world of middle-class men.

Social psychology in the first period of corporate liberalism was at least in part a scientific technical force of production; in the second period, it describes interaction as a series of interpersonally mediated events at a time when a reduced proportion of everyday life is in fact interpersonally mediated, when the interpersonal mediations have a decreased impact on the organization of social relations. Social psychology becomes ideological — obscuring the form and content of social interaction. It can accomplish this obscuring by placing people in artificial laboratory situations, which as a sample of social situations represents more the social ideals of a specific historic class than actual life conditions of the mass of people. Then, the 'research findings' are applied, selectively, as general real-life laws. Similarly, the interpersonal situational social psychology of affiliation, altruism, cooperation and mutual adaptation obviously represent the experienced social dynamics of only a small segment of the population. Finally, and most import-antly, social psychology reverts more and more to the subjective, communicative and cognitive aspects of social relations precisely as those social relations have become increasingly objectified as commodities, and the mediations between people can be better seen as exchanges of abstract values, than as interpersonal relations.

At the time that social interaction is being increasingly objectivized, abstracted, and rationalized, social psychology retreats from interpersonal situationism toward the sublimation of its most subjective aspects as characteristic and determining interaction. The earlier social psychology of interaction had emphasized social roles – the naturalization (as I have argued in chapter 6) of an alienated social division of labor – as the key mediating concept of social interaction. Despite acknowledging the positional or structural aspect of social relations through the concept of role, the normative, expectation aspect of role was specifically emphasized. In general, interaction is, 'basically a communication process,' (Hollander, 1976, pp. 209–47). Here are some selected bold type assertions about social interaction which appear in a popular, recent social psychology text:

Interaction depends upon shared expectancies.

The biggest difference between formal and informal interaction is that the latter depends more on individual dispositions and satisfactions.

Social interaction can be vital in providing support and reducing stress.

Understanding the outlook of others is an essential feature of interaction.

Cooperation and competition are not necessarily opposite, because competition often involves cooperative elements.

As corporate liberalism, still dominant, moves from ascension to decline, social psychology further abstracts the social from social interaction. Attribution theory and other revised versions of cognitive and attitude theories increasingly ignore the entire process of social interaction – except as an added external variable, or in describing only the cognitive and subjective aspects of social interaction. This is the familiar disassociation of aspects of mind from social relations. Along with the new idealism of social psychology, there is a current return to an additional method for the denial of social interaction. This method focuses on individual traits. The revival of individual trait theories occurs through the current importance of various models of moral and cognitive development. The hegemonic operation of the idealizing and individualizing culture of social psychology is evidenced by its capacity to incorporate oppostion and to shape it to its own image. Now, 'dialectical reasoning' becomes an unfolding individual developmental characteristic of mind (Basseches, 1980).

Sociological social psychology follows the same course. Symbolic interactionism enjoys an academic renaissance, both in the United States and England (Rock, 1979), and its competing paradigmatic successor, ethnomethodology, further limits social interaction to the most immediate, linguistic communications of the proximate and structurally abstracted situation. Schegloff's (1979, pp. 23-78) analysis of telephone conversations, whatever may be its interest, and the value of ethnomethodology in redeeming the most concrete aspects of social interaction from abstractive, marketizing, and commodifying tendencies, is ideological because it regards that work as completely constitutive of the study of social interaction. Schegloff writes (1979, p. 24): 'The work in which my colleagues and I have been engaged is concerned with the organization of social interaction.' The abstraction of language and its careful description, which might make ethno-methodological activity a dereifying social psychology is obviated by the increasing goal of formalizing abstracted patterns of conversational analysis. Psathas observes (1979, p. 1): 'Each of the contributors is engaged in the serious quest of discovering the properties of repeatable and recurrent usages and working toward a formal descriptive-analytic account of these discovered properties.'

Decline becomes crisis for corporate liberalism. The technicization of the organizational forms of corporate production (Edwards, 1979), deskilling (Braverman, 1974; Zimbalist, 1979), and the intensification of Taylorist methods as attempts to improve productivity, intensify the rate of exploitation of labor and so, according to traditional Marxist economics (Castells, 1980), are necessary to counteract the tendency of the falling rate of profit. All this sets the stage for the return of an ungraded utilitarian logic, both in everday culture and among academic social psychologists. The utilitarianism, which appears in Homan's (1961) work for example, buttresses the atomized social imagery of possessive individualism with the language of modern cost accounting and the psychology of behaviorism. Equity theory is one of the more sophisticated and academically well-received instances of the return of utilitarianism as the social psychology of exchange.

Taken together, the subjectivization and economization of social psychology represent a familiar cultural method of social denial. The possibility of a social psychology of the interactive social production of social relations is avoided by dividing the social world of human beings into the subject and the object. Interaction as a simultaneously self and collectively transforming activity is dissipated as a social form and as a mode of thought by this division between the objective and the subjective.

Once a theory has seized one pole of subjectivity/objectivity as a starting-point, it must proceed to fabricate the other pole. Ironically, in the case of equity theory, this means that the objectivizing economization tendency of social psychology leads beyond its own naive naturalization of commodity relations of abstract exchanges as causal and fundamental. It makes an effort to understand the production obscured by the commodity form, the human activity which makes products and exchanges possible. When an objective exchange model encourages the analysis of social interaction as an aspect of a more general economic process, then the study of production returns to the subjective and objective social relations of human activity as interaction that I suggest is disappearing from the language of social psychology. A critique of equity theory can return us to the underlying social reality which the theory both reveals and falsifies: the liberal culture and social formation which has nurtured this social psychology and now divides between technical, instrumental rationality, on the one hand, and idealistic moral fundamentalism and individual subjectivism, on the other.

Critique of equity theory: the social psychology of possessive individualism

Although equity theory has been debated and discussed, criticisms and qualifications have been made only from competing social psychological paradigms for interaction study, or from the perspective of equity theory itself. For positivism, theoretical statements are simply attempts to correlate observed independent events. Thus the overriding question is always, how well does equity theory predict interactive behavior?

I intend to view equity theory in its larger cultural role — its ideological role. A theory can be analyzed as a particular kind of cultural statement. It advertises a particular imagery, a particular mode of thought, a particular view of what is going on in the world. Interpretive intervention is required to grasp the meaning of a theory; it must literally be read. Social psychologists refuse to see this theoretical surplus meaning at a point when many textbooks are written as if they were an advertising copy.

Beyond interrogating theory for its everyday commonsense messages, I wish to read equity theory as a theoretical production, the result of the textual work of a set of interpretive practices (for a theory of textual production, see Eagleton, 1976). I shall try to describe how these interpretive textual practices perform the work of translating a whole series of unstated assumptions about the character of social reality into explicit social psychological theory. This is not a disinterested structuralist exercise in theory reading, but a demonstration of how social psychology functions to produce social ignorance. All the textual practices work together to remove social production from social interaction.

Cultural critique

What is the general cultural message of equity theory? It offers consolation. It reassures us that individuals can achieve happiness by rational calculation. It does so during a time when traditional bases of everyday social forecasting appear less reliable. It reasserts the value of justice, but as a naturalized trait, and not as a social goal of human activity. It promises that violations of fairness do not go unpunished. According to the theory, those who get more than what their efforts merit will be unhappy, even though, in reality, the distribution of psychological burdens indicates that happiness is more determined by socially conditioned life chances than by individual effort. Egotism is posited as an innate motive. Then the effects of egotism are mitigated by suggesting that there is a companionate motive, 'fairness.' Equity theory thereby reduces questions of fundamental social contradiction and conflict to subjective, normative regulation. 'Deservingness' regulates the social disorder of natural egotism.

At a time when market mechanisms are transformed by bureaucratic-political management, equity theory revives the imagery of a society constituted of separate individuals who are motivated by the pursuit of private gain and are limited largely by a natural propensity to strike fair bargains. At a time when social analysts see a crisis of public rationality and an autonomous ego (Habermas, 1975), equity theory resuscitates private rationality and the utilitarian view of a society of individual entrepreneurs. It puts all social relations into the marketplace, just as the free market of individual exchanges fades as an economic reality and social-theoretic metaphor.

Then it turns around and puts social relations back in the head. In the society that it imagines, social conflicts are subjective individual matters. Contradiction and conflict are regulated naturally by a need for subjective cognitive balance. Social harmony is accomplished by individual accommodation and adjustment.

Equity theory combines the perspective of the eighteenth century, the ideology of the 1950s, and the social interests of contemporary middle-class status anxiety. It crystallizes the new forms of individualized subjective reaction against the social change movements of the 1960s, while claiming these movements for its own. It accepts and includes demands for self-expression and redistribution, but it denies the origins and premises of these demands in social structure and class conflict. Equity theory is an emblematic modern social psychology; it consoles and reassures by abstracting the individual from social, collective interests, and removing society from social history. It is a cultural statement, but it speaks the language of ethics and science, which helps to obscure its real content. Equity theory systematizes and rationalizes culture during times of social reaction. It updates the philosophy of possessive individualism (MacPherson, 1962) to accommodate liberal culture in its decline.

As an unstated social theory, the social psychology of equity theory is a regression behind even conservative sociology. Sociology began in response to the theoretical failures of utilitarianism and the practical problems of early capitalism (Parsons, 1937; Therborn, 1976). The first science of society, classical political economy, universalized the concerns and practices of the early bourgeoisie. All social relationships were viewed as free exchange in the emergent marketplace. But the universalization of conscious voluntary trading as a dominant image is an ideology even for the eighteenth century. The marketplace itself was created through forceful appropriation, violence and coercion. Its continued operation is made possible by social domination, which lies close beneath the surface rhetoric of free exchange. Marx's assertion that (1967, p. 760): 'If money, according to Augier, "comes into the world with a congenital blood-stain on one cheek", capital comes dripping from head to foot, from every pore, with blood and dirt,' has been well documented by contemporary economic historians (Hilton, 1976).

105

Analysis

The central metaphor of utilitarian social theory which idealizes the marketplace of early capitalist society as a general model of social interaction is possessive individualism. On this view, 'society consists of relations of exchange between proprietors . . . its possessive quality is found in its conception of the individual as essentially the proprietor of his own person or capacities, owing nothing to society for them' (MacPherson, 1962, p. 3).

Even Durkheim's conservative sociology rejects this view. Durkheim argued that exchanges exist within and are determined by a broader social context. Inter-individual interactions are meaningless fictions without a description of the environment which shapes their form and gives them content. For Durkheim the social is the shared symbols, the collective conscience, which makes exchange possible. These symbols are produced and reproduced through collective rituals which may appear irrational. But without symbolic rituals there would be no society.

The individual social actor is an historical product of a collectively produced and transmitted symbolic structure, and of the social and ecological morphology upon which it is based. In Durkheim's functionalism, the individual is not a proprietor who is driven by a logic of self-interest. The individual is an embodiment of the collective conscience.

Marx shares Durkheim's views on social context, but creates a more specific and critical theory. For Marx, the decline of the ancient regime and the transformation of feudalism extracted the individual from one set of corporate identities and replaced him into a new set of collective relations. In contradistinction to feudalism, in early capitalism the individual is seen as free or socially abstracted. In fact, freedom to exchange is defined by the altered collective organization of social relations in the process of economic production. Freedom and equity of economic exchange and their political aspect, in individual right, are formal rather than substantive. The real conditions of exchange are forced. The choice of the wage laborer is exploitation or starvation.

What distinguishes capitalism from feudalism is not the end of the collective determination of individuals, but the transformation of the social patterning of constraint, and the individualizing of the rhetoric of social domination. The commodity form makes opaque not only the unequal exchange of labor power for wage, which falsely presents itself as a contract, freely entered upon, but also the social character of the labor process itself. Human relations of production interdependence appear as 'relations among things' (Marx, 1967, pp. 71-83). For Marx, then, only one class of people are proprietary entrepreneurs. Their profits are not generated by striking sharp bargains with equals, but through the coercive and socially mystified exploitation and domination of another class, whose productive labor is the actual source of profit. The marketplace image of political economy reflects the world view, not of the new captains of capital, but of their historical predecessors, the shopkeepers and traders. These petit bourgeoisie cannot survive in trading with the development of an accumulative and centralizing process of social control, one based on the socially organized exploitation of the producers. The marketplace metaphor is nostalgia.

The new producers, the wage laborers, are proprietors only of their own labor power. This labor power is socially constituted, transformed, and ultimately robbed and diminished in the labor process. That is the more limited meaning of alienation. The ideology of capitalism, in utilitarian philosophy, in political economy and in bourgeois morality, propounds a society of free individuals. In fact, there are only class individuals, whose interchanges are defined by their membership in antagonistic social groups, or classes. The social fabric is held together neither by shared symbols, nor by selfish trading moderated by an external, neutral state, but by internally generated patterns of domination which are based on economic exploitation, political oppression, and the ideological mystification of these forms of domination. That is the role which the 'free individual' plays in capitalist society!

Equity theory returns to the ideology of the petit bourgeoisie.

Textual critique

In reading through the propositions of equity theory, we can specify the theoretic operations involved in constructing this ideological picture of the world. One finds four interpretive practices through which the denial of the social is accomplished: desocialization; deproblematization; deinstitutionalization; and, dehistoricization. I will read through and explicate the theory, interpolating a general description of each textual practice as it arises.

Desocialization

'Proposition I: Individuals will try to maximize their outcomes.' But

107

in equity theory selfishness is not unlimited. It is contained by individuals' need for a sense of fairness subject to equity. Rewards can only be enjoyed if they are based on proportional efforts. This individual and subjective basis of regulating conduct is apparently a transhistorical human trait. 'Proposition III: When individuals find themselves participating in inequitable relationships, they will become distressed. The more inequitable the relationship, the more distress individuals will feel.' This 'equity motive' is based on the first proposition. Since, 'if we consistently try to snatch more benefits than we deserve we will get caught and punished. We soon learn that the most profitable way to be selfish is to be "fair" ' (Walster, Walster and Berscheid, 1978, p. 15).

In equity theory, which offers itself as a 'general theory of social behavior,' the classic utilitarian dilemma of the socially disruptive consequences of boundless egotism is resolved by positing an individual need for self-regulation. Although equity theorists asserts that this motive is socially acquired, through socialization, its operative theoretical status is that of a natural human tendency. This theoretical status is displayed by a lack of empirical attention to historical, social, and, to a lesser extent, even individual variability in the distribution of the equity motive ('individuals evidently do generally feel that it is in their best interest to act fairly, for they generally do so' Walster, Walster and Bernschied, 1978, p. 16). The process of the sociohistorical production, distribution, and meaning of the motive remains undescribed.

The view of the individual which is presented in equity theory is the Skinnerian reinforcement model, joined to a marketplace metaphor by the linguistic equation of rewards and profits, punishments and costs. Despite the translation of all statements of relationships among variables into the synthesized language of behaviorist psychology and capitalist economics, activation of reinforcements is predicated on an anterior model of individual functioning: the need to maintain cognitive balance.

Fairness or equity appears as the motivational norm of human conduct. It is the equilibrium point of the individual organismic system. Deviation from it leads to behaviors which return the organism to its optimal state. Equity theory is a drive theory, based on the maintenance of cognitive balance around individuals' need for a subjective sense that their relationships are equitable. 'Equity' then means that their perceived 'returns' for their 'investments' are proportionally equivalent to the ratio of the returns to the effort of those with whom they are interacting in the language of the theory, their 'partners'. Proposition IV: Individuals who discover they are in an inequitable relationship will attempt to eliminate their distress by restoring equity. The greater the inequity that exists the more distress they will feel, and the harder they will try to restore equity.'

Explaining human interactions by the positing of drives and motives, in this instance, cognitive consistency, is an example of the cultural practice of desocialization. Desocialization works by first abstracting the individual from her generative social context. Then the abstracted individual is recontextualized, but in a way which denies social constitution. The person appears within social interaction, but what occurs in the interaction emanates from the individual. The interaction of individual emanations determines social relations. In this way, the individual is socially stripped and constitutive social processes present themselves only in a hieroglyphic of individual, natural tendencies.

Desocialization is a method of reification (Lukács, 1971). In religious reification, humanly created images of the non-human and extraterrestrial become seen as sources of human powers and this wordly events. Secularization, science, and changing social relations have altered the terms of reification. The gods are replaced by the individual. Supernatural forces are replaced by human nature, or traits and natural tendencies. The result is an occlusion of social processes which are collapsed into individual motives, but an appearance of a social explanation. The appearance of a social explanation occurs here because the reified clusterings of social dynamics, the individual, are then repositioned in a social interaction. As an ideological practice, desocialization supports the ethos of individualism. It helps contain explanation within social psychology by eclipsing the relation between social structure and social interaction.

Deproblematization

Individualizing social relations, and describing social interaction outside of social structure is made possible only in part by translation of social process into individual motive. Ironically, a society of desocialized individuals is theoretically upheld by a theory that has usually been labeled as anti-individualistic, structural functionalism. Structural functionalism is never openly explicated. But behind the metaphor of the marketplace, beneath the apriorism of individual needs, unreminded of a sociology which pushes the concepts of culture and socialization to the fore, there is a social theory behind the social psychology: functionalism.

Equity theory translates individual utilitarianism to the societal level: Proposition IIA: 'Groups can maximize collective reward by evolving accepted systems for equitably apportioning resources among members. Thus, groups will evolve such systems of equity, and will attempt to induce members to accept and adhere to these systems.'

Lest there by any doubt that the equity motive is a natural tendency of social aggregates as well as individuals, Proposition IIB underlines that: 'Groups will generally reward members who treat others equitably, and generally punish (increase the cost for) members who treat others inequitably.'

The structure of social relations enters equity theory in a way which makes it unproblematic. The deproblematizing of social relations, and their interchanges, is theoretically accomplished by seeing the social component as an entity — society — rather than as social structures, relations among contending groups, or concrete social processes. Society becomes the personified entity which acts with a single will, mirroring the rational, fair, self-seeking, isolated individual: 'Proposition IIA simply states that societies will act in their own self-interest, and will hammer out a set of rules for allocating community resources' (Walster, Walster and Berscheid, 1978, p. 8).

Social conflict, internal societal contradiction, and social change can be ignored as determinants of social interchanges. In equity theory, the social makes itself known only as the undifferentiated entity, society acting and evolving toward equity. Social dynamic parallels individual dynamic. Both are driven by an ahistorical, socially unconstituted and undescribed self-interest, pushing toward the individual equilibrium of perceived equity, and the social equilibrium of equitable distribution of rewards.

As the *sotto voce* social theory of equity, this rationalistic, socially undifferentiated version of functionalism relegates social processes to the realm of the automatic. Although equity theory shares with functionalism a concern with equilibrium and social harmony, it neglects efforts of functional theorists to describe the social processes and the shared symbolic structures through which harmony is accomplished. By appropriating the teleological equilibrium logic of functionalism, without its description of the processes of social balancing (Parsons, 1951), equity theory illustrates how the social can be denied while it appears to be included.

110

Deinstitutionalization

Equity theory is also constructed upon a theory of distribution which states that unequal social distribution exists because it is in the self-interest of society. This has been a traditionally held worldview of privileged social classes. The belief that social inequality is a societal virtue or necessity has also been articulated by functional theorists in sociology. They have argued that social inequality promotes societal stability and survival. Those who have the most talent must be motivated to contribute most to societal functioning through the lure of greater and unequal rewards (Davis and Moore, 1945).

Equity theory modifies a bald assertion of the rewards of unimpeded egoism. While fairness is rewarded because it ultimately serves self-interest, the view that inequality is socially justified on the basis of differential individual performance is rejected by defining social contribution as equitable behavior. The ideology of reward for individual merit is ideologically mitigated, just as the social relations of entrepreneurial capitalism were transformed into a set of interconnections between business, government, social reformers and the new social professionals of corporate liberalism (Weinstein, 1968). The social analysis of the corporate liberals was that socially unregulated pursuit of profit would be unprofitable. In the long run, reform is a surer road to continuing profit. The ideology of the new corporate capitalism is public spirited.

Just as the social relations of profit seeking were broadened to include education and welfare, individual merit now includes acting fairly and taking account of others' claims to deservingness. Individual profit, like corporate profit, entails social responsibility.

A third interpretive practice, deinstitutionalization, is involved here. It affirms the absence of social determination by externalizing it. We see no interaction between the person and the institutions of corporate capitalism, no interiorization of specific meanings from the social array.

The utilitarian philosophies of possessive individualism ignored societal structures except as an afterthought, as a conflict regulator brought in by individuals to adjudicate collective egoism. Society or state appear on the theoretical scene as *deus ex machina*, while individuals remain the self-constituted 'possessors of their own capacities, owing nothing to society for them.' Equity theory maintains the fiction of a socially unconstituted individual through its portrayal of exchanges as socially unmediated and decontextualized. Social

111

environment determines inter-individual interchanges, but not as an interplay between the interiorized collective symbolic structure of the individual and structured constraint. Rather the environment is an external force, an intervention. The non-mediation of exchanges is affirmed by locating social determination in outside agencies. Social determination is described through the effects of interventions on perceptions of equity, and not as an understanding of social influences within exchange processes themselves. Once again, the appearance of the social is maintained, and its external impact assessed, but in a process which is fundamentally both natural and individual.

When the social constitution of individual interaction is theorized as an intervention of legal agencies and 'third parties' rather than as itself the individualized embodiment and the transformation of social processes then the subjective side of social determination is externalized in the concept of 'scrutineer.' Subjectivity is socially grounded, but outside the relationship. *The social struggle over definitions is not theorized as a basic aspect of the exchange process itself.* Instead, society determines inputs and rewards on the basis of power. Individuals perceive on the basis of these social definitions, so that the crux of the equity process is adaptation to perceptions of equity or inequity rather than conflict over the determination of meanings. In this way, objective social factors are admitted as abstract power and subjective perceptions are seen as ultimately objectively socially determined, while the ongoing process of the relation between social resources and subjective definition is ignored. We get the abstractions 'culture' and 'society' instead of social interaction.

Dehistoricization

In equity theory, behavior is explained as an effort to achieve, maintain, and restore equity or, failing to do that, to rationalize inequity. This behavior is motivated by a need to perceive social relations as equitable or 'fair.' While definitions of specific inputs and outcomes are culturally determined, and rooted in power relations, the general belief in fairness is posited as a universal, natural trait, and is exempted from the socio-historical process of the production of meanings.

Reporting the research of Lerner cited in Walster, Walster, and Berscheid (1978, p. 220) they note that 'theorists have observed that *people* [emphasis added] possess an intense need to perceive this as a fair and equitable world,' and that: 'Exploiting another violates the *normal* [emphasis added] person's ethical principles and conflicts with his self expectations' (Walster, Walster and Berscheid, 1978, p. 23). But if fairness means that a person's rewards should be proportioned to his/her efforts, it seems to be more of an idealized social rule of modern capitalist societies than any universal human trait. Equity theory dehumanizes and dehistoricizes a social rule.

History is full of examples of belief systems which justify exploitation, and accord legitimacy to reward on the basis of supernatural grace, divine rights, original sins, or simply, class and caste origins. Historical differences are homogenized by saying that they represent variable inputs. But that recasts historically variant norms into the mold of a currently prevalent distribution norm, and denies the specificity of the underlying equity formula: reward for effort. In the present historical period, belief in equity as a social rule is, I suggest, an extension of the ideology of merit from the world of work to the broader sphere of social interactions.

By ignoring the sociohistorical constitution and social location of the norm or expectation of fairness in changing socio-economic structures and processes, equity theory serves as a scientized legitimation of the dominant mode of false consciousness. Instead of explaining the social basis and historical reasons that the expectation of fairness has become so prevalent in social interaction, equity theory naturalizes this important social rule as a basic human motivation. It presents social reality as the result of natural, individual motives. Naturalizing historical developments buttresses the *status quo*. Where the natural replaces the historical, thinking of social change becomes less possible.

The absence of production

But equity theory does describe some social reality. What it portrays is that the present social formation is so intractable as to defy collective transformation, so implacable as to appear eternal and natural, and so overpowering as to make individual accommodation of action and thought seem the most viable strategy. Equity theory is an affirmation of present social order and the loss of historical consciousness and objective powerlessness, which is both its antecedent and consequence.

All these interpretive practices — desocialization, deproblematization, deinstitutionalization, and dehistoricization — are in a sense instances of still another and more fundamental aspect of an ideology which equity theory represents: the admission of the social and the economic while denying social production. This is particularly ironic since equity theory is often accused of importing economic models to

113

the study of social interaction (Rubin, 1973). The economic metaphor that equity theory uses is based on exchange, on the distribution of rewards as the determinant of social interaction.

This economic view in equity theory is descriptively insightful. It systematizes and scientizes our rationalizations. It affirms the prevalent economic ideology of consumerism, the view that we are living in a market economy governed by individual choices and consumer sovereignty. Equity theory, in applying an economic model to social interaction, accepts this everyday commonsense view instead of explaining it. It imagines a society without economic production. At the micro level of social interaction also, there is no productive activity. Outcomes are always the result of exchanges and never of production. Interactions are explained in terms of proportionalities of inputs to outcomes, both for the individual, and in social relationships. Interactional products — intimacy, liking, distress — are the results of exchanges from which the intervening transformative process of human labor has been omitted. Equity theory economizes society, only to remove process and production from social interaction.

Restoring production and exploitation

A critical social psychology of social interaction would begin with the question of labor power. The central aspect of social interaction is the continuous production of labor and the conditions for its reproduction. The dependence of specific characteristics of labor power on social relational interaction for their production is historically variable. If Marcuse, Braverman, Ewen and others are right about the extension of the market dynamic of abstract exchange value then the production of labor power requires a fairly standard repertoire, and a reduced amount of social interaction with other people. Decreased relevance of the category of interaction in social psychology and its displacement by the importance of subjective individual processes and objectivised exchanges of abstract utilities is the theoretical expression of this historical abstraction and fragmentation of social interaction.

Not only labor power, but the social characteristics and conditions of its production are created in social interaction. For characteristics of labor power like docility, interpersonal cleverness, and skilled self advertisement, the social psychological question is what the social interactional dynamics are that make this type of labor power possible.

If labor power is seen as including not just the workplace behaviors of the individual, but the characteristics of the personal formation as a whole, the economic categories take on a deeper meaning. It is not only that labor power is exploited in the process of economic production, with the capitalist appropriating the surplus product and surplus value. Rather, exploitation occurs interactionally in the very constitution of labor power. Where labor becomes a kind of capital, then exploitation occurs in the process of its constitution.

Marx's theory of exploitation might well be describing: the destruction of the family scapegoat for the ego aggrandizement of the others; the appropriation of the social space of discourse by the language of men against women; or the cognitive incapacitation of students by those with more bourgeois class origin, in the name of academic achievement. In his view (Bottomore and Rubel, 1956, p. 156):

> We have also seen that capital (the capitalist is merely capital
> personified and functions in the process of production as the agent
> of capital), in the social process of production corresponding to it
> . . . surplus labour for which no equivalent is returned and which
> always remains essentially forced labour.

This exploitative production of the specific characteristics of labor power as a multidimensional interaction process is ignored by conventional social psychology.

Social psychology ignores exploitation as well as production. Exploitation is based on antagonistic interests, and the fact that somebody benefits at the expense of somebody else. The success of the few is built upon the losses and social-psychological expropriation of the many. In social psychology, this possibility is only peripherally acknowledged in game studies. But exploitation is no game. It is a central sociopsychologic of capitalism, which the social movements of the 1960s and 1970s have brought to the fore as a basic aspect of social interaction in this society. But social psychology acknowledges these processes only by emptying their antagonistic, critical assumptions, and their practical social applications. It replaces them with interactionally generalized cost benefit analyses such as equity theory, and the practices of interpersonal management. The irony of this exploitative production of labor power is that in commodifying human characteristics and in realizing their production only as abstract exchange value — without intersubjective interaction — the human capacities which

115

constitute labor power are being diminished. I think that is the specific meaning of 'alienation' in Seve's (1978) and Garai's (n.d.) Marxist psychologies.

While social interaction, as practice and content, is being dissolved between the ideologies and practical methods of subjectivism and objectivism, this dissolution is being fought against in everyday life. The task of a critical social psychology is not only to describe generalized production and exploitation, but also to describe the everyday strategies that are being developed by the exploited to counteract the end of social interaction.

8
The new self:
breakdown or breakthrough?

The new self is commodified and approaches madness as a limit. To display the nature of the new self and the modern form of madness, which hides under the ahistorical abstractions of conventional social psychology, I will follow the program for a critical psychology advanced in earlier. First, the commodification of production will be described; second, I will work through the concept of self in terms of current historical contradictions; and, third, I will restore the class relations of the self abstraction. The argument is prefaced by a negative, critical moment, a critique of an 'historical' view of the self; and concluded by a positive utopian moment, the anticipation of the social psychology beyond self. The accent, in this chapter, is on the substantive, theoretical moment.

Critique of an historical approach to the changing self

Against the predominantly ahistorical social psychological views of the self, Ralph Turner (1976) has offered the hypothesis that the organization and processes of the self are historically variable. His argument is that there has been a shift from an institutional to an impulsive basis of the self. More people in the United States, especially younger ones, seem to locate their 'real selves,' the core of their self-definitions, in the satisfaction of 'non-institutional impulses.' The characteristics of the impulsive self are: spontaneous action, self-discovery, decreased 'self-control,' expression of 'human frailties,' and distrust of rules which appear arbitrary. Social control becomes increasingly problematic as the locus of self-definition shifts away from the perception of institutionalized values and conformity to them as the criterion of self-validation and adequacy.

117

The social theory which Turner implicitly criticizes is the moral integration model. Social order is possible because individuals share moral commitments which are enacted as conformity to the role prescriptions embedded in social institutions. Though Turner offers a number of examples to demonstrate a new self, 'the impulsive self,' anchored outside the bases of the old 'institutional self,' and then describes a number of hypotheses which could explain a historical shift in the United States during the past several decades from institutional to impulsive self, his effort is handicapped by continued use of the very social theory which he criticizes.

Three characteristics of the moral integration model are: its concern with social control; its tendency to dichotomize society and social needs, and individual needs; and explanation of social phenomena in terms of morality, ideas and conceptions. Turner recapitulates these tendencies. He formulates his problem in terms of social control – the shift in self-anchorage leads to loss of social control. He separates individual and society as two sets of concrete commitments and self-definitions, the 'impulsive' and the 'institutional.' Though he observes that each self-definition has aspects of both the individual and the social, and though he shifts the level of analysis from norms and values, typical of the moral integration model, to self-definitions, he still reprises the individual/society split. Finally, though Turner assumes that 'self-conception . . . is most usefully viewed as a variable intervening between some aspect of social structure and the working of the same or another aspect' (1976, p. 990), his conception of social structure overemphasizes role definitions, sentiments, values, norms and rituals.

The alternative to Turner's view is to reground the nature of the self in concrete historical social relations, in lived interaction, and in relation to the social structure of production. First, I think that a strong case could be made that the components of institutional self-anchorage, which now seem so absolute that it is easy to slide into identifying them with society, were themselves once part of a broad set of social structure and self-definitional changes which appeared to threaten society (which Turner recognizes but does not develop). The characteristics of the institutional self that Turner mentions, seem to me, remarkably similar to the virtues of the rising bourgeoisie, especially when abstractions like 'volition,' 'achievement,' 'morality,' and 'altruism' are seen in terms of their constituent institutional behaviors. Viewed concretely, they represent the self-definitions of

118

the 'free market' individual and the historically developed loyalties to occupational specialization and nuclear family.

Second, the complex and changing interactions between aspects of social structure and self-definitions must be reinserted into the organization of interactional networks constituting social structure. Turner believes that 'few of the instigations and sensations that people experience as impulse are not institutionally conditioned and generated' (1976, p. 1012). Yet, the particular set of self-anchorages to be explained, the impulsive self, is seen as outside of society or, more precisely through metaphorically, as a player, waiting in the wings, who can appear on stage only when the play breaks down (the 'lower inhibitions' of the repressed 'impulses,' 'mad desire') or has been fully enacted. When Turner does discuss social structure in terms of production and exchange relationships, it is only after production problems are routinized or 'resolved' that the 'impulsive self' appears. Social relations can influence the impulsive self as a trigger or catalyst, but its apparently static core consists of 'deep, unsocialized, inner impulses.'

The impulsive self like the institutional self can be regrounded in historical social relations and lived interactions rather than abstracted from them and reified. There is no more reason to see the specific characteristics of the institutional self as being society. To some extent, all these behaviors are rooted in the capacities of the organism, and all are subject to social construction. I see self-anchorage more fully as a constituent of social process.

Third, the self must be understood in terms of the structure of production. The emphasis on norms, values, and culture typical of conventional social psychology must be replaced with a more accurate view of the nature of social structure. It is very difficult for both the social actor and the social analyst to see the impulsive self as connected to social structure and, even further, as a process of social control. But that is precisely because of the form which social production increasingly takes in advanced capitalism, and the difficulty of seeing highly individualized needs with an enormous stress on self-gratification as an aspect of social control is indeed one of the major socially patterned defenses for the maintenance of the current system. This apparently contradictory process can be better comprehended by an analysis which begins with the tradition of 'commodity fetishism' (Marx, 1967; Lukács, 1971; Marcuse, 1964; Gorz, 1967) rather than with the moral integration approach.

This is, again, the three dimensions of the program for a critical

119

social psychology. When we have worked through them, we will have a more adequate conception of the self which breaks free from the ideological boundaries of the moral integration approach. We will see the current situation of the self in its contradictory potentiality. Negatively, the 'impulsive self' represents not a breakdown in social control, but a new form of social control, which tends to the limit of complete schizophrenization. Positively, this new self opens human possibilities only glimpsed by the radical madness theorists of the 1960s.

Commodification and the self

The bourgeois self is in the process of dissolution. Turner's 'impulsive self' is one of a number of formulations of an historically new self. This new self has been labeled other directed (Riesman, 1950), protean, (Lifton, 1968), mutable (Zurcher, 1977), multiple, boundless and lacking individualization (Wheelis, 1958; Sampson, 1975). All these theorists represent reified and ideological views of the contemporary processes of self-formation.

My view is that the new self is one instance of an historical personal formation — a lived moment in social relations — of which the schizophrenic is the extreme, ideal typical case. The connection between the new self and the schizophrenic is denied by theory and by social practice. The new self is explained, as we saw in the case of Turner's analysis, as a result of rapid rates of normative change and societal complexity. Schizophrenia is increasingly offered as an instance of the biological determination of behavior (Ratner, 1981). Conceptual compartmentalization is complemented by geographical segregation in everyday life. Even the deinstitutionalized insane remain socially segregated (Brown, 1982). Yet, the schizophrenic, as our archetypical mad-person, is still recognizable as the extreme of the new self. He casts the mirror to that self in process: the bourgeois self in dissolution. Of course, it is easier to deplore or laud (Turkle, 1980, pp. 150-83) the condition of our wrecks than it is to acknowledge how much they and we are really alike. There is now, along with an opposing tendency toward effective voluntary and enforced repression, a collapsing of this space, and a bringing of the similarities between normal and crazy to the surface.

The process of this dissolution is part of a changing set of production relations. The popular ideologies that champion and condemn it, as well as the theories which seek to capture it, are themselves part of these changing social relations of production. To understand this new self means to locate both its appearance and cultural representation in the general logic and specific history of capitalist production. In ordinary social relations, a new self is being produced, one which cannot be contained except through repression. First, I want to review and elaborate upon the meaning of commodification, and to show how it is related to the self — the subjective moment of class conflict — during a period, when as Horkheimer wrote (1947): 'The theme of this time is self preservation, while there is no self to preserve.'

Each aspect of the social relations of capital contributes in a different way to the production and transformation of the self. The most general of these relations is the commodity form. The commodity form originated in the organization and regulation of the labor process. Commodification as a more general form of social relations has extended well beyond the narrow economic sphere. I repeat Lukács's observation (1971, p. 83): 'the problem of commodities must not be considered in isolation or even regarded as the central problem in economics, but as the central, structural problem of capitalist society in all its aspects.' It is a social form in which: a product of human labor, which need not be a material product, but any result of human interaction, is separated from its producers and standardized to such an extent that the product becomes confused with the social process in which it is produced (Marx, 1967, pp. 72-3). People not only fail to recognize human labor in the things they exchange, but they ascribe causation to those products rather than to themselves or to other people. The world is perceived as an externally controlled place to adapt to rather than a product of collective human activity. Social relations become commodified as all human activities assume a social form in which the product, or its abstract representation, becomes more important than the development of the human capacities by which it is made (Perlman, 1968). The specificity of human effort and activity is replaced by standardized calculable units of abstract labor time. In the workplace, social relations of production display the commodification which includes the rationalization and overspecialization described by Weber and Marx.

The evidence is persuasive that this actually occurs now in the organization of all types of work (Braverman, 1974; Zimbalist, 1979). Separation of product from process, attribution of causal efficacy to the product (or its representation) and measuring human activity against abstract standards, are now typical in many domains of social interaction. When learning (Apple, 1980; Pinar, 1980), sexuality (Lewis and Brisset, 1967), and even illness (Illich, 1976) occur in the form of the commodity — externalized, objectified, abstracted human social interaction — then it makes sense to speak of a commodified society.

Participation in the social relations of such a society shapes the dynamics of the self. Continuous adaptation to external control leads to atrophy and devaluation of the potential capacity for intentional, self-directed behavior. Objective powerlessness combines with the perception of external causation to foster the idealization of the power of parent figures, earthly and transcendant lords, movie stars, and less accessible abstractions like 'the system.' The objective power-lessness and perceptual acceptance of the commodity appearance make the possibility of ego — intentional, transformative activity less likely.

In a commodified society individuals evaluate themselves according to the accumulation of abstract values, of which money is only an early example. The process of defining the self by reference to commensur-able, institutionally rational abstract values instead of specific, contextual social interactions, attaches internal self dynamics to the external, impersonal law of commodity exchange. If the accumulation of these abstracted values becomes the reference point of self-validation, then self-processes follow one of the organizing rules of commodity capitalism: accumulation without regard to need. When the criteria of self-definition are abstracted values rather than social interactions, and when self-validation requires continuous accumulation of these abstracted values to feed this market ego (Fromm, 1947), then the concrete stimuli of immediate social contexts are made less important for self-functioning. The result is that the abstracted accumulative self loses the capacity to make sensible discriminations in and adaptions to immediate contexts of stimulation. The information processing categories, recognitory prototypes (Carver, 1979, p. 1255), become so standardized and rigidified that the perceptual space for environmental input scanning is reduced. Abstract accumulation as the basis of self-definition diminishes the capacity for experiencing the world.

The new impulsive sensory hungry self is not, from this point of view, simply the symptom of declining institutional constraint and amorality. It cannot be cured by restoring social authority. Rather, the quest for experience is a result of an impoverishment of the capacity to experience. In its earliest historical appearance in the commodity life of the bourgeoisie, the general social logic of accumulation also became a guide for the organization of personal life. In the face of the imperative to accumulate abstract values, especially money, any emphasis on the experiential gratification of the particular moment was redefined as indulgence. It was this nineteenth-century social character that Marx was describing when he wrote (quoted in McLellan, 1973, p. 105):

> The less you eat, drink, buy books, go to the theatre or to balls,
> or to the public house, and the less you think, love, theorize, sing,
> paint, fence, etc., the more you will be able to save and the greater
> will become your treasure which neither moth nor rust will corrupt
> – your capital. The less you are, the less you express your life, the
> more you have, the greater is your alienated life and the greater is
> the saving of your alienated being.

In the twentieth century, this bourgeois character became the anal compulsive of psychoanalysis, the engineer and the victim of commodity relations. As abstracted accumulation becomes the preoccupation and standard of self-organization, the capacity to be gratified by the intense specificity of the immediate situation declines. It is replaced by an addictive obsession which aims to capture the gratification of specific sensuousness by pursuing those products of commodified social relations which are the very source of the deprivation. Addiction, not desire, becomes the mode or organism-environment relation when connection to the immediate environment is replaced by pursuit of a decontextualized abstraction (Schneider, 1975, pp. 122, 130).

The search for intensified experience which typifies the impulsive self of the late twentieth century is evidence that the need for immediate experiential stimulation and gratification has not been extinguished by commodity relations. Rather, it has become more desperate, searching out compensatory resources to restore the immediacy which the abstractness of accumulation debilitates. The sad irony of this search is that the lack of concrete experiential gratification within the course of social relations – an effect of commodification – impels the seeker toward substitute object gratifications, toward commodities. Even when the objects of gratification are themselves not commodities, they are prone to incorporation in commodified social relations and their abstracted rationalizing procedures (Marcuse, 1964). The commodity that can itself no longer satisfy desire has now attached to it additional abstracted symbolic promises of gratification.

With the further abstraction of the commodity-as-symbol, the self passes from the repressed, hoarding collector of objects of value, to the sensory hungry, addicted consumer of things, to the contemporary wandering stimulus receiver. This new self is searching for the symbolic beam in a world of abstract representations. S/he is pursuing symbols which have been removed from both their objectification as products and from the social relations of their original production. This incipient new self takes another turn in the road toward a chaotic symbolic market as the place in which to realize a desire stimulated by its lack in the ordinary production of everyday life (Haug, quoted in Schneider, 1975, p. 218).

When these effects of commodified social relations on the self are taken together, they portray a society which is producing madness as a fundamental social psychological tendency. The sociopsychologic of commodification leads to self-destruction. The madness that we now like to call schizophrenia is the result of: a powerlessness that induces ego dissolution; an abstractness that atrophies concrete discriminatory capacities; and a symbolic addiction that decontextualizes meaning and confuses, through incorporation, internal desire with external object, person and symbol. This is, I think, a more specific literal understanding of what Deleuze and Guattari (1977) envision as the collective social production of madness.

In America, Terry Kupers (1976) independently suggested the same hypothesis: schizophrenia is the quintessential self-product of the social relations of late capitalism and commodity relations, in particular. Kupers lists five typical aspects of schizophrenia: fragmentation of experience with bizarreness; fusion or confusion of the imaginary with the real; loss of boundary around ego or self; perception of self as object or thing; terror, fragility, and isolation. In his view (1976, p. 117): 'The very structure of capitalist society is "schizophrenic".' Reified social relations create the psychological conditions for the development of schizophrenia. The majority of the population is spared from this madness only at the cost of numbing their awareness. Those who refuse to be numbed fall prey to the viciousness of the social labeling process (Kupers, 1976, p. 119):

> they are denied validation in the areas where their beliefs contradict
> the conventional consciousness . . . devaluation can create areas
> where these people are unable to evaluate the truth or merit of their
> own perceptions and beliefs . . . . If they refuse to surrender or
> alter their course . . . they may become unable to differ with the

increasingly consolidated attribution by others that they are first different, then strange, and finally mad.

Socialization to numbness is only one method by which a potentially more widespread expression of the schizophrenic potential of commodification is inhibited. The psychological effects of commodified social relations are not randomly distributed. Part of the reason that not everyone is manifestly schizophrenic is that different social segments of the population experience different effects of commodification. The evidence is fairly consistent (Roman and Trice, 1967; Dohrenwend and Dohrenwend, 1969) that labeled and incarcerated schizophrenics are most likely to be poor. This is yet another instance of the human costs of commodity capital production being placed on the backs of those who are least able to pay.

Beyond the punitive, socially stratified labeling of psychiatric social management, there remain differences in how people in different social classes experience and express the psychological effects of commodification which, when taken together, constitute schizophrenia. The effects of powerlessness are most evident among the members of a working class which has the least power in producing its life, on and off the job. Commodity attributes of fitting in and valuing conformity to external standards are more likely among people who have little control and determination over their own work (Kohn, 1969). In this society, production powerlessness and the invidious status differences which are attached to it decrease the possibility for personal effectiveness, cognitive flexibility and self-esteem (Fried, 1973, pp. 200-24; Kohn and Schooler, 1978). Not surprisingly, powerlessness damages self-regard and the confidence necessary to act effectively. The rationalization and powerlessness of commodity ruled work experiences reappears in dream life (Wallraff, quoted in Schneider, 1975, p. 176). The powerlessness and lack of self-confidence and expansiveness that result from prolonged participation in commodity relations decrease feelings of well-being and general mental health (Gurin, 1960; Kornhauser, 1965; Bradburn and Caplovitz, 1965).

The older middle class still suffer the neurotic hysteria and psychosomatic complaints that result from the overregulation which develops in the pursuit of abstract accumulation (Manning and Zucker, 1976, pp. 35, 74). Commodification leads the so-called new middle classes to sensory searching in sex, drugs, and head tripping. Unlike working-class youths who suffer the invalidation of self that comes with powerless-

125

ness (Willis, 1977), upper-middle-class high school students feel a lack of meaning, and report boredom as their most common experience (Larkin, 1979). The full effects of commodification, which we now see only in their extreme version as schizophrenia, are blocked from expression through this class compartmentalization of the psychological consequences of commodification. But this pattern is not fixed. If class and social production relations change in ways that coalesce the separate aspects of commodity psychology, then there emerges a volatile collective madness, which may be turned against the social relations in which it is produced. Commodification is only the most general form of these social relations.

An historical note

The self that is being commodified — deflated, abstracted and decontextualized — is itself an historical product. The social history of this self, as Horkheimer observed (1947, p. 130), still remains to be written. We are still reading it indirectly, out of the silences of theoretic cultures, like social psychology.

The personal organization and social ideology of the self first developed with the rise of capitalist social relations. Personalized interiorization of social relational space, ascription of social cause to private intention, and unconscious incorporation of social need as individual motive are, as collective patterns, relatively recent historical developments. While Sappho already used the confessional 'I,' Socrates, Horkheimer asserts (1947, p. 134), 'was the true herald of the abstract idea of individuality, the first to affirm explicitly the autonomy of the individual.' The term autobiography does not appear until the beginning of the nineteenth century (Lyons, 1978, p. 55). But popular belief in detailed individual particularity, embodied in the novel, 'the translation from the objective, social and public orientation of the classical world to the subjective, individualist and private orientation' (Watt, 1962, p. 176) belongs to the social formation of early capitalism. A reorganization of social energy, and its channeling as the private internally regulated self, is expressed in literature, art, architecture and design (Lukács, 1970, pp. 191-200). During this period, the social uprooting and rearrangement of the population (Hilton, 1976) results in narrowing the social bases of personal reference and anchorage.

The rise of the self is the subjective aspect of capital accumulation.

The internalization of the social discipline of capital and labor as self-regulation and self-ideal, an internalization resisted by workers up until the present, is, however, more than the simple personalized reflection of changes in the organization of social production. The development of the self is accomplished also by a restructuring of social rules and a rearrangement of mediating social institutions. A reclassification and redeployment of the population occurs in which all behavior that interferes with production efficiency is labeled as different, abnormal or inferior (Foucault, 1965). At the same time, the everyday rules of the social interactions which occur in production are either abstracted as moral values or personalized as internal individual characteristics. This recoding has been so successful that even today psychology defines the self as a set of universal attributes and processes, rather than as an abstraction of the production rules of the early bourgeoisie. That is the basis of my objection to Turner's historical analysis of the self.

The establishment of internal discipline as the fundamental criterion of self occurred through the personalization of historical rules of social reframing, as well as through the reification of production relations as morality. The nuclear family reinforced these changes and gained new importance as a basis of social grounding, laying claim to the work of self development (Shorter, 1975; Zaretsky, 1976). Earlier, more extensive social involvements and rituals were in part displaced by a set of abstract rules that were used to sort and stigmatize the unproductive population, to fuse external work with self-evaluation, and to elevate the repression of sexuality as personal virtue. Both these rules of social regulation and the rules of production were called morality. Sexual guilt and morality helped displace attention from the fact that accumulation was the basis of self-discipline, and that introjection of the social needs of capital was the social reason for maintaining integrity of the self. Self is an historically new social coding which succeeds in: abstracting the person or monad from the production formation which constitutes it; ignoring the social policy rules of classification which enclose it; and enabling the sexual repression of the family to function as the false signifier of the source of repression. This historically produced organization of social energy, the individual bourgeois self, is now being challenged from within the very social relations that it has functioned to obscure.

The worker was forced into selfhood. In the unwillingness to accept the external discipline required to make wealth for others, workers have resisted all kinds of social domination (Gutman, 1976). Opposition to

127

external domination exists now also within the workplace (Aronowitz, 1978) and, less evidently, in the process of self-formation. One indication of this resistance is the refusal to internalize external domination as a natural principle of self-organization. Freud described this class difference of internalized constraint, but hardly from the viewpoint of class conflict and resistance (Cuddihy, 1974, p. 29).

In the class struggle over the self, family culture has played a constitutive and mystifying role. It has helped produce, for the bourgeoisie, the kind of guilt ridden self-integrity that fueled early capitalism. This dominant class generalized its model of the family, and tried to recruit the proletariat to its characterological banner (Zaretsky, 1976). For the working class, the socially enforced family and school were the public modes of subjective regulation, and the functional equivalents for the private guilt of the bourgeoisie. Through these institutions, and the social methods of enticement, coercion, and propaganda, the dominant group sought to universalize and naturalize its ideology. The working class fought back, and resisted imposition of production rules and class interests that were translated into moral values, and personality ideals. State action supported, if it did not simply implement, this class imposition of the self through schools (Nasaw, 1979) and families (Donzelot, 1979).

Even now, but in the neutralized language of science rather than one of morality and personality, the bourgeois self ideal is used as a standard by which to inferiorize any working-class subjectivity that resists its hegemony. Attributions of working-class external superegos (Gekas, 1979) and weak egos (Fried, 1973) can be interpreted as empirical evidence of subjective exploitation, a cost of commodity life. On the other hand, they are also signs of a refusal to accept the bourgeois ideals of internalized self-regulation as an organizing rule of interpersonal relations. The lack of belief in internal control is certainly no bar to social action. Research indicates that it may be one of its psychological prerequisites (Gurin, Gurin and Morrison, 1978, p. 290).

Despite these differences and continuing conflicts, the bourgeois self was established as the objective standard of personal organization. A self-ideology did develop among workers. But it was based less on the fear of sexuality, and more on the fear of industrial discipline, hunger and poverty, and falling down on the job (Gutman, 1976). The kind of self-blaming individual useful for exploitative production was provided by schools which trained for dependability, predictability and submission (Bowles and Gintis, 1976, pp. 125-48), and by families which so thoroughly accepted their dominated work lives that they represented the character of their submission as a social value (Kohn, 1969).

As the social organization of production changed, this socially imposed and largely established bourgeois self also changed. In the middle period of capitalism, the socially disciplined, internally regulated, private self was socially generalized, organizationally routinized, and more deeply commodified. Later, the commodified self began to become undone. The first period of early capitalism left an inheritance of its accomplishments for succeeding generations: a continuing belief in personalized attributions of cause and responsibility; a blurred fusion of social constraint and individual self-discipline; and an overarching conviction that an historically specific crystallization of social energies is a universal organismic attribute of the species. Early capitalism bequeathed to us the ideology of the self.

Production, class and the self

The psychological effects of commodification are differently experienced at different points in history and among different social classes. During the early period of capital accumulation, self-denying internal regulation and its familied displacement as sexual guilt were typical for the bourgeois self. The working class, despite resistance, was subjectively colonized, in schools and families. The powerlessness dimension of commodity effects had historically had the greatest impact on this class. During the middle stage of capitalism, there developed a contextual sensory deprivation of commodification, and substitution of the commodity for the lack of experience. With the rise of symbolic markets, the commodity self has become more decontextualized.

More importantly, the new self now appears to combine the psychological processes that have been historically and socially differentiated: powerlessness, abstractness and decontextualization. These general effects of commodification are supplemented by specific changes in the social relations of production. The specific changes lead toward a socialization – a deprivatization – of the self that originated in privatization. Not only are there changes in self-production, but also in the modes of self-regulation. There are small signs of a decline in the traditional modes by which self-processes are repressively regulated. Socialization as moral imposition and the social compartmentalization

129

of psychological labor no longer seem natural and inevitable.

These subjective changes are part of changes in the social organization of production. In the second stage, middle capitalism, the organization of work is more rationalized, specialized and centrally regulated. The development of scientific management, corporate ownership, state liberalism, and technical control of the labor process characterize this period (Edwards, 1979; Dowd, 1977;. Weinstein, 1968). During this middle capitalism, the ideology of the internal, private self is first put in question — in the name of industrial progress (Fine, 1956, Wiebe, 1967). Social changes begun then, during the Progressive period of American history, in the organization and management of the labor process, the technology of production, and the distribution of the labor force, further modify the social conditions of self-production. Not only do popular and academic ideologies begin to question the bourgeois ideal of selfhood, but the organization of social relations begins to recode the social grounds of its production.

Scientific management is increasingly accompanied by human relations management (Bendix, 1956). Despite the continuing domination of capital, this change does represent some movement toward an interactional, socialization of the production process. Production performance is mediated through social negotiation rather than exclusively by the machine pacing and technical control of the middle period. Changing forms of organizing production control systems also have implications for the organization of social energy as self. Bureaucratic management, intentionally and explicitly increases the range of self-processes which are considered production relevant. Some social analysts have criticized this mode of management as totalitarian (Edwards, 1979, p. 148). But the other face of bureaucratic rather than purely technical domination is its encouragement of social interaction. Even in its distortion of human relations, it does increase the importance of social communication. Explicit demands that private life, behavior earlier classified as personal, should follow corporate directives and production needs, brings out into the open the process by which the self is shaped in production. In its most sophisticated forms, the capital dominated bureaucratic encouragement of social interaction as a necessary aspect of production and management may itself be surpassed by cybernetically controlled systems. Interaction gives way to exchange.

Although work autonomy remains limited within corporate capitalism, the changing job demands of the newer working class

130

require a continuing attachment to the self ideal of the earlier period. Self-representation as job requirement, especially in the sales, service and management sectors, builds on the historical residue of a belief in the private self. But this newer self of interpersonal management only uses the private internal self as an emblem, while it is being constituted by social relations which depend on social interactional, interpersonal and symbolic negotiation and field dependence, rather than self-regulation. The content of selfhood is redefined along with changing job requirements which begin to value flexibility and disposability more than the moralized reifications of earlier production relations, such as integrity and responsibility.

The relation between changing job requirements and their translation into criteria of self-definition is evident in the history of education. Bowles and Gintis (1976, p. 137) describe the self-ideals communicated by schools as mirroring the alienated labor requirements of capitalist production. But the characteristics which they find valued (perseverance, dependability, consistency) and used as criteria of social differentiation seem more typical of the self-ideology of an earlier capitalism. If the new self is truly an aspect of the changing social relations of production, then schools are not preparing labor power efficiently. The progressive education movement, with its valorization of cooperation and social sensitivity, was an effort to translate the specific social relational production requirements of the new corporate capitalism into a school culture in which the psychology of the new self could be produced (Spring, 1972). Middle-class complaints about the failures of schools and families may be due less to working-class resistance to the imposition of class-alien standards, and more to an adaptive inability of schools and families to match the faster turn around times of the changing self-cultures attached to the technology and social requisites of production.

Several results of these changes are becoming apparent. First, changing requirements of production lead to a change of ideal self characteristics. Bourgeois virtues are now openly challenged, from within the middle classes, by those sectors of the labor force who represent the more flexible interpersonal rules of their working conditions as a culture of freedom. This change is ordinarily explained by social critics and scientists as the result of conflicts in life styles, moralities, demographic shifts, and faster rates of social change. It is not considered as class conflict mediated through cultural and psychological recodings of lags and contradictions in production relations.

131

Analysis

The threat of replacing families and schools with mass culture and internal corporate education, as psychological training centers for labor power, should increase the likelihood of theoretical awareness of connections between the needs of capital and the modes by which social energy is organized as self.

The second important development is that not only does the content of self change, but also the process by which self is formed through social production. The generalization of exploitation beyond the factory walls and the change in the subjectivity of work skills, from accumulative internal regulation to the symbolic social negotiation of privately owned capital which is produced through social interaction, represents a change in the mode of self-production. *The contradiction between a high degree of self-representation and a negotiated socially sensitive field-dependent self is a modern psychological version of the classic contradiction between private ownership and social production.* This contradiction, which is currently debated in terms of the merits of old and new cultures and selves, is the structural source of myriad private struggles to shore up a continually receding sense of self against the wave of social psychological dependency. One cost of this struggle is a mass, but privately experienced, self-fragility or identity anxiety. Attempts to develop social solutions to this shared but privatized struggle spawn mental health industries and popular movements to achieve psychological restoration through renewed familism and sexual regression. The social structural conditions of contradictory self-production are left unnoticed and unchanged.

The third development is the possibility of becoming aware of this relation between self-dilemmas and production contradictions. Marcuse (1964) foresaw the extension of corporate commodity relations to the farthest reaches of language, imagination, and desire. However, this commodification includes the possibility of its own demystification. Academic theories of socialization and popular social movements continue to attempt to locate self-formation in the family-sex grid. Nevertheless, the connection between self-formation and social production is pressed upon consciousness by the continuing demand for profit maximization and production efficiency. There are other ways than morality and family by which social stability can be assured. The need for a labor force psychological matching between self and production is an explicit task of industrial psychology (Baritz, 1960). As the leash on personal energy required for continued capital accumulation gets shorter, it becomes harder to deny the connection between the psychology of the organism and the social relations of production.

In the historical time of its dissolution, as at its origin, the self is not simply a direct personalized mirror of the social relations of production. The self is redefined by the application of rules of social framing. While such rules may be based in production, they are represented and made effective through a variety of cultural expressions and social movements. The development of the ideal and enacted social category of self – simultaneously cultural meaning and social practice occurred, in part, through the cultural generalization and practical social application of social rules which translate efficiency into functionally autonomous morality. Social relational characteristics, including age, sex, class and region, were effectively recoded, stratified, and accepted as personal attributes.

The translation of social relational attributes into personalizing and stratifying ones and the acceptance of this ascription of responsibility by the individual is a major accomplishment of the culture of capitalism. Weber (1958) claimed this accomplishment for religion. But Foucault (1965; 1970; 1972) and his school have attempted to demonstrate the importance of science, public institutions, and families in the cultural task of self-demarcation. The family was especially important to the extent that the rule of self-regulation was made in its name, simultaneously legitimating sexual repression and capital accumulation. The translation of extensive social relations into abstract rules of social classification, and the increased importance of smaller family groups, reduced the range of concrete social referents available for self-definition. Persons were increasingly differentiated and distanced from the wider social field. Later, in the twentieth century, psychologists abstracted and universalized this historical process of differentiation and its ontogenetic recapitulation as the concept of ego strength.

In late capitalism, the tendency toward social differentiation is reversed. The cultural call of the times is for the removal of rules which differentiate persons on the basis of their positions in social relations. While this culture of equality only occasionally threatens the frame of capital domination, it does represent a continuing pressure for social dedifferentiation and declassification. The diminution of recognizable sortable differences and the declining importance of age, sex, and ethnic insignia is an example of a loosening of the boundaries of the frames of social classification. Framing rules and job requirements together press toward weakening the traditional boundary between organism and environment, deregulating the self.

The deregulation of the self is the combined result of the psychological effects of the commodity form, the specific changing social organization of production, and the transformation of social rules. The process of self-deregulation is also effected by changes in specialized social modes of self regulation. These social modes are the methods — society's social psychological police — by which explosive subjective expressions of social contradictions are ordinarily contained. In late capitalism subjective contradictions are most evident in the externalized opposition between the new self (field dependent, social, associational, sensory hungry, relatively powerless, detached from integrated meaning), and the old self (internal regulation, linear thought, self-referential, and moral certainty). This contradiction develops as a result of a number of social psychological processes. These include:

a lag between personalized ideology and social production;

contradictory production demands of the need for self presentation, standardizing effects of commodity relations, and the interactional communicative competence required by newer organizational and production routines;

class differences in labor power psychology which are universalized as cultural disagreements;

the heightening of self-referential behavior induced by the use of self appeals in mass culture and advertising, within a context of mass consumption that presses toward self dedifferentiation.

Traditionally, socialization as moral training assured internal self-regulation through a carrot-and-stick based introjection of the self-ideals of the powerful. A social division of psychological labor assured external regulation of the self by subdividing a suppressed shared psychology into class specific psychological attributes. Any transcendence of the contradiction between new and old selves, any freeing of the psychological potential contained within the oppressive commodity psychology and new self worklife depends on the transformation of these modes of self-regulation.

One hint of a change in the mode of self-regulation is provided by current challenges to established concepts of socialization. Ethnomethodologists (Garfinkel, 1967; Turner, 1974) oppose the traditional view of socialization as the imposition of fixed rules by powerful parents. They emphasize, instead, the tentative character of rule constituted negotiations and particularly the reciprocal quality of the child/parent interactions (Douglas, 1970; MacKay, 1973). Feminist theory (Benjamin, 1978) opposes the moral imposition internalization model. That socialization model of learning presents male domination as natural learning. Empirical demonstrations of historical and class variability in socialization patterns (Bernstein, 1975; Kohn, 1969) also contribute to the delegitimation of socialization as a natural, universal description of self-formation.

Each of the major assumptions in the socialization model — identification, stability of personal characteristics, personal attachment to significant others, and integral core self — can be viewed as the reification of historically specific conditions. Social change invalidates the applicability of the model and suggests an alternative way of understanding the relation between person and social context. The concept of identification as a fixed emotional attachment may be only a particular instance of a more general social informational process by which identity is formed. Informational signals may be more important for conformity than internalization of morality. The social importance of Turner's moral integration analysis is that it shows how socialization models of self rationalize the ideals of the *gemeinschaft*, familied society, at a time when that mode of self-regulation begins to be acknowledged as practically ineffective.

The continuation of self-regulation through a compartmentalization of commodity psychology into class character is put in question by changes in class structure. A critical social psychology includes, along with an analysis of general social psychological tendencies and historically specific institutional and class contradictions, also an attempt to articulate the unspoken social psychology of emergent classes. Gouldner (1979, pp. 7, 8) as we saw, underlined the importance of the historic emergence of a new class of technical intelligentsia and humanistic intellectuals. They 'are seen as an embryonic new "universal class" — as the prefigured embodiment of such future as the working class still has. It is that part of the working class which will survive cybernation.' The new class is still relatively powerless and economically insecure, blocked in its aspirations for social and economic ascendance. It lives through symbolic work, the work of writing, talking, and calculating. It is committed to a 'culture of critical discourse (that) is characterized by speech that is relatively more situation-free, more context or field "independent",' (1979, p. 28). Members of the new class value work autonomy and are part of the new sectors of production requiring the communicatively competent self. In these sectors, self-representational needs conflict with the social decentering of the self. The new class appears to be in an objective social location that coalesces previously socially segregated psychological aspects of commodity relations and new production requirements. Under these conditions, the divide and conquer mode of self-regulation through social psychological compartmentalization becomes less effective.

If the new class is the working class of the future, then the battle over the new and old selves is not an intra-class cultural disagreement between old and new segments of the upper classes. The battle over the new self belongs to the wider class conflict between a propertied minority and an educated majority who possess only their cultural skills. Whether new self tendencies − powerlessness, abstractness, decontextualization, social field dependence, symbolic interactional competence, high self-representation combined with low self-production − will be repressed and compartmentalized in new ways, or whether they will become the basis for a truly new self, will be resolved in the course of this class conflict.

The unspoken social psychology of the future: beyond the self

Radical social theory, which promises an alternative, scants the importance of a critical social psychology. Marxist positivists are busy doing the valuable work of documenting interlocking political economic elite networks, or are trying to measure the rate of exploitation. Critical theorists have discovered culture, and are analyzing the texts of mass culture with the logos of high culture, and vice versa. Contemporary radicalism has its own brands of psychological restorationism and its own seductions which lead to an avoidance of critical social psychology. For example, the watchword of current hopes is the discovery of 'resistance' in every domain of social activity. Resistance means that workers develop autonomous cultures against the domination of rationalized capital, that students fight through boredom and withdrawal the education practices which incorporate them into a competitive world of stratifying inferiorization, inauthenticity, and powerlessness. Families too can be thought of as resistance against the bureaucratizing state and its ever growing therapeutic apparatus. Social analysis now pays hommage to political economy as abstracted empiricism, discourse, and the search for comforting pockets of resistance and social solidarity — while personal energies are further commodified and routed into the cycle of capital accumulation.

While the cognitive voice of this radicalism proclaims a critique of society, it hides (when it is not dreaming of bygone days) behind its mothers' apronstrings and in its fathers' laps. I mean that the subjective basis of cognitive radicalism draws whatever strength it has from nostalgic familism and social organicism. Reich (1972, p. 295) expressed it this way: 'When, during the November 1911 revolution, the masses were demonstrating in the Tiergarten in Berlin, most of the demonstrators took great care not to walk on the grass.'

The familism and organicism of the radical self, or at least the self behind the voice of radical social science and critical theory is expressed in the topic of counter-moralities. But the concrete alternative to the subjective traditional self that speaks the voice of a moral radical social theory is going through and beyond the psychological effects of the commodified, socializing and deregulating society in order to be able to create new forms of personal energy, social collectivity, thought, emotion, and imagination. The psychological work of going through the subjective experience of capitalism — awake and aware — is the rational redemption of the symbolic unconscious. Doing this means to develop the unspoken social psychology of the future that is currently repressed and ignored. To speak of the schizophrenic and the breakdown that is a breakthrough is not to romanticize so-called mental illness. Rather, it is an emblematic denial of the bourgeois and authoritarian leanings of the old self of the old left. It is the rallying slogan of a subjective alternative. The schizophrenic is only a progressive freak when he/she refuses to play the specialized social role of either heroic martyr or garbage pail victim (one, the romanticization of anti-psychiatry and the other, the brutalization of conventional psychiatry).

The tendency of the new self to approach the schizoid state is the other, opening side of commodification. When all traditional attachments are loosened, when the self is desocialized energy, when meaning systems are not hammered in place — then the human social organism is in a subjective position to remake itself and the social world. The dramatic unfreezing of socially hardened character defenses is the extreme of a process that is now occurring slowly and generally through the operation of everyday social relations. The subjective crisis is becoming an everyday matter. The commodity relation renders the ideal of autonomy less credible in a social environment which in fact enables relatively little powerfulness. It crushes the illusion of sensory maintenance through aesthetic attachment in a social environment which minimizes the possibility of creating sensitizing objects. It flattens the texture of differences in meaning in a social environment where meaning outweighs the possibilities of its use, and where its codes return social sectarianism for the price of personal security. The dialectic of commodification resides in the shattering of ego, sense, and meaning which frees energy for possibilities beyond current forms of self-organization.

We have already had glimpses of this subjective condition and precarious advertisements of its fortunes. The incipient, aborted cultural revolution of the sixties had elements of this self-unfreezing. High, mystical, natural, and transcendent, the self was experimentally dissolved in the social machinery of accumulation and routinized exploitation. But, this liberated open self was soon reincorporated, through the pathway of private satisfaction, into the prevailing social arrangements. The open self is open also to the possibility of an intensified and deeper exploitation of personal energy, and a more thorough harnessing of desire to the social apparatus which both needs and destroys it. ('But what they deterritorialize with one hand, they reterritorialize with the other,' Deleuze and Guattari, 1977, p. 257).

Among the alternate social psychologists, Schneider is more optimistic, and does not see the socially reincorporated exploitation of the decoded destroyed self, but its future freedom (Schneider, 1975, p. 270):

> This very dissolution, that is, weakening of the classic bourgeois
> ego contains the 'revolutionary ferment' of a new collective ego
> structure, of a kind of group ego structure based on the cooperation
> of numerous individual egos within the division of labor. Such 'free
> association' of many individuals with 'weak egos' thus creates the
> prerequisite for a new collective 'ego strength', for a cooperative
> instinctual structure which is the psycho-sexual pendent for the
> collective acquisition of production.

Language and meaning are also loosened from their rigid connotative places by the communicative, field dependent demands of production, and the object-detached, associative meaning grids which are an aspect of the mass producing of consumers. Class languages merge. The linguistic precision of the middle classes becomes more vulnerable to associative meaning, while the unarticulated voice of the working class becomes educated. Without a structural recoding, the potential linguistic

resource of decontextualized meaning implodes upon itself in the over-
subjectivized language of schizophrenia. Symbolically richer open
languages are resegregated among job specific social clusterings within
the new working class. The promise that a culture of critical discourse
(Gouldner, 1979) can create a collective public is betrayed by the rise
of professional corporatism which uses linguistic competence to
insulate and restratify itself. The effective universalizing use of language
and denotative symbols is limited to private industry advertising, which
universalizes by transforming socially diverse receivers into standardized
buyers.

Even in the face of this process in which socially loosened energy
and meaning is systematically rechanneled back into a production
system ruled by private ownership, the importance of a critical social
psychology still goes unrecognized, by the old left of political economics and the new left of cultural theorists.

The denial of a social psychology is also a characteristic of a radical
social crisis. Social structuralism, culturalism, and scientism are favored,
precisely at a time when applied social psychology serves as the right
arm of social domination. A counterpractice that includes a critical
social psychology would grasp the social psychology of domination
and reverse it. This requires a theoretical and empirical understanding
of contemporary social psychological processes from within the context
of social production. Intimacy, interpersonal attraction, exchange,
socialization, attribution – all the current categories of academic
psychological understanding need to be reinterpreted in ways which
demonstrate how psychological infrastructure enables current social
relations to be maintained. The unconscious is not simply a repository
of family scenarios, but of all socially repressed activities and their
symbolic representations. The use of sexual symbolism in commercial
advertising is a small example of how collective social mobilization
depends on the ability to map this social unconscious, and to develop
the codes and cues by which it can be activated. Now, the social unconscious is being used for capital, through the commodity. As traditional
self-regulation decreases, the rush of energy is opened to absorption by
demagogues who know better than to dismiss the unconscious as a
bourgeois construct. The use of language to effect social change implies
a lot more than being able to create a rational discourse where justificatory claims are respected. The real power of language is in its capacity
to organize irrationality, to bring to the surface incompletely repressed
preconscious awareness and to rouse the blocked wishes and fantasies

139

which move between private delusion and collective illusion (Freud, 1957, p. 53).

A socially deregulated self finds new regulation in commodity symbols which effectively channel stored associations into the behavioral enactment of system demands. Semantic cuing begins to replace person attachment as the basis of self reproduction and regulation. This semantic power, like other means of production, is privately owned (Golding and Murdock, 1979). The possibility of social freedom must then involve a democratic reclamation of a linguistically cued social unconscious, which, in effect, is also privately owned. A counterpractice which tries to overcome symbolic domination will have to work through the self. The collective ego and collective control of meaning production may only develop after a period of collective, but privately experienced, self-transformation. Especially during this period, however, there exists the possibility of a massification of psychological energy under the rule of a new pseudosocial, supraprivate ego — the mass corporate leader. This is the danger of the Fascism which moves underneath and behind the shield of commodified social relations.

9
Intimacy:
the contraction of the social

Social psychology is haunted by the private, the personal, 'intimacy.' The reification and compartmentalization of interaction between subjective individualism and market economic objectivism is only one type of dichotomization that occurs with the polarization of liberal social psychology. The personal and the social are now separated – as whole domains of study. The individual-society dichotomy which characterizes theorizing in social psychology is now institutionalized as disciplinary specialization, and in this institutional separation, the study of the personal is emerging as the ascendant tendency. The social, however, has not disappeared. It is simply reexpressed in the language of the personal and even further hidden and beclouded.

The aim of a critical social psychology, beyond critique, beyond substantive theory, is the articulation of concrete everyday experience in a way which recovers the suppressed social. In this chapter, the accent is on the concrete.

The social psychology of intimacy

Intimacy is the new and popular topic for social psychology. In everyday, popular culture also, there is an outpouring of books with prescriptions for how to have intimate relations (a well-known intimacy expert, Rubin (1974, p. 166) defines intimacy as 'close and confidential communication between two people'), creative intimate combat, and even simply on how to live with another person. In the how-to mass literature, success and family books are now joined by didactic intimacy. Along with freedom, and success, it is becoming one of our favorite commonsense categories for collapsing social relational understanding into private and personal matters.

Analysis

Academic research and publications follow the same trend, with a flurry of books on personal, close, intimate and interpersonal relations (Huston, 1974; Levinger and Raush, 1977; Murstein, 1971; Walster and Walster, 1978; Huston and Levinger, 1978; Duck and Gilmour, 1981). These works share the view of intimacy as a special kind of meeting, a self-disclosing communication within a dyad. The most recent of these works begins the publication of a series of volumes, and claims the establishment of a new encompassing category for social psychology — personal relationships. (Duck and Gilmour, 1981, pp. 7, 8):

> The study of personal relationships is thus clearly destined to establish itself firmly as an important new area that transcends, though it draws from, a number of existing lines of work . . . . In the last decade, interest has grown vigorously in the development of relationships, in the real-world meanings and events of relationships, and in the sociocognitive processes that occur once two people start interacting as acquaintances.

Two by now familiar models stand behind much of the research in intimacy and, by its more modish designation, 'personal relationships': utilitarianism and functionalism. The metaphor of society as marketplace, still underlies current intimacy research (Berscheid and Walster, 1978; Walster, Walster and Berscheid, 1978; Huston and Levinger, 1978). As in *laissez-faire* economics, individual trades and transactions sum to collective output. Attraction is a result, an analogue of profits which result from exchange. Exchange is a matter of private negotiation and decision making. Social determination is restricted to influencing the cultural definitions of valued traits. In such an imaginary society-without-structure, intimacy is easily reduced to attraction between individuals — as a congeries of traits.

This market model results in a typical explanatory sequence. The individual is uprooted from social relations and history. The process of interaction is, according to what I have called the 'social psychology (modifying MacPherson's apt phrase) of possessive individualism,' reduced to individual trait matching. Huston and Levinger, for example, (1978, pp. 145, 119), in their review of one of the staples of the intimacy field, interpersonal attraction research, have observed: 'More than two-thirds of the studies reviewed dealt with impressions and encounters, usually removed from their social context,' and further, that 'societal and cultural influences on attraction have also received little systematic attention.' Their solution shows how deeply ingrained

142

is the separation of individual behavior from the social interactional process of its production. The individual, or some behavior of individuals is reified, socially abstracted and then the social is added on later — as a set of variables. Huston and Levinger (1978, p. 146) suggest the need for more 'research on the effects of power and wealth on sexual attractiveness.' Again, the class factor is reified, added on, and then peddled as a structural, social or even radical approach to social psychology.

The second familiar but silent background social theory for social psychology is functionalism. In functionalism, the imagery is not of society as marketplace, but as organism. In functional theory, the structured whole is greater than and different from the sum of its individual parts. Holism's politically and socially engaged interests are displayed in the many functionalist analyses of the negative consequences of the decline of the ideal of feudal communalism (Nisbet, 1966; Durkheim, 1951). When the functionalist metaphor is applied to the study of intimacy, it is this particular view of the social — an integrative and organicist one — that defines a social approach to intimacy.

Durkheim's (1954) emphasis on study of the socially patterned methods by which social integration and stability are accomplished is an appropriate counterpoint to Freud's assertion of a natural antagonism between the individual and the social (Freud, 1949, 1960). Parsons (1955) tries to combine the perspectives of functionalism and psychoanalysis. In this view, the egotistically driven individual monad must be bound to the needs of the group through a history of personal identification, common ritual, and shared morality. Anything less than internalized 'socialization' is a threat to the survival of the society.

This characteristic functionalist assumption of an opposition between the instinctually anarchic individual and the integrative social is present in the more sociological approaches to intimacy. For example, intimacy as dyadic withdrawal (Slater, 1974) or as signalling the decline of the public person (Sennett, 1977) counterposes the personal and the private and asocial. Its prevalence is evidence of social fragmentation and disintegration. The social psychology of intimacy that develops in this second model is an effort to explain the social control of intimacy. It is a replay of the familiar scenario of the triumph of social integration over centripetal tendencies, like intimacy.

The research problematic which flows from this view — the opposition between the personal and the public and the interest in social integration

— is how the intimate dyad becomes social. Goode (1974, p. 143) for example, offers a sociological analysis of love that emphasizes 'the structural patterns by which societies keep in check the potentially disruptive effect of love relationships.' He concludes a functionalist analysis of love with the statement (1974, p. 156): 'The theoretical importance of love is thus to be seen in the socio-structural patterns which are developed to keep it from disrupting existing social arrangements.' Intimacy is social only because there are social patterns, particularly values and rituals, which control it.

Intimacy and social contradictions

The alternative view that I suggest is that what we call intimacy is fundamentally and constitutively social. Intimacy is not a magnetic formula for two separate individuals' instinctual passion which becomes social through the operation of social control rituals. Rather, it is a particular historical and structurally regulated process by which specific aspects of the social relations of the totality are segregated out and given a special designation, one which is then experienced phenomenologically by the participants as a private dyadic matter.

The nature of intimacy depends on the specific sociohistorical contradictions of a given society. And these contradictions are quite variable. Mao argued (1971) that: there are a variety of principle and secondary contradictions in any context; and each has to be studied and described within its context.

There is no overall formula, although the contradictions between capital and labor and between socialized forces of production and privatized relations of production are of obvious importance. One attempt to describe the specific contradictions within United States society is Castells's analysis of the current social crisis (1980, p. 177). He includes in his discussion of concrete contradictions such familiar (to Marxists) antinomies as: the requirements of innovation and flexibility for the development of the productive forces, on the one hand, and the constraints of hierarchical, bureaucratic organizational social relations in production, on the other; service and profit needs, contradictions of the public sector, etc.

I want to suggest as an orienting introductory approach three general tendential contradictions. They will be familiar to general social science readers, and at the same time, do not require a complete social analysis of the US, England, France or other capitalist social formations in order to see their applicability. We can simply interpret each of the best known classical social theories as descriptions of major social tendencies which remain operative in contemporary society. Then we can note the countertendencies which constitute contemporary social contradictions. Next, both process and category of interaction can be described as developing out of the interplay between tendencies and countertendencies. Finally, these interrelationships can be understood only in relation to both the social whole and particular dilemmas of concrete individual lives.

Durkheim, Weber, and Marx each emphasized one of the central historic social tendencies. Durkheim (1964) saw in modern society a process of social fragmentation and the development of an excessive individualism which loosened the individual from the necessary social bonds of the collective. Weber tried to show how modern society was tending toward rationalization and routinization, a 'disenchantment of the world,' in which all aspects of social relations became instrumentalized (Gerth and Mills, 1964; Weber, 1963). For Marx (1967), capitalism is characterized by powerlessness, alienation, and the exploitation of the producers of social wealth. In daily production, people reproduce the conditions of their lack of control over their own life conditions, the diminution of their capacities, and the projection of their own potential capacities unto others.

Alongside these well-known large scale social tendencies, there are, in modern society, also countertendencies, oppositional processes, contradictory patterns. Despite socially disintegrative individualism, there are also collective and communal tendencies. Against rationalization, there is also a socially patterned need and desire for spontaneity, play and transcendance. Counter to powerlessness, there remains the desire and social possibility for power and personal efficiency.

These counter or oppositional tendencies are social patterns, produced, along with the dominant tendencies, in the course of collective life. The ethos of unlimited individual consumption, despite its object of commodity emphasis, contains also the message of a continuing valuation of personal expression. While the individuation and fragmentation of work tasks continues, so also does the work which demands conscious cooperation and communication. The same socioeconomic organization which thrives on the overall powerlessness of the individual producers, requires and fosters the desire for self-direction and efficiency, within the limits of that organization.

145

Analysis

The oppositional tendencies are simultaneously developed and suppressed and inhibited along with the major social tendencies. There are examples of this from a variety of contexts. The suppressed aspects —collectivity play, and powerfulness — are seen in the so-called informal organization, the underlife of social organizations. Against and within the individualism of the school, the plant and the office are created coffee cliques, gangs and clubs. Even in the navy, bureaucracy has 'another face' (Page, 1946). Aronowitz (1973; 1978) describes how, within the heart of routinized factory production, there is game playing, innovativeness and creativity. Sociologists of education know that powerlessness within schools is countered by the establishment of alternative and autochthonous criteria of self-validation. Standards of academic performance are replaced by those of students' physical prowess and toughness as the basis of a counter subculture (Levy, 1970; Willis, 1977).

The existence of counter social tendencies can be seen not only in the underlife of the powerless, but also in the efforts of organizational elites and managers to harness and utilize what they perceive as the potentially disruptive effects of these expressions of the suppressed sides of social contradictions. The solidarity needs of office workers are channeled into the company picnic. Game playing is made production relevant. The alternative criteria of rebellion against powerlessness are translated into the officially sanctioned norms of achievement.

The wider social importance of intimacy, and its rationalized legitimation in social psychology, is not, I believe, simply the march of academic science toward the discovery of a science of personal relations. Rather, the study of intimacy becomes more important as the actual social contradictions intensify and polarize within concrete social institutional contexts, like factories, offices, schools, and other public institutions. The reaction against the further suppression of the suppressed takes a number of forms, the various historically familiar guises of the carrot and the stick. One method of containing contradictory social tendencies is to shift their expression out of the concrete institutional contexts in which they are produced. Specifically, the socially developed oppositional tendencies are increasingly shifted out of the most central organizational context of production and reproduction into the domain of the personal, private life in intimate and personal relationships. These social phenomena therefore take on a new-found importance, which social psychologists ascribe to their own theoretical innovativeness. Without denying that a host of additional and not unimportant new contradictions are continuously developing in the creation of dyadic relationships, I think that we can describe how social contradictions, and especially their socially suppressed aspects, are played out in an altered and transformed manner as intimate, personal relations.

Personalization

The deflection of social contradictions from public sources into the realm of the more personal and intimate is not a structural automatism. The development of a personalized appropriation of social experience is an historical development. Zaretsky attempts to show how (1976, pp. 9, 10):

> the rise of industrial capitalism, while destroying the traditional
> form of family life, gave rise to a new search for personal identity
> which takes place outside the division of labor. In a phrase:
> proletarianization gave rise to subjectivity.

However, experiencing and collectively defining aspects of the fractured social whole, as purely private matters, is the result of social and cultural patterns which reproduce personalization.

The reproduction of personalization is accomplished through processes that translate and transform collective organization and contradiction into individualized terms. Aspects of collective social organization are seen and experienced as individual. Personalization is one socioculturally patterned method of social denial: it diverts critical attention from the social sources of personal desire and encourages seeking the realization of social incompletions outside public social life. Social contradictions are indeed personally experienced, as individual and interpersonal dilemmas. Intimacy is not, as for functionalism, a threat to social control. On the contrary, personalization of socially patterned contradictions as the private dilemmas of intimacy is a method by which the social *status quo* is maintained.

Three examples of how personalization is ordinarily accomplished are: family socialization, role socialization, and mass communication. The very term family socialization is ironic, because it means the acquisition of a personalized, privatistic social character in the family formation. Middle class socialization is seen as superior, because it encourages privatism, self directedness as opposed to working-class conformity (Kohn, 1969) – or a non-positional language (Bernstein, 1975). Language that is more socially than personally centered is taken as a sign of cultural and cognitive deficiency. Research on class differences in socialization is really testimony to the greater degree of personalization among the middle classes (Gekas, 1979). But, for all social classes, family socialization is not only inculcating shared social ideals, but also a structural process of learning to privatise affection and perception.

The identification of personalization with socialization is so un-examined that the personalized social character is simply assumed to be an objective standard of normality. The mature person, according to the commonly accepted therapeutic vision, is differentiated or autonomous. Crystallization of the personalization process as an objective standard which begins in the family is, I suspect, more generally reinforced by the criteria of evaluation in public institutions.

Personalization of collective life is accomplished also by the freezing of the social division of labor into roles and identities. The collective basis of the division of labor is constantly translated into the language of individual performances. The engagement of social actors in their roles becomes identity and obscures any vision of the script, the socially structured center out of which the parts are constructed. Motivationally, competition underlines both the need for personalized identities and assures the acquisition of cognitive structures of persona-lized credit and blame.

This institutionalized mode of obscuring the social character of social production – the deeper personalization of alienated roles – only becomes evident at the extremes, in the show and the outcast. In Hollywood, as at the office, the social division of labor and production is denied. At awards time, the gracious star thanks all those who have contributed. This is the familiar afterthought that adds to the social. The star is really the example most socially constructed and the most apparently personal, the extreme of the personalizing aspects of a hier-archical, alienated division of social labor.

The outcast, too, serves to translate the hidden, ambiguous, and undesired aspects of the social whole into the more familiar terms of personal idiosyncracy and evil. As Erickson (1966) has shown, changing definitions of what is publicly considered a deviant behavior can be traced to alterations in the organization and conflicts of the whole society. By continuing to reproduce the socially problematic as deviance, the personal hierarchization of social processes, from the winning star to the losing deviant, is accomplished.

Even the apparently non-hierarchical aspects of the social division of labor manifest personalization, through creating the specialist. Task specialization is accompanied by an only partly technically justified privatization and compartmentalization of information and communication. The category of specialist is a fitting complement to those of star and deviant, for she/he legitimates partial knowledge as socially valuable. The partialization of information gives an objective veneer to a socially patterned incapacity to depersonalize — to see from private appearance to social production and organization.

Personalization is also accomplished through the social organization of symbols, particularly the mass media. Its importance for the process of personalization lies not only in its semantic content and social modeling, but also in the way that it organizes experience. Mass communication demonstrates that heightened forms of arousal and stimulus reception (key aspects of perception) are private matters. The social relations in which perception occurs assimilates personalization to the very structure of knowing. Although we may also identify counter messages, oppositional tendencies and contradictions within this cultural sphere, both the form and content of the prevailing mass culture affirm a social organization of personalism (Brenkman, 1979).

A dialectic of intimacy

The disjunction between social production and individual realization is generalized, institutionalized and comes to appear as natural. The privileging of individual realization and the denial of social production is the phenomenal meaning of capitalism. In economics, this means exploitation; collective production and private appropriation (Marx, 1967). Profit is the term which naturalizes and obscures the disjunction. In philosophy, culture and ideology, this means reification; lack of awareness of collective creation (Lukács, 1971). In hierarchical social organizations, in formulized symbolic communications, in family interactions, 'identity,' 'fun,' and 'love' operate, respectively, as the naturalizing linguistic glosses, the undefined terms that obscure social production, and elevate personal realization to a fact, rather than a social accomplishment.

Intimacy is a type of social sublimation. Unlike art, madness or consumption, it is an effort to realize the suppressed sides of social

149

contradictions in a way that is neither other-wordly, egocentric nor commodified. If intimacy is self-centered, from a collective social point of view, it is a self-centeredness that reaches outward to others for its realization. While it is vulnerable to commercial standardization, intimacy is still not thoroughly commodified. Therefore, as a social form, I suggest that intimacy stands between purely personalized, commodified existence and a conscious social, collective realization of those desires which are socially generated; for a society in which spontaneity, efficiency and solidarity are attainable with the social patterns of public life. It is the cultural and social expression of con-tradiction as a form of life; intimacy includes both the possibility of further personalizing efforts to realize socially produced individual needs, and the potential to build outward toward wider social con-nectedness and collective consciousness. Intimacy is at once less than full socialness, because it privatizes desires — and more than com-modified personalism, because the realization of desire requires the valuation of another human being. Intimacy is at the moving center of an overriding structural contradiction between personalization and socialization.

The social motives of intimacy are the personally translated exper-ienced representations of those aspects of the social which are simul-taneously socially produced and socially suppressed: the social needs and personal desires for spontaneity, play, transcendance, interpersonal efficacy and collective solidarity. Ethnographies and everyday accounts portray intimate relations precisely as efforts to realize these aspects of what is socially suppressed (Walster and Walster, 1978; Davis, 1973; Berman and Weiss, 1978).

The romantic is the contra-routine that revels in the playfulness of non-surveilled activity and untimed mutual innovation and surprise. Attractiveness attests the continuing human power to move others, the power to control the human environment not by calculation, but through simple presence — an effectivity without performance. No less important is the power to be moved. In the face of the powerlessness of anonymous fragmentation, the power of surrender to a human integral is also an expression of relative powerfulness. In intimacy there is renewed activated memory of human bonding, of mutuality which is not even yet destroyed by stylized adaptation and reproduction for the purposes of doing business. The hope of intimacy is the realization of capitalist society's other face.

Intimate relations are not, however, simply a presonalized reproduc-

150

tion of the relatively suppressed aspects of social contradictions. Nor is intimacy merely a complementary alternative to the world of work (Kantor, 1977). The life course of relationships reveals that in intimate relations there is a tendency toward a 'return of the social,' a reassertion of dominant social patterns. For example, sex-as-transcendence can become sex-as-work (Lewis and Brisset, 1967). The solidarity of mutual recognition gives way to what Bergman portrays in his film as the 'Shame' of a couple's competition for individual survival in a war-filled world. The subjective sense of efficacy attained by the impact of presence may be corroded by objective interpersonal impotence. The rewardingness of adoration is then openly supplanted by what was at every step its hidden rule, as it is in every social idolatry, the bond between romantic love and sadism – dominate and submit. The major tendencies of social contradictions – whirlpool like-individualism, instrumentalizing rationalization, alienated powerlessness – are also expressed within intimate relations. *The dialectic of intimacy is a reversal of social contradictions: the social is personalized, and suppressed aspects of social contradictions become the primary motives, hopes and themes of intimacy, while pervasive social tendencies are now the reasserted underside, intimacy's underlife.*

This socially generated tension, between the desires and behaviors of transcendent collectivity and solidarity, spontaneity and play, efficacy and power, versus individualization, routinization, and powerlessness, is the contradictory social matrix of intimacy.

Social contradiction and personal ambivalence

This view of intimacy – as against the utilitarian and functionalist models – needs to be empirically examined. The reports of family therapists are a valuable source of evidence. They often describe intimacy as the expression of personal ambivalencies. These ambivalencies are usually attributed, by therapists, to the crisis of personal development and family histories, and not to societal contradictions (Goldstine *et al.*, 1977; Shor and Sanville, 1978). Yet, the ambivalencies described closely parallel what I have described as personalized social contradictions.

For example, the larger social question of individualism or personalization in relation to solidarity needs and collectivizing tendencies is phrased as a dyadic dilemma of individuation and fusion (Napier,

1977). The opposition between rationalization and play is described in personal and psychoanalytic terms as a conflict between the needs for security and excitement in relationships. Issues of power and alienation are stated in terms of family conflicts and individual struggles for autonomy, in the psychoanalytic language of dependence and control (Sluzki and Vernon, 1977). From the therapeutic perspective, ambivalence is rooted in the needs of the individual. Ambivalencies are not regarded as personal dilemmas that are mediated through family communications but which are only made personally pressing because they represent fundamental contradictions in social organization.

Patterns of intimacy and the containment of contradictions

Variations in the patterns or forms of intimate relationships can be analyzed as alternative methods by which people respond to and try to manage personalized, but socially structured contradictions. Although the selection of methods of contradiction coping is itself socially variable, here I suggest only an ideal typical description of interactional methods through which personalized social contradictions — experienced as ambivalencies — are contained.

Post-relationship revelations, 'I had no idea; I never loved you' show that intimacy, however optimistic the academic definition, is not characterized solely by self-disclosure.

Walter Mitty's solution to a social world of conflicting ideals and contradictory demands is to create an inner life of fantasy, where all that is externally unrealizable can be accomplished inwardly, in dream and imagination. The *interiorization* of one aspect of a contradiction allows external relations to run smoothly, at least temporarily. It is precisely when what is hidden in personal mythology is expressed that the relationship becomes the scene of battles. The ultimate strategy of transferring the costs of solutions of social antagonisms to the individual, interiorization, collapses, forcing back toward an interactional rather than private solution. But even this forced recognition of interpersonal opposition can be redefined by the participants, and their psychological consultants, as an individual personality disagreement or incompatability.

The dyad represses contradiction, not through the creation of

152

fantasy life — although there are certainly dyadic mythologies — but through the *patterns of differential association and specialization.* Common patterns of intimacy, which are central in the definition of life style and personal identity, become the basis of social networks and structures of association. Association is the demographic base of identity, which is then embellished with a justificatory ideology (why our way is best). Social compartmentalization and segregation on the basis of intimacy patterns, forged through both association and ideology, is another way that manifestations of social contradictions in personal life are avoided. As in the world of work, the totality is partialized, creating a false specialization which becomes the defended fortress of identity. Married people, singles, gays and swingers avoid interactions with those others who have crystallized their identities about a different aspect of the larger contradictory social processes. Some become specialists in security, others in play, potency, passivity, gregariousness or detachment. The contradictions of intimacy are denied by specialization, and the interactional analogue to repression — associational selection and social segregation.

Avoidance of consciousness about social contradictions in intimate relations is also accomplished by various forms of alternation, or interactional juggling. for example, in the multiple relationship pattern, specializing characterizes individuals rather than dyads. The importance of intimacy specialization for social control is that as long as difference and opposition can be attributed to particular other persons, or even types, instead of being understood as internal contradictory elements of oneself, or of the social context, there is less of a perceived need for confrontation and change. In simultaneous multiple relationships, the division of intimate labor follows the larger tendency of social labor toward increased specialization. A second and more familiar pattern of intimacy specialization is *sequentializing and serializing* relationships. In longer term relationships, this may be simply taking turns enacting relational roles. Multiple relationships, sequentializing and turn taking are all methods, interactional strategies, that handle clashes of the internally contradictory demands of intimacy by spacing, diffusing and scheduling. Social contradictions are less likely to be actively faced when they can be distilled into types of people, and then serially and separately sorted and collected.

Social relationships built on contradictory patterns can also be maintained by occasional *ritualized admissions* of their contradictory character. The tension, for example, between the needs of separateness and closeness, the personalizing and collectivizing tendencies, is temporarily alieviated by the ritual or symbolic admission of that aspect of the contradiction which is most suppressed. The self-enclosed separateness of many marriages is punctuated by the activation of solidarity myths; retelling, for example the story of 'our meeting,' and, in a more technicized milieu, a replay of the old slides and movies. The relatively suppressed is ritually enacted, to insure its non-disturbing demarcation as relief rather than change. The love grows cold syndrome of routinization is broken by the vacation, the second honeymoon. The need for excitement, play, and transcendence is admitted, but only realized outside of the normal geographical and interpersonal boundaries of the relationship. These are the stylized *mardi gras* which renew the ideological hope of intimacy against rationalization, while serving as the exotically packaged repair shops for the preservation of an instrumentalized social existence.

Breaking the containment

Not all patterns of intimacy repress, segregate, compartmentalize, serialize and mythologize conflict and contradiction, and thereby contribute to maintaining the social *status quo*. Interpersonal conflicts are being made explicit as integral aspects of intimate relations. The rise of relational contractuality acknowledges the antagonistic elements of intimacy, but interprets these oppositions as differences in personal needs and values which can be resolved through interpersonal negotiation (Sager, 1976). This popular effort is the practical parallel to the academic metaphor of intimacy as private negotiation in the marketplace. Like the conceptual model of exchange which legitimates it, contractuality stops at the level of interpersonal conflict. It ignores the social structure which generates conflict, and the collective social action which might transform that structure.

The largely unrealized alternative in intimate relations is socialization rather than personalization. It entails recognizing that private ambivalencies and interpersonal conflicts are connected to contradictions that are fundamental to the collective organization of the social whole. Conflict does not have to be an occasion for striking the best bargain. It can be the occasion of mutual recognition of the common social source of private-seeming antagonism.

Whether one attributes the putative failure of couples therapies, communications and intimate encounter groups to the personal or the social is important. As long as intimacy remains the focus for the intense personalization of contradictory social processes, it will function, in this society, as a successful socially patterned deflection and, in that way, as a basic method of social control. Development of a practice for the socialization of the dilemmas of intimate relations opens the way toward social change. As the women's movement begins to assert that 'the personal is not political enough,' (Fox-Genovese, 1979-80) awareness of the social patterning of personal ambivalences becomes a first step toward change. But, social psychology presently seems more intent upon glorifying and promoting 'personal relationship.'

In everyday life, the transfer of social costs and uncertainties of love into individual ascriptions adds to an already heavy burden that the ideologies of success and achievement have placed on the individual. Because it is difficult to realize privately as intimacy what is both present and reinforced in the public life of capitalism — competition and achievement (rationalization, alienation and unlimited individuation) — and also what is relatively absent and socially suppressed, the quest for intimate satisfaction has a high rate of failure. Failure in intimacy corrodes even the self-respect which remains after the daily onslaught of invidious ranking and the 'nightmare of failure' (Henry, 1963), which is the message of public life. The ego is puffed and de-puffed along with the oscillations of social change. The social tendencies shaping individual lives are kept opaque by ideologies of freedom, success, and now intimacy.

The reproduction of individualism in ideology and social character is not intimacy's only outcome. As social contradictions push further into the cathectic core of private selfhood, social domination is increasingly masked by a misleading and caricatured ideology of individualism. But this very inclusiveness of social control and domination pushes toward a consciousness of the connection between personal and social. The social psychological dialectic of socialization-personalization is expressed in a simultaneous elevation and reduction of private selves.

In intimate relations, solutions to the conditions of contradictory social existence range from the most interior privatization to the conscious socialization of personal ambivalencies. This socializing practice goes beyond the development of social consciousness, to the practice of socially realizing playfulness, transcendence, personal potency, and participatory effectiveness. The present dissolution of

155

intimacy (social psychologists, like Minerva's owl, seem always to be spreading their wings at dusk) back into familism, sexism and fundamentalism also opens the possibility of returning from personalization to social solidarity.

10

Conclusion: social psychology and social change

Introduction

I have argued that social psychology is part of a wider culture and that it plays a social role. Social psychologists appeal to a superordinate norm, the ideal of scientific autonomy, to justify their experiences and actions as professional and socially neutral. But professionalism (Larson, 1977) is hardly historically transcendent or socially disinterested. Indeed, professionalism may itself be the new ideology for the mystification and denial of the social character of knowledge.

The social constitution and functions of social facts, like professional knowledge, become most apparent during crises. Crises of the individual, the culture, and the social formation can, as Horkheimer and Adorno often wrote, 'break the spell of the taken-for-granted.' But the crisis is only an invitation to identify the constituent tendencies and to create from them something different and better. The crisis in social psychology is just such an invitation. In this chapter, I develop the anticipatory moment of a critical social psychology.

The crisis discourse can be arrested at the methodological level or at the point of introducing new concepts, or even at suggesting alternative paradigms. Such solutions accept the much deeper assumptions which the crisis offers an occasion to display and to challenge: the separation between theory and practice, between theoretic culture and the social tendencies and dilemmas of everyday life, and the totality to which it belongs.

It is the refusal of this separation which opens the way toward understanding, not only the academic crisis but also its relation to structural and experiential crises. The renewal of theory and method — if it is not going to remain a cosmetic surface ritual — must go through the cultural milieu, the social lives, the collective struggles, and the structural tendencies out of which social psychology is built. The future of social psychology depends on the outcome of these personal, cultural, and social struggles. But in order to understand this, one must first see social psychology in historical society, deeply implicated in social history, and not take it at its idealized word as somehow up above and beyond the social world of ordinary people.

Social psychology in society

My argument is that social psychology is part of a liberal culture, and that the academic crisis is only one sector of the much wider crisis of the culture and the society. There is by now a fair amount of evidence that social science, at least in the United States, has, since its beginnings, been tied up with organized social interests. We can see the connections between social science and the general culture by doing cultural comparisons, or by tracing the relation between changing theories and sociohistorical events, or even, as Eakins (1966) and Silva and Slaughter (1981) have done, by documenting the actual positional interconnection and communication among the leaders of social science and business and government leaders. One reason why social psychology has been so successful in convincing its practitioners, audience, and clients of its disinterested professionalism is that little research has been done about the cultural and socially formative connections and interactions of the academic discipline.

Franks (1975), Cina (1981) and others working with Dana Bramel and Ron Friend (Bramel and Friend, 1981) have made some inroads toward a social analysis of social psychology, but on the whole very little research is yet available to give fuller documentation to the argument. It is encouraging that David Ingleby (1982) believes that: 'nowadays it is only in the most stagnant backwaters of academe that a concern with the wider social context of science is seen as a reprehensible diversion from "real" research.' Perhaps we shall soon be able to claim more empirical instances of realizing this changed attitude. While I endorse Ingleby's hopefulness, I am not so sure that the current social situation, perhaps more so in the US than in the UK, will enable the realization of the attitude that encourages a more detailed empirical sociological and historical analysis of social psychology.

Social psychology and social change

The breakup of the liberal culture and crises in the social formation in which it is rooted have indeed historically preceded the crises of the social sciences. This provides some further, macrohistorical evidence for the argument that changes, particularly crisis changes in social psychology, are due not simply to internal patterns of epistemological doubt nor to the latest anomaly which yet needs to be explained. The crisis of the 1960s — protest against the Southeast Asian war, the Black movement, the beginnings of the women's movement, and the international student revolt — was the first recent historical event to send shock waves through the academy and ultimately to create, at least for a few brief years, a greater tolerance for Marxist, critical, phenomenological and existentialist approaches as token alternatives to the reigning abstracted positivist empiricist culture of the academies. The theoretical results of that crisis were at first generally encouraging.

But the crisis of the 1970s and early 1980s is another matter. The cultural crisis and revolts of the 1960s occurred within the safe zones and against the hegemony of the corporate liberal class and its social institutional fiefdoms. But the more recent crisis is a crisis of that corporate liberalism itself. The current economic crisis is the development, as O'Connor has argued, of a fiscal crisis of the state (1973); as Castells (1980) suggests, a structural crisis of the system, with the tendential falling rate of profit at its center. This crisis has consequences which are not so sanguine, nor protected within corporate liberalism. The former sites of protest have been fiscally decimated, and what we now see, at every level, is the ascendance of the rightist tendency in personal, cultural and social formations. The challenge to the corporate liberal state does not have automatically progressive results. The dissolution or at least the current crack in the liberal hegemony — of which the crisis in social psychology is a localized moment — opens the way for a polarized expression of the internal contradictions of that social regime which were there and contained all the while.

One central social role of social psychology, which has brought it support and believers, has been to maintain that liberal center by denying and avoiding its internal contradictory character. That denial has been accomplished by what I have called the 'social production of ignorance.' Social psychology has surrounded itself with the legitimating aura of scientifically transcendent inviolability, which establishes its protection both institutionally (Cina, 1981) and metanormatively in methodological procedures which make a virtue of its scientific insularity and empirical ritualism. I have tried to argue in this book that neither its methodology nor its social infrastructure provide an adequate basis for critique. One must start with the content of social psychology in order to illustrate the ways that the containment of cultural contradictions is accomplished. The central method has been the denial of the social — of any understanding of individual social-collective mediations which would enable professionals and students to understand their realities in some way other than what is best likely to reproduce it. Social psychology is an ideology of the corporate liberal period.

The political importance of social psychology as a specific ideology has been that it claims for itself the description — alas, even the explanation — of the relation between the individual and collective social organization. Social changes occur in part because people are able to articulate the dissatisfactions of their everday lives in relation to the sources of their problems in general social conditions. In the past, various kinds of other-worldliness and cosmologies of individual virtue and sin have blocked this awareness. In a secular period with a fair amount of social consciousness, it is not easy to deny the very existence of the social. The blockage of social awareness occurs by simultaneously admitting the social, and denying it in social psychology.

Social psychology retains the ideology of individualism — the deep, reified denial of the social relational character of existence essential to a social formation such as capitalism. But it dresses this denial in social clothing. It provides a more socialized outlook than an earlier Social Darwinist individualism, but stops short of examining the social dynamic that brings the social to the fore, or the structuring principles of collective association. That is why it makes perfect sense for social psychology to study immediate situational factors and remain restricted to laboratory experiments. The usual criticism of laboratory experiments — which are currently being challenged for their lack of 'ecological validity' (Bronfenbrenner, 1979) — is that they are simply imitative efforts at being scientific. This criticism misses the point — the conceptual content of this type of research. It is social, but only at the face-to-face, and so in practical interaction (whatever its simulation claims) remains removed from the larger structure of society.

I have chosen three examples of conceptual containment, and have tried to show how the containment is culturally accomplished in each case. The dissolution or the inadequacy of those concepts to the present social reality develops because the reality is changing. The liberal society, which social psychology defends, changes and polarizes. I have tried to criticize each of those concepts and then to provide alternative ways of grasping the changing character of social relations, and the social psychology which emerges from those changes. The growing transparency of the categories of theory in social psychology is the result of actual changes which make those categories increasingly ideological — increasingly distortions of actual social life and the character of the mediations between individual and collective, which is the subject matter of social psychology.

This theoretical and critical reading of social psychology and the effort to develop an alternative theory is partly in advance of social events. I try to augment and amplify what I perceive as developing tendencies in social relations and in social psychological processes. Trying to see behind the surface of the present, I draw from informal experience and observation, on the one side, and from a more articulated theoretical tradition of Marxism and critical theory, on the other. What results is the outlines of a critical social psychology.

But there is only so far one can go in theory. The new social psychology is being created in everyday life. But the social psychology of corporate liberalism still reigns. My hypothesis about the current social role of this social psychology is that it has become a diffuse set of cultural rationalizations, providing a more rationalized cultural production of everyday methods for covering over the incipient tendencies that so-called facts contain. It is a major source of social type understandings which substitutes for a structural understanding and insures that a critical theory of the social is left out of academic supplying of popular consciousness. The fight over and the blockade against a critical social psychology is not a purely theoretical academic question.

I argue that social psychology rationalizes and reinforces the deep assumptions of popular consciousness while improving on its factual errors within the assumptions. If this is so, then the suppression of an alternative paradigm, and of the conditions of its production — even the limited immediate conditions of its production in academe, for example (Lubek, 1980) — is political.

The struggle is over theories which 'become a material force,' theory as popular consciousness. Despite Ingleby's assurance that only in the academic backwaters is a social and political view of psychology unacceptable, the fact remains that there is no systematic research on the diffusion and dissemination of social psychology adequate to support or refute the hypothesis that it is a resource for popular ideologies that maintain mass ignorance. There is research about the industrial uses of psychology and military uses of social psychology. But, the broader cultural role of social psychology, which I think can be documented by studies in the diffusion and translation of knowledge — particularly between academic fields and popular guide-to-living books, and newspaper, magazine, and television presentation — remains virtually unexplored.

Social psychology and social movements

The development of an alternative in social psychology is itself the result of historic changes outside of academic knowledge producing routines. In chapter 5 I tried to show that some of the alternate viewpoints, social psychologies, were the cultural aspects of historic social movements. What are the prospects in the social present?

The polarization of liberalism is at once a practical and theoretic event. For example, the bifurcation of the concept of the self between theories of authority as formatively necessary and theories which argue for a collective subject is also a practical historic and contemporary social struggle. Theorists of the collective subject have developed along with the concrete practical activities of the anti-psychiatry movement (Ingleby, 1980; Brown, 1981). On the other side, the later Frankfurt School view is being revived by Lasch (1977) and others. It argues that family authority is necessary for the development of strong egos resistant to mass movements and has its cruder practical analogue on its social right. The current reassertion of an older work ethos, individual competition, and the uncritical acceptance of the accumulation of ego capital is both one of the most prevalent expressions of the underlying economic crisis and the right wing social movements which herald a return to the 'good old days.' Obviously, the theorists are not necessarily spokespeople for the movements, although they may be. The movements and the theories interact and develop as different types of responses to the same historical conditions.

During the current social and theoretic crisis, all the categories of social psychology and the phenomena which they refer to split into antagonistic tendencies. For the self, there is the theory and practice of familied authority versus the theory and practice of collective subjectivity. The category of interaction has split into subjective and market economic tendencies. The current liberal practice of inter-personalism and its stylized, ideal typical appearance in sensitivity groups, gave way to a practical change that the dissolution of the category of social interaction is only now just beginning to acknow-ledge. The subjectivization of social interaction was the step beyond the encounter movements, a step expressed in this and other wordly forms, as diverse as Roszak (1969) and Ram Dass (1971). The corpora-tizing tendency, the rationalization of 'fellowship' of the Progressive culture of the corporate liberal period into self-management and self-programming – in a phrase, the Taylorization of social interaction – is a much more recent development.

The fight over these tendencies is not just theoretical. The empathic friendliness model of the individual-collective mediation is currently being fought over on the terrain of feminism, and the anti-feminist reaction which is currently so powerful in the US (Evans, 1980). Radical feminism denies the personalistic veneer, the friendly inter-personalism of surface, false liberal egalitarianism in order to explore the centrality of exploitation as the central category and practice of so-called social interaction. The theoretical articulation of this program includes the analysis of domestic exploitation, the super-exploitation of women, and the wider conditions of social production which make that possible. The analysis of interaction as exploitation is then not an imagining of the critical social psychological theorist, but an historically mystified aspect of a category representing the mediation between the individual and the collective which the women's movement is bringing to the surface (Saffioti, 1978; Kuhn and Wolpe, 1978; Dalla Costa and James, 1973). But as the polarization of interaction uncovers the traditional secret – exploitation, so too do movements of the right reassert the privatized domestic ideology which, along with 'fellowship,' has occluded the exploitative character of everday life. The new familism joins the new economics in its campaigns against abortion rights and for the reintroduction of a culture of sexism (Jaffe, Lindheim and Lee, 1981). Against this alternative, what the women's movement has foreshadowed is the possibility of collective, rational organization of activity as the substitute for an ideology of social interaction.

Intimacy is the crucial barrier between the public and the private as the self is the cultural frontier that stands between the normal and the mad. The regime of liberalism is the admission of a minimum amount of affective relation, the necessary cathexis of human relations management. The crisis of the 1960s and its cultural revolution insisted on the extension of affective behaviors ordinarily associated with the family, or at best, private life, as an integral aspect of all social connection, whatever its institutional site. This challenge to the commodification of the self and interaction and the alienating fragmentation of the social whole underlined the socially contradictory character of the category and practice of intimacy. On the one hand, intimacy is a method of containment, shuffling the socially suppressed aspects of public life into a private realm. On the other hand, the acknowledgment of a cultural category of behavior that extends the affective beyond traditional institutional sites, such as the family, challenges the boundaries of the institutionally regulated division of expressive labor. Intimacy is the furthest reach of human relations, functioning at once to contain the distance between the public and the private, but also to explode it.

Gender division reinforces the alienating fragmentation of human capacities. The social division of labor, while it accomplishes super-exploitation through hierarchized and stigmatized social roles, also divides capacities by gender. The challenge to intimacy as a compartmentalizing category develops when the affective instrumental distinction is no longer gender-linked. The gay movement poses such a challenge and also questions the linkage of gender and the public and private by challenging the affective neutrality of the same-sex workplace or school (Pinar, 1981). The reduction of gender differences in the gay movement is currently the object of rightwing action from religious fundamentalism which insists on the segregation of differences, and opposes a same-sex emotional and physical bonding, which offers a possibility of overcoming repression and competition with social solidarity.

Social psychology: from containment to mobilization

The historical success of conventional academic social psychology was tied to the success of the corporate liberal class for whom, intentionally or unaware, it functioned as a regiment in the army of its organic intellectuals. The decomposition of that class, and its reconstitution as new right free enterprisers, on the one side, and a variety of separate, splintered opposition groups, on the other, removed the social ground out from under contemporary social psychology. I have tried to show exactly how this historical social realignment is expressed within the concepts of social psychology, and also what it means for the development of an alternative conceptual representation of the future.

I suggest that social psychology will now try to hold its center line, despite the obvious social polarization which surrounds and engulfs its academic sites of intellectual, or more accurately, ignorance production. The current economic crisis reinforces the use of professionalism as an excuse for more selective stratified sorting, and the exclusion of anything or anyone who is different. The right backlash that has been developing in society for the past ten years will, I think, discount efforts to develop beyond the so-called crisis literature. The crisis, for social psychologists, will fade into memory, and the earlier attacks will no longer have to be debated — merely excluded as unproductive ideas dreamed up by unaffordably risky people during this time of fiscal retrenchment of the entire public sector. At the same time, the cultural function of social psychology, contradiction containment by social moronization, will become less important. People no longer need the legitimations of the academy to deceive themselves. Besides, the money is on the military.

It is during this time, when the smoke of the crisis has cleared and liberal, internal critics have moved to safer terrain, now that the social polarization gets increasingly fought out in the open without the benefit of academic refereeing, that the possibility of a critical social psychology is most apparent. The right does not need a social psychology. Its viewpoint is already embedded in the logic of advertising and the pre-liberal ideologies of religion and family. It becomes possible for critical social psychology to turn active, and to complete its critique of liberalism by articulating the social psychological preconditions for attaining the goals of the currently fragmented, dissenting cultural and social movements. Instead of the critique of domination in the sublimations, repressions, and denials of social psychology, the task becomes the articulation of the possibilities for the active appropriation of current contradictory possibilities.

Social psychology then becomes openly what it has been all along — a theoretic moment in the conflict of classes. It no longer serves the ruling class by perfecting everyday methods of destroying social consciousness. Instead, it takes the part of the oppressed and ascending classes. As a transformative social practice, the early tasks of an alternative, mobilizing social psychology are to understand: What are the social psychological requisities of the undoing of repression? How can psychological mobilization be accomplished?

I want to offer several brief suggestions for this future of an alternative social psychology that ceases to be simply critical. After the critiques and then the construction of the categories through which sense can be made of existing mediated domination, social psychology can become a description of enabling mediations. How can the individual be related to the collective in ways which facilitate both individual and collective transformation? Critical social psychology has had enough of balance and adjustment theories.

The theoretic task of an alternative social psychology has already begun in practice. Its first step is the articulation of individual dis-satisfaction around particular points of oppression to develop possi-bilities for collective action. I have tried (Wexler, 1981b; Wexler and Whitson, 1981) to indicate how that oppositional activity becomes formed and what is required to prevent its appropriation into the formation of the hegemonic class. Such action requires an analysis and a practice at the cultural, interactional, organizational, and personal levels.

There are a number of efforts to describe the necessary conditions for collective action of different sorts (Smelser, 1963; Wallace, 1961). There is, as Wallace suggests in his analysis of revitalization movements, a sequence which change movements pass through. Wallace, (1961, pp. 143-4) defines revitalization movements as 'organized attempts by some members of a society to construct a more satisfying culture by rapid acceptance of multiple innovations.'

Alternatively, one can see revitalization movements as examples of a more totalizing process of psychological mobilization that begins with more specific and limited aims. Piven and Cloward (1977, pp. 3, 4) suggest the social stages which people's movements go through:

First the 'system' — or those aspects of the system that people experience and perceive — loses legitimacy . . . . Second, people who are ordinarily fatalistic, who believe that existing arrangements are inevitable, begin to assert 'rights' that imply demands for change. Third, there is a new sense of efficiency: people who ordinarily consider themselves helpless come to believe that they have some capacity to alter their lot.

From a specific mobilization develops a general mobilization. This second aspect of psychological mobilization depends on the specific character of the dissatisfaction and its relation to a more general

166

mobilization for change. This second stage, which depends on the prior particularity of constituent collective movements, is the coalescence of the specific mobilizations into a more general collective movement for social transformation.

Critical social psychology requires a theory which can comprehend and facilitate social change movements. It will then become a social psychology of the undoing of domination — one which begins with the recognition of deprivation and domination but moves toward the realization of denied forms of life. Such a practical and articulated social psychology of specific and general mobilization has not yet developed, but there are signs of both specific and general cultural mobilization. For each of the sociocultural movements that I have indicated as key to the development of a critical social psychology, there are what we might call moves toward the transformation of the whole, but (unlike the late Frankfurt School) a concrete whole, specified — economically, culturally and socially — in theory and in practice. There are current examples of this concrete movement toward the historically specific social whole.

In an analysis of the situation of feminism in the US during the current right reaction. Riddiough urges the building of coalitions, in a tone not heard very often during an earlier period of the movement (1981, p. 50). 'An important factor will be whether a progressive coalition of women, labor, blacks and other groups develops . . . . Work in the ERA has already led to alliances between feminists and labor, alliances that can be expanded.' Writing about gay and lesbian life, in describing the current political situation in San Francisco, D'Emilio echoes the same particularly based movement toward the historical social whole (1981, p. 103): 'The enemy is the same: corporations, banks, and real estate developers . . . sexual orientation is not a sufficient basis of unity for our politics, for moving us toward liberation.'

Similarly, in her description of the anti-psychiatry movement in France, Turkle (1980) describes the role of the psychotics, the mental patients, and the ex-mental patients as an organizing locus for a much larger social-political protest (p. 181):

psychiatric issues are frequently presented as the most appropriate vehicle for mobilizing political energies that were frustrated after 1968. Why? . . . in the eyes of the state, the citizen, *like the madman and like the political dissident*, is in a perverse relationship to the normal order. The citizen and the radical have every reason to

167

identify with the psychotic — on a basic level the state relates to them all on the same terms . . . . The psychotic's symptom is considered as an expression of a socially-shared malaise. By reflecting on the psychotic's situation, the political activist will better understand his own.

The simultaneous articulation of a series of social movements, and increasing consciousness of their interrelation, combines with a situation in which the fundamental categories of cultural representation and containment become increasingly less believable. Fernandez describes this situation in a cross-cultural analysis of revitalization movements (1981, p. 23): 'It is the falling apart of these relational structures of ordering — these "structural replications" in different domains — that produces the epistemological crisis which is one of the chief motives for attempts at revitalization by returning to the whole.'

All these efforts to transcend existing practical and theoretical social psychologies are at first met with stigmatization. The articulation and organization of opposition also involves struggle against pervasive labeling processes of political deviantization (Schur, 1980, p. 13). In this society, the desire for wholeness is considered a thought disorder, a symptom of madness. That is why the current irrationality can only be reversed by a mobilization and transformation of the whole.

Bibliography

Adorno, T. W. (1967), 'Sociology and psychology,' *New Left Review*, vol. 46, pp. 67-80.

Adorno, T. W. (1968), 'Sociology and psychology – II,' *New Left Review*, vol. 47, pp. 79-97.

Adorno, T. W., Frenkel-Brunswik, E., Levinson, D. J. and Sanford, R. N. (1964), *The Authoritarian Personality*, New York, Wiley.

Allport, F. H. (1924) *Social Psychology*, New York, Houghton Mifflin.

Allport, G. W. (1968), 'The historical background of modern social psychology,' in G. Lindzey and E. Aronson (eds), *The Handbook of Social Psychology*, 2nd edn, vol. 1, Reading, Mass., Addison-Wesley, pp. 1-80.

Altbach, P. G., Laufer, R. S. and McVey, S. (eds)(1971), *Academic Super Markets*, San Francisco, Jossey-Bass.

Althusser, L. (1969), *For Marx*, London, Allen Lane.

Althusser, L. (1971), 'Ideology and ideological state apparatuses (notes towards an investigation),' in *Lenin and Philosophy and other Essays*, New York, Monthly Review Press, pp. 127-86.

Althusser, L. and Balibar, E. (1970), *Reading Capital*, London, New Left Books.

Anderson, P. (1976), *Consideration on Western Marxism*, London, New Left Books.

Apple, M. W. (1980), 'Curriculum form and the logic of technical control: building the possessive individual,' in L. Barton, R. Meighan and S. Walker (eds), *Schooling, Ideology and the Curriculum*, Sussex, The Falmer Press, pp. 11-27.

Archibald, W. P. (1978), *Social Psychology as Political Economy*, Toronto, McGraw-Hill Ryerson.

Armistead, N. (ed) (1974), *Reconstructing Social Psychology*, Baltimore, Penguin.

Aronowitz, S. (1973), *False Promises: The Shaping of the American Working Class Consciousness*, New York, McGraw-Hill.

Bibliography

Aronowitz, S. (1978), 'Marx, Braverman and the logic of capital,'
The Insurgent Sociologist, vol. 3, nos. 2 and 3, fall, pp. 126-47.

Baldwin, J. M. (1897), *Social and Ethical Interpretations in Mental
Development*, New York and London, Macmillan.

Baldwin, J. M. (1913), *History of Psychology*, New York and London,
Putnams.

Baritz, L. (1960), *The Servants of Power: A History of the Use of
Social Science in American Industry*, Middletown, Conn., Wesleyan
University Press.

Basseches, M. (1980), 'Dialectical schemata: a framework for the
empirical study of the development of dialectical thinking,' *Human
Development*, vol. 23, pp. 400-21.

Baumgardner, S. R. (1977), 'Critical studies in the history of social
psychology,' *Personality and Social Psychology Bulletin* (4), 3, fall,
pp. 681-7.

Baxandall, R., Gordon, L. and Reverby, S., (eds) (1976), *America's
Working Women: A Documentary History – 1600 to the Present*,
New York, Vintage.

Bendix, R. (1956), *Work and Authority in Industry*, New York, Wiley.

Benjamin, J. (1978), 'Authority and the family revisited: or a world
without fathers,' *New German Critique*, no. 13, winter, pp. 35-57.

Bennis, W. G., Berlew, David E., Schein, Edgar H. and Steale, Fred I.
(1973), *Interpersonal Dynamics; Essays and Readings on Human
Interaction*, 3rd edn., Homewood, Illinois, Dorsey.

Berman, S. and Weiss, V. (1978), *Relationships*, New York, Hawthorn.

Bernbaum, G. (ed) (1979), *Schooling in Decline*, London, Macmillan.

Bernstein, B. (1975), *Class, Codes and Control: Towards a Theory of
Educational Transmissions*, vol. 3, London, Routledge & Kegan Paul.

Berscheid, E. and Walster, E. H. (1978), *Interpersonal Attraction*, 2nd
ed, Reading, Mass., Addison-Wesley.

Biddle, B. J. (1979), *Role Theory*, New York, Academic Press.

Biddle, B. J. and Thomas, E. J. (eds) (1966), *Role Theory*, New York,
Wiley.

Blackburn, R. (1973), *Ideology in Social Science: Readings in Critical
Social Theory*, New York, Vintage.

Bottomore, T. B. and Rubel, M. (eds) (1956), *Karl Marx: Selected
Writings in Sociology and Social Philosophy*, New York, McGraw-Hill.

Bowles, S. and Gintis, H. (1976), *Schooling in Capitalist America:
Educational Reform and the Contradictions of Economic Life*, New
York, Basic Books.

Bradburn, N. M. and Caplovitz, D. (1965), *Reports on Happiness: A
Pilot Study of Behavior Related to Mental Health*, Chicago, Aldine.

Bramel, D. and Friend, R. (1981), 'The theory and practice of psychology in the US,' in B. Ollman and E. Vernoff (eds), *The Left Academy:*

170

Marxist Scholars on American Campuses, New York, McGraw-Hill.

Braverman, H. (1974), *Labor and Monopoly Capital: The Degradation of Work in the Twentieth Century*, New York, Monthly Review Press.

Breines, P. (ed) (1972), *Critical Interruptions: New Left Perspectives on Herbert Marcuse*, New York, Herder & Herder.

Brenkman, J. (1979), 'Mass media: from collective experience to the culture of privatization,' *Social Text*, vol. 1, winter, pp. 94-109.

Brewster-Smith, M. (1977), 'A dialectical social psychology? Comments on a symposium,' *Personality and Social Psychology Bulletin* (4), 3, fall, pp. 714-24.

Brigham, J. C. and Wrightsman, L. S. (eds) (1977), *Contemporary Issues in Social Psychology*, 3rd edn, Belmont, California, Wadsworth.

Bronfenbrenner, U. (1979), *The Ecology of Human Development: Experiments by Nature and Design*, Cambridge, Harvard University Press.

Brown, B. (1973), *Marx, Freud, and the Critique of Everyday Life: Toward a Permanent Cultural Revolution*, London, Monthly Review Press.

Brown, P. (1982), 'Anti-psychiatry and the left,' *Psychology and Social Theory*, no. 2.

Burawoy, M. (1978), 'Toward a Marxist theory of the labor process: Braverman and beyond,' *Politics and Society*, vol. 8, nos. 3 and 4, pp. 247-312.

Carey, J. T. (1975), *Sociology and Public Affairs: The Chicago School*, Beverly Hills and London, Sage.

Cartwright, D. (1979), 'Contemporary social psychology in historical perspective,' *Social Psychology Quarterly*, vol. 42, no. 1, pp. 82-93.

Carver, C. S. (1979), 'A cybernetic model of self-attention processes,' *Journal of Personality and Social Psychology*, vol. 37, no. 8, August, pp. 1252-81.

Castells, M. (1980), *The Economic Crisis and American Society*, Princeton University Press.

Cina, C. (1981), 'Social science for whom? A structural history of social psychology,' PhD dissertation, State University of New York at Stony Brook.

Cohen, H. (1980), *You Can Negotiate Anything: How to Get What You Want*, Secaucus, New Jersey, Lyle Stuart.

Connerton, P. (ed) (1976), *Critical Sociology*, Harmondsworth, Penguin.

Cooley, C. H. (1902), *Human Nature and the Social Order*, New York, Scribners.

Cooley, C. H. (1909), *Social Organization*, New York, Scribners.

Cooper, D. (1971), *The Death of the Family*, New York, Random House.

Bibliography

Cuddihy, J. M. (1974), *The Ordeal of Civility: Freud, Marx, Levi-Strauss, and the Jewish Struggle with Modernity*, New York, Delta.

Dalla Costa, M. and James, S. (1973), *The Power of Women and the Subversion of the Community*, Bristol, Falling Wall.

Davis, K. and Moore, W. E. (1945), 'Some principles of stratification,' *American Sociological Review*, vol. 10, no. 2, April, pp. 242-9.

Davis, M. S. (1973), *Intimate Relations*, New York, Free Press.

D'Emilio, J. (1981), 'Gay politics, gay community: San Francisco's experience,' *Socialist Review*, Number 55, vol. 2, no. 1, January-February, pp. 77-104.

Deleuze, G. and Guattari, F. (1977), *Anti-Oedipus: Capitalism and Schizophrenia*, New York, Viking.

Dohrenwend, B. P. and Dohrenwend, B. S. (1969), *Social Status and Psychological Disorder: A Causal Inquiry*, New York, Wiley.

Donzelot, J. (1979), *The Policing of Families*, New York, Pantheon.

Douglas, J. (1970), 'Understanding everyday life,' in J. Douglas (ed), *Understanding Everyday Life: Toward the Reconstruction of Sociological Knowledge*, Chicago, Aldine, pp. 3-44.

Douvan, E. (1977), 'Interpersonal relationships: some questions and observations,' in G. Levinger and H. L. Raush (eds), *Close Relationships: Perspectives on the Meaning of Intimacy*, Amherst, University of Massachusetts, pp. 17-32.

Dowd, D. F. (1977), *The Twisted Dream: Capitalist Development in the United States Since 1776*, Cambridge, Mass., Winthrop.

Duck, S. and Gilmour, R. (eds) (1981), *Personal Relationships: Studying Personal Relationships*, vol. 1, London, Academic Press.

Durkheim, E. (1951), *Suicide*, New York, Free Press.

Durkheim, E. (1954), *The Elementary Forms of Religious Life,* New York, Free Press.

Durkheim, E. (1964), *The Division of Labor in Society*, New York, Free Press.

Dwyer, W. W. (1978), *Pulling Your Own Strings: Dynamic Techniques for Dealing with Other People and Mastering Your Own Life*, New York, Avon.

Eagleton, J. (1976), *Criticism and Ideology: A Study in Marxist Literary Theory*, London, New Left Books.

Eakins, D. W. (1966), 'The development of corporate liberal policy research in the United States, 1885-1965,' PhD dissertation, University of Wisconsin.

Edwards, R. (1979), *Contested Terrain: The Transformation of the Workplace in the Twentieth Century*, New York, Basic Books.

Erickson, K. (1966), *Wayward Puritans: A Study in the Sociology of Deviance*, New York, Wiley.

Eros, F. (1974), 'Review of L. Garai's *Personality dynamics and social* existence,' *European Journal of Social Psychology*, vol. 4, no. 3, pp. 369-79.

Evans, M. S. (1980), 'Saving the family: family protection act,' *National Review*, vol. 32, no. 101, January, pp. 25-80.

Ewen, S. (1976), *Captains of Consciousness: Advertising and the Social Roots of the Consumer Culture*, New York, McGraw-Hill.

Fernandez, J. W. (1981), 'The experience of returning to the whole,' unpublished manuscript, Princeton University.

Fine, S. (1956), *Laissez-Faire and the General Welfare State: A Study of Conflict in American Thought, 1865-1901*, Ann Arbor, University of Michigan.

Fitzgerald, F. (1979), *America Revised: History Schoolbooks in the Twentieth Century*, Boston and Toronto, Little, Brown.

Foucault, M. (1965), *Madness and Civilization: A History of Insanity in the Age of Reason*, New York, Pantheon.

Foucault, M. (1970), *The Order of Things: An Archaeology of the Human Sciences*, New York, Vintage.

Foucault, M. (1972), *The Archaeology of Knowledge and the Discourse on Language*, New York, Harper & Row.

Fox-Genovese, E. (1979/80), 'The personal is not political enough,' *Marxist Perspectives*, vol. 2, no. 4, winter, pp. 94-113.

Frankfurt Institute of Social Research (1956), *Aspects of Sociology*, Boston, Beacon.

Franklin, B. (1974), 'The curriculum field and the problem of social control, 1918-1938: A study in critical theory,' PhD dissertation, University of Wisconsin.

Franks, P. E. (1975), 'A Social History of American Social Psychology Up to the Second World War,' PhD dissertation, State University of New York at Stony Brook.

Freud, S. (1922), *Group Psychology and the Analysis of the Ego*, New York, Boni & Liveright.

Freud, S. (1924), *A General Introduction to Psychoanalysis* (Boni & Liveright), New York, Washington Square Press, 1952.

Freud, S. (1949), *Civilization and Its Discontent*, London, Hogarth.

Freud, S. (1957), *The Future of an Illusion*, New York, Doubleday Anchor.

Freud, S. (1959), *Collected Papers*, vol. V, New York, Basic Books.

Freud, S. (1960), *Group Psychology and the Analysis of the Ego*, New York, Bantam.

Freud, S. (1962), *The Ego and the Id*, New York, Norton.

Fried, M. (1973), *The World of the Urban Working Class*, Cambridge, Mass., Harvard.

Fromm, E. (1947), *Man For Himself: An Inquiry into the Psychology of Ethics*, New York, Rinehart.

Gadlin, H. (1977), 'Private lives and public order: A critical view of the history of intimate relations in the United States,' in G. Levinger and H. L. Raush (eds), *Close Relationships: Perspectives on the Meaning of Intimacy*, Amherst, University of Massachusetts, pp. 33-72.

Garai, L. (n.d.), 'A new theoretical approach to human motivation,' unpublished English language manuscript, courtesy of Ferenc Eros, Institute of Psychology, Hungarian Academy of Sciences, Budapest, Hungary.

Garfinkel, H. (1967), *Studies in Ethnomethodology*, Englewood Cliffs, New Jersey, Prentice-Hall.

Gekas, V. (1979), 'The influence of social class on socialization,' in W. R. Burr, R. Hill, F. I. Nye and I. L. Reiss (eds), *Contemporary Theories About the Family*, vol. 1, New York, Free Press, pp. 365-404.

Gergen, K. J. (1971), *The Concept of Self,* New York, Holt, Rinehart & Winston.

Gergen, K. J. (1973), 'Social psychology as history,' *Journal of Personality and Psychology*, vol. 26, no. 2, pp. 309-20.

Gerth, H. and Mills, C. W. (1964), *Character and Social Structure: The Psychology of Social Institutions*, New York, Harcourt, Brace & World.

Gilder, G. (1981), *Wealth and Poverty*, New York, Basic Books.

Goffman, E. (1959), *The Presentation of Self in Everyday Life*, Garden City, New York, Doubleday.

Golding, P. and Murdock, G. (1979), 'Ideology and the mass media: The question of determination,' in M. Barrett, P. Corrigan, A. Kuhn and J. Wolff (eds), *Ideology and Cultural Production*, New York, St Martins, pp. 198-224.

Goldstine, D., Larner, K., Zuckerman, S. and Goldstine, H. (1977), *The Dance-Away Lover: And Other Roles We Play in Sex and Marriage*, New York, Ballantine.

Goode, W. J. (1974), 'The theoretical importance of love,' in R. L. Coser (ed), *The Family: Its Structures and Functions*, 2nd edn, New York, St Martins, pp. 143-56.

Gorz, A. (1967), *Strategy for Labor: A Radical Proposal*, Boston, Beacon.

Gouldner, A. W. (1970), *The Coming Crisis of Western Sociology*, New York, Avon.

Gouldner, A. W. (1979), *The Future of Intellectuals and the Rise of the New Class*, New York, Seabury.

Gramsci, A. (1971), *Selections from the Prison Notebooks*, New York, International.

Gurin, G., Veroff, J. and Feld, S. (1960), *Americans View their Mental Health*, New York, Basic Books.

Gurin, P., Gurin, G. and Morrison, B. M. (1978), 'Personal and ideological aspects of internal and external control,' *Social Psychology*, vol. 41, no. 4, pp. 275-96.

Gutman, H. G. (1976), *Work, Culture, and Society in Industrializing America: Essays in American Working-Class and Social History*, New York, Knopf.

Habermas, J. (1970), *Toward a Rational Society: Student Protest, Science, and Politics*, Boston, Beacon.

Habermas, J. (1975), *Legitimation Crisis*, Boston, Beacon.

Hall, S. (1981), 'Moving right,' *Socialist Review*, no. 55, January-February, pp. 113-37.

Harré, R. and Secord, P. F. (1972), *The Explanation of Social Behavior*, Totowa, NJ, Rowman & Littlefield.

Harvey, J., Ickes, W. and Kidd, R. F. (1978), *New Directions in Attribution Research*, vol. 2, Hillsdale, NJ, Lawrence Erlbaum.

Held, D. (1980), *Introduction to Critical Theory: Horkheimer to Habermas*, Berkeley, University of California Press.

Henry, J. (1963), *Culture Against Man*, New York, Vintage.

Henry, J. (1973), *Pathways to Madness*, New York, vintage.

Hilton, R. (1976), *The Transition from Feudalism to Capitalism*, London, New Left Books.

Hollander, E. P. (1976), *Principles and Methods of Social Psychology*, 3rd edn, New York, Oxford University Press.

Homans, G. C. (1961), *Social Behavior: Its Elementary Forms*, New York, Harcourt, Brace & World.

Horkheimer, M. (1947), *Eclipse of Reason*, New York, Oxford University Press.

Horkheimer, M. (1972), *Critical Theory*, New York, Herder & Herder.

Horkheimer, M. and Adorno, T. W. (1972), *Dialectic of Enlightenment*, New York, Herder & Herder.

Howard, D. and Klare, K. E. (eds) (1972), *The Unknown Dimension*, New York, Basic Books.

Huston, T. L. (ed) (1974), *Foundations of Interpersonal Attraction*, New York, Academic Press.

Huston, T. and Levinger, G. (1978), 'Interpersonal attraction and relationships,' *Annual Review of Psychology*, vol. 29, pp. 115-56.

Hymes, D. (ed) (1972), *Reinventing Anthropology*, New York, Random House.

Illich, I. (1976), *Medical Nemesis: The Exploitation of Health*, Toronto, Bantam.

Ingleby, D. (1974), 'The job psychologists do,' in N. Armistead (ed), *Reconstructing Social Psychology*, Baltimore, Penguin, pp. 314-28.

Ingleby, D. (ed) (1980), *Critical Psychiatry: The Politics of Mental Health*, New York, Pantheon.

Ingleby, D. (1982), 'The politics of psychology: review of a decade,' *Psychology and Social Theory*, no. 2.

Israel, J. and Tajfel, H. (eds) (1972), *The Context of Social Psychology: A Critical Assessment*, London, Academic Press.

Jacoby, R. (1975), *Social Amnesia: A Critique of Conformist Psychology from Adler to Laing*, Boston, Beacon.

Jaffe, F., Lindheim, B. L. and Lee, P. (1981), *Abortion Politics: Private Morality and Public Policy*, New York, McGraw-Hill.

Kamin, L. J. (1974), *The Science and Politics of I. Q.*, Potomac, Md., Lawrence Erlbaum, distributed by Halstead Press, New York.

Kantor, R. M. (1977), *Work and Family in the United States: A Critical Review and Agenda for Research and Policy*, New York, Russell Sage Foundation.

Kantor, D. and Lehr, W. (1975), *Inside the Family*, San Francisco, Jossey-Bass.

Karpf, F. B. (1932), *American Social Psychology*, New York, McGraw-Hill.

Klapp, O. E. (1978), *Opening and Closing: Strategies of Information Adaptation in Society*, Cambridge University Press.

Kohn, M. L. (1969), *Class and Conformity: A Study in Values*, Homewood, Illinois, Dorsey.

Kohn, M. L. and Schooler, C. (1978), 'The reciprocal effects of the substantive complexity of work and intellectual flexibility: a longitudinal assessment,' *American Journal of Sociology*, vol. 84, no. 1, pp. 24-52.

Kornhauser, A. (1965), *Mental Health of the Industrial Worker*, New York, Wiley.

Kovel, J. (1980), 'The American mental health industry,' in D. Ingleby (ed), *Critical Psychiatry: The Politics of Mental Health*, New York, Pantheon, pp. 72-101.

Krueger, M. and Silvert, F. (1975), *Dissent Denied: The Technocratic Response to Protest*, New York, Elsevier.

Krueger, M. (1976), 'Notes on a materialistic theory of interaction,' *Cornell Journal of Social Relations*, vol. 2, no. 1, spring, pp. 97-104.

Kuhn, A. and Wolpe, A. (1978), *Feminism and Materialism: Women and Modes of Production*, London, Routledge & Kegan Paul.

Kupers, T. A. (1976), 'Schizophrenia and reification,' *Socialist Revolution*, Number 29, vol. 6, no. 3, July-September, pp. 105-24.

Laddis, A. (1979), 'Dialectical materialism and psychology,' unpublished manuscript, Madison, Wisconsin.

Ladner, J. (ed) (1973), *The Death of White Sociology*, New York, Random House.

Laing, R. D. (1959), *The Divided Self: An Existential Study in Sanity and Madness*, Harmondsworth, Penguin.

Laing, R. D. (1968), *The Politics of Experience*, New York, Ballantine.

Larkin, R. W. (1979), *Suburban Youth in Cultural Crisis*, New York, Oxford University Press.

Larsen, K. S. (ed) (1980), *Social Psychology: Crisis or Failure*, Monmouth, Oregon, Institute for Theoretical History.

Larson, M. S. (1977), *The Rise of Professionalism: Sociological Analyses*, Berkeley, University of California.

Lasch, C. (1977), *Haven in a Heartless World: The Family Besieged*, New York, Basic Books.

Levinger, G., and Raush, H. L. (eds) (1977), *Close Relationships: Perspectives on the Meaning of Intimacy*, Amherst, University of Massachusetts.

Levy, G. (1970), *Ghetto School: Class Warfare in an Elementary School*, Indianapolis, Pegasus, Bobbs-Merrill.

Lewin, K. (1951), *Field Theory in Social Science*, New York, Harper.

Lewis, L. S. and Brisset, D. (1967), 'Sex as work: a study of avocational counseling,' *Social Problems*, vol. 15, no. 1, pp. 8-18.

Lifton, R. J. (1968), 'Protean man,' *Partisan Review*, no. 35, Winter, pp. 13-27.

Lubek, I. (1980), 'The psychological establishment: pressure to preserve paradigms, publish rather than perish, win friends, and influence students,' in K. S. Larsen (ed), *Social Psychology: Crisis or Failure*, Monmouth, Oregon, Institute for Theoretical History, pp. 129-57.

Lukács, J. (1970), *The Passing of the Modern Age*, New York, Harper & Row.

Lukács, G. (1971), *History and Class Consciousness: Studies in Marxist Dialectics*, Cambridge, Mass., MIT Press.

Lyons, J. O. (1978), *The Invention of the Self: The Hinge of Consciousness in the Eighteenth Century*, Carbondale and Edwardsville, Southern Illinois University Press.

MacKay, R. (1973), 'Conceptions of children and models of socialization,' in H. P. Dreitzel (ed), *Recent Sociology: Childhood and Socialization*, no. 5, pp. 27-43.

MacPherson, C. B. (1962), *The Political Theory of Possessive Individualism: Hobbes to Locke*, London, Oxford University Press.

Mandel, E. (1978), *The Second Slump: A Marxist Analysis of Recession in the Seventies*, London, New Left Books.

Mannheim, K. (1936), *Ideology and Utopia: An Introduction to the Sociology of Knowledge*, New York, Harcourt, Brace & World.

Manning, P. K. and Zucker, M. (1976), *The Sociology of Mental Health and Illness*, Indianapolis, Bobbs-Merrill.

Marcuse, H. (1962), *Eros and Civilization: A Philosophical Inquiry into Freud*, New York, Vintage.

Marcuse, H. (1964), *One-Dimensional Man: Studies in the Ideology of*

Bibliography

Advanced Industrial Society, Boston, Beacon.

Marcuse, H. (1968), 'The affirmative character of culture,' *Negations*, Boston, Beacon, pp. 88-133.

Marx, K. (1967), *Capital: A Critique of Political Economy*, vol. 1, New York International.

Marx, K. (1973), *Grundrisse: Foundations of the Critique of Political Economy*, New York, Vintage.

McDougall, W. (1908), *Introduction to Social Psychology*, London, Methuen.

McGuire, W. (1973), 'The yin and yang of progress in social psychology,' *Journal of Personality and Social Psychology*, vol. 26, no. 3, June, pp. 446-56.

McLellan, D. (1973), *Karl Marx: His Life and Thought*, New York, Harper & Row.

McVey, S. (1975), 'Social control of social research. The development of the social scientist as expert, 1875-1916,' PhD dissertation, University of Wisconsin.

Mead, G. H. (1934), *Mind, Self and Society from the Standpoint of a Social Behaviorist*, Chicago University Press.

Meltzer, B. N., Petras, J. W. and Reynolds, L. T. (1975), *Symbolic Interactionism: genesis, varieties and criticism*, London and Boston, Routledge & Kegan Paul.

Merton, R. K. (1957), *Social Theory and Social Structure*, Glencoe, Ill., Free Press.

Meszaros, I. (1970), *Marx's Theory of Alienation*, London, Merlin.

Miles, M. W. (1971), *The Radical Probe*, New York, Atheneum.

Mills, C. W. (1943), 'The professional ideology of social pathologists,' *American Journal of Sociology*, vol. 49, September, pp. 168-80.

Moscovici, S. (1972), 'Society and theory in social psychology,' in J. Israel and H. Tajfel (eds), *The Context of Social Psychology: A Critical Assessment*, London, Academic Press.

Murstein, B. I. (ed) (1971), *Theories of Attraction and Love*, New York, Springer.

Napier, A. Y. (1977), 'The rejection-intrusion pattern: a central family dynamic,' unpublished manuscript, School of Family Resources, University of Wisconsin-Madison.

Napier, A. Y. and Whitaker, C. A. (1978), *The Family Crucible*, New York, Harper & Row.

Nasaw, D. (1979), *Schooled to Order*, New York, Oxford University Press.

New York Times (1980), 3 June, section 11, p. 12, col. 1.

New York Times (1980), October, section IV, p. 19, col. 2.

Nicolaus, M. (1973), 'Foreward,' in Marx, K., *Grundrisse*, New York, Vintage, pp. 7-63.

178

Nisbet, R. A. (1965), *Emile Durkheim*, Englewood Cliffs, New Jersey, Prentice-Hall.

Nisbet, R. A. (1966), *The Sociological Tradition*, New York, Basic Books.

Nisbet, R. A. (1974), *The Sociology of Emile Durkheim*, New York, Oxford University Press.

Noble, D. F. (1977), *America by Design: Science, Technology and the Rise of Corporate Capitalism*, New York, Knopf.

Noble, D. W. (1958), *The Paradox of Progressive Thought*, Minneapolis, University of Minnesota.

O'Connor, J. (1973), *The Fiscal Crisis of the State*, New York, St Martin's.

Ollman, B. (1971), *Alienation: Marx's Conception of Man in Capitalist Society*, London, Cambridge University Press.

Page, C. H. (1946), 'Bureaucracy's other face,' *Social Forces*, vol. 25, pp. 88-94.

Parenti, M. (1980), 'Political bigotry in academe,' *Chronical of Higher Education*, vol. 19, no. 18, January, p. 56.

Parker, L. (1981), 'Neopositivism and dialectics,' *Psychology and Social Theory*, no. 1, Spring/Summer, pp. 12-26.

Parsons, T. (1937), *The Structure of Social Action*, Glencoe, Free Press.

Parsons, T. (1951), *The Social System*, Glencoe, Free Press.

Parsons, T. and Bales, Robert F. and others (1955), *Family, Socialization and Interaction Process*, New York, Free Press.

Pepitone, A. (1976), 'Toward a normative and comparative social psychology,' *Journal of Personality and Social Psychology*, vol. 34, pp. 641-53.

Perlman, F. (1968), *Essay on Commodity Fetishism*, Somerville, New England.

Petras, J. W. (1970), 'Images of man in early American sociology, part I: the individualistic perspective in motivation,' *Journal of the History of Behavioral Sciences*, vol. 6, July, pp. 231-40.

Pinar, W. F. (1980), 'The abstract and the concrete in curriculum theorising,' in H. Giroux, A. Penna and W. F. Pinar (eds), *Introduction to Curriculum*, Berkeley, McCutchan.

Pinar, W. F. (1982), 'Curriculum as gender text: notes on reproduction, resistance and male-male relations,' *Journal of Curriculum Theorizing*, vol. 4, no. 2, Summer.

Piven, F. F. and Cloward, R. A. (1977), *Poor People's Movements: Why They Succeed, How They Fail*, New York, Pantheon.

Psathas, G. (ed) (1979), *Everyday Language: Studies in Ethnomethodology*, New York, Irvington.

Ram Dass, B. (1971), *Remember Be Here Now*, San Cristobel, New Mexico, Lama Foundation.

179

Bibliography

Rappaport, L. (1977), 'Symposium: towards a dialectical social psychology — Introduction,' *Personality and Social Psychology Bulletin*, pp. 678-80.

Ratner, C. (1981), 'A critique of the genetic theories of madness,' *Psychology and Social Theory*, fall/winter, no. 2 (in press).

Reich, W. (1970), *The Mass Psychology of Fascism*, New York, Farrar, Straus & Giroux.

Reich, W. (1972), *Sex-Pol: essays 1929-1934*, New York, Vintage.

Resler, H. and Walton, P. (1974), 'How social is it?,' *Reconstructing Social Psychology*, N. Armistead (ed), Baltimore, Penguin.

Riddiough, C. R. (1981), 'Women, feminism, and the 1980 elections,' *Socialist Review* Number 56, vol. 11, no. 2, March-April, pp. 37-52.

Ridgeway, J. (1968), *The Closed Corporation*, New York, Random House.

Riesman, D., Denney, R. and Glazer, N. (1950), *The Lonely Crowd: A Study of the Changing American Character*, New Haven, Yale University Press.

Rock, P. (1979), *The Making of Symbolic Interactionism*, London, MacMillan.

Roman, P. and Trice, H. M. (1967), *Schizophrenia and the Poor*, Ithaca, Cayuga Press.

Rose, A. M. (ed) (1962), *Human Behavior and Social Processes: An Interactionist Approach*, Boston, Houghton Mifflin.

Rosnow, R. L. (1981), *Paradigms in Transition: The Methodology of Social Inquiry*, New York, Oxford University Press.

Ross, E. A. (1908), *Social Psychology*, New York, Macmillan.

Roszak, T. (1969), *The Making of a Counter Culture: Reflections on the Technocratic Society and Its Youthful Opposition*, Garden City, New York, Anchor.

Rubin, Z. (1973), *Liking and Loving: An Invitation to Social Psychology*, New York, Holt, Rinehart & Winston.

Rubin, Z. (1974), *Doing Unto Others: Joining, Molding, Conforming, Helping, Loving*, Englewood Cliffs, New Jersey, Prentice-Hall.

Saffioti, H. (1978), *Women in Class Society*, New York and London, Monthly Review Press.

Sager, C. (1976), *Marriage Contracts and Couple Therapy*, New York, Bruner Mazel.

Samelson, F. (1977), 'World War I intelligence testing and the development of psychology,' *Journal of the History of the Behavioral Sciences*, vol. 13, pp. 274-82.

Sampson, E. E. (1971), *Social Psychology and Contemporary Society* New York, Wiley.

Sampson, E. E. (1975), *Ego at the Threshold*, New York, Delacorte.

Schegloff, Emanuel A. (1979), 'Identification and recognition in telephone conversation openings,' in George Psathas (ed), *Everyday Language: Studies in Ethnomethodology*, New York, Irvington, pp. 23-78.

Schneider, M. (1975), *Neurosis and Civilization: A Marxist/Freudian Synthesis*, New York, Seabury.

Schur, E. M. (1980), *The Politics of Deviance: Stigma Contests and the Uses of Power*, Englewood Cliffs, New Jersey, Prentice-Hall.

Schwartz, J. (1977), *The Subtle Anatomy of capitalism*, Santa Monica, California, Goodyear.

Schwendinger, H. and Schwendinger, J. R. (1974), *The Sociologists of the Chair: A Radical Analysis of the Formative Years of American Sociology, 1883-1922*, New York, Basic Books.

Sedgwick, P. (1974), 'Ideology and modern psychology,' in N. Armistead (ed), *Reconstructing Social Psychology*, Baltimore, Penguin, pp. 29-37.

Secord, P. F. (1977), 'Social psychology in search of a paradigm,' *Personality and Social Psychology Bulletin*, vol. 3, no. 1, winter, pp. 41-50.

Seeman, M. (1975), 'Alienation Studies,' *Annual Review of Sociology*, vol. 1, pp. 91-123.

Sennet, R. and Cobb, J. (1973), *The Hidden Injuries of Class*, New York, Vintage.

Sennett, R. (1977), *The Fall of Public Man*, New York, Knopf.

Seve, L. (1978), *Man in Marxist Theory: And the Psychology of Personality*, Sussex, Harvester.

Shames, C. (1980), 'The scientific humanism of Lucien Seve,' *Science and Society*, vol. 45, no. 1, spring, pp. 1-23.

Shepard, Jon M. (1977), 'Technology, alienation and job satisfaction,' in *Annual Review of Sociology*, vol. 3, Palo Alto, Annual Review, pp. 1-21.

Sherif, M. (1977), 'Crisis in social psychology: some remarks towards breaking through the crisis,' *Personality and Social Psychology Bulletin*, vol. 3, summer, pp. 368-82.

Sherman, J. A. and Beck, E. T. (eds) (1979), *The Prism of Sex: Essays in the Sociology of Knowledge*, Madison, University of Wisconsin.

Shor, J. and Sanville, J. (1978), *Illusion in Loving: A Psychoanalytic Approach to the Evolution of Intimacy and Autonomy*, New York, International Universities.

Shorter, E. (1975), *The Making of the Modern Family*, New York, Basic Books.

Shostak, A. B. and Gomberg, W. (1964), *Blue-Collar World: Studies of the American Worker*, Englewood Cliffs, New Jersey, Prentice-Hall.

Silva, E. T. and Slaughter, S. A. (1981), 'Prometheus/bound: knowledge, power and the transformation of American social science,' 1865-1920, unpublished MS, University of Toronto.

Slater, P. (1974), 'Social limitations on libidinal withdrawal,' in Rose Laub Coser (ed), *The Family: Its Structures and Functions*, 2nd edn, New York, St Martin's, pp. 111-33.

Sluzki, C.E. and Veron, E. (1977), 'The double bind as a universal pathogenic situation,' in P. Watzlawick and J. Weakland (eds), *The Interactional View*, New York, Norton, pp. 228-48.

Smelser, N. J. (1963), *Theory of Collective Behavior*, New York, Free Press.

Smith, D. N. (1974), *Who Rules the Universities?*, New York, Monthly Review Press.

Soffer, R. N. (1978), *Ethics and Society in England: The Revolution in the Social Sciences*, 1870-1914, Berkeley, University of California Press.

Spring, J. H. (1972), *Education and the Rise of the Corporate State*, Boston, Beacon.

Stryker, S. (1980), *Symbolic Interactionism: A Social Structural Version*, Menlo Park, California, Benjamin/Cummings.

Steiner, I. N. (1974), 'Whatever happened to the group in social psychology?,' *Journal of Experimental Social Psychology*, vol. 10, pp. 94-108.

Stone, G. P. (1962), 'Appearance and the self,' in A. M. Rose (ed), *Human Behavior and Social Processes: An Interactionist Approach*, Boston, Houghton Mifflin, pp. 86-118.

Sutton, F. X., Harris, S. E., Kaysen, C. and Tobin, J. (1956), *The American Business Creed*, New York, Schocken.

Sullivan, E. V. (1977), 'A study of Kohlberg's structural theory of moral development: a critique of liberal social science ideology,' *Human Development*, vol. 20, pp. 352-76.

Therborn, G. (1976), *Science, Class and Society: On the Formation of Sociology and Historical Materialism*, London, New Left Books.

Tse-tung, Mao (1971), 'On contradiction,' *Selected Readings from the Works of Mao Tse-tung*, Peking, Foreign Language Press.

Turkle, S. (1980), 'French anti-psychiatry,' in D. Ingleby (ed), *Critical Psychiatry: The Politics of Mental Health*, New York, Pantheon, pp. 150-83.

Turner, R. H. (1976), 'The real self: from institution to impulse,' *American Hournal of Sociology*, vol. 81, March, pp. 989-1017.

Turner, R. (ed) (1974), *Ethnomethodology*, Harmondsworth, Penguin.

Veblen, T. (1918), *The Higher Learning in America: A Memorandum on the Conduct of Universities by Business Men*, New York, Hill & Wang.

Wallace, A. F. C. (1961), *Culture and Personality*, New York, Random House.

Walster, E. and Walster, G. W. (1978), *A New Look at Love*, Reading, Mass., Addison-Wesley.

Walster, E. L. and Walster, G. W. and Berscheid, E. (1978), *Equity: Theory and Research*, Boston, Allyn-Bacon.

Watt, I. (1962), *The Rise of the Novel: Studies in Defoe, Richardson and Fielding*, Berkeley and Los Angeles, University of California Press.

Weber, M. (1946), 'The social psychology of the world religions,' in *From Max Weber: Essays in Sociology*, H. H. Gerth and C. W. Mills (eds), New York, Oxford University Press, pp. 267-301.

Weber, M. (1958), *The Protestant Ethic and the Spirit of Capitalism*, New York, Scribners.

Weber, M. (1963), *The Sociology of Religion*, Boston, Beacon.

Weinstein, J. (1968), *The Corporate Ideal in the Liberal State*, Boston, Beacon.

Wexler, P. (1976), *The Sociology of Education: Beyond Equality*, Indianapolis, Bobbs-Merrill.

Wexler, P. (1981a), 'Toward a critical social psychology,' in *Psychology and Social theory*, no. 1, spring/summer, pp. 52-68.

Wexler, P. (1981b) 'Body and soul: sources of social change and strategies of education,' *British Journal of Sociology of Education*, vol. 2, no. 3.

Wexler, P. and Whitson, T. (1981), Hegemony and Education (unpublished manuscript).

Wexler, P., Whitson, T. and Moskowitz, E. (1981), 'De-schooling by default: the changing social functions of public education,' *Interchange*, vol. 12, nos. 2-3.

Wheelis, A. (1958), *The Quest for Identity*, New York, Norton.

Wiebe, R. H. (1967), *The Search for Order, 1877-1920*, New York, Hill & Wang.

Willis, P. (1977), *Learning to Labour: How Working Class Kids Get Working Class Jobs*, Westmead, England, Saxon House.

Wright, E. O. (1979), *Class Crisis and the State*, London, Verso.

Zaretsky, E. (1976), *Capitalism, the Family and Personal Life*, New York, Harper & Row.

Zeitlin, M. (ed) (1980), *Classes, Class Conflict, and the State: Empirical Studies in Class Analysis*, Cambridge, Mass., Winthrop.

Zimbalist, A. (ed) (1979), *Case Studies on the Labor Process*, New York and London, Monthly Review Press.

Zurcher, L. A., Jr. (1977), *The Mutable Self: A Self-Concept for Social Change*, Beverly Hills, Sage.

Index

Philip Wexler is the Michael Scandling Professor of Education and Sociology and Dean of the Warner School at the University of Rochester. He is the former Editor of the American Sociological Association Journal, *Sociology of Education*. Among his publications are: *Sociology of Education: Beyond Equality*; *Social Analysis of Education*; and *Becoming Somebody*. He is the co-editor, with Richard Smith, of *After Postmodernism: Education, Politics and Identity*.